Defense Policy and the Presidency

Other Titles of Interest

Presidents, Secretaries of State, and Crises in U.S. Foreign Relations: A Model and Predictive Analysis, Lawrence Falkowski

U.S. Policy in International Institutions: Defining Reasonable Options in an Unreasonable World, edited by Seymour Maxwell Finger and Joseph R. Harbert

Congress and Arms Control, edited by Alan Platt and Lawrence D. Weiler

Crisis Resolution: Presidential Decision Making in the Mayaguez and Korean Confrontations, Richard Head, Frisco Short, and Robert C. McFarlane

U.S.-Japan Relations and the Security of East Asia: The Next Decade, edited by Franklin B. Weinstein

Communist Indochina and U.S. Foreign Policy: Postwar Realities, Joseph J. Zasloff and MacAlister Brown

National Interests and Presidential Leadership: The Settling of Priorities, Donald E. Nuechterlein

Arms Transfers to the Third World: The Military Buildup in Less Industrial Countries, Uri Ra'anan, Robert Pfaltzgraff, Jr., and Geoffrey Kemp

Political Leadership in NATO: A Study in Multinational Diplomacy, Robert S. Jordan

Psychological Models in International Politics, edited by Lawrence Falkowski

Lend-Lease, Loans, and the Coming of the Cold War: A Study of the Implementation of Foreign Policy, Leon C. Martel

Westview Special Studies in National Security and Defense

Defense Policy and the Presidency: Carter's First Years
edited by Sam C. Sarkesian

This book examines the role of the president in the defense policy process, focusing specifically, but not exclusively, on the administration of President Carter. Contributors discuss such current concerns as the NATO-Warsaw confrontation and attitudes of European allies, U.S.-China-Japan defense relationships, and the issues of military intervention. In examining the broader aspects of defense policy, they focus on the style of leadership and world view of the president and his immediate national security staff and on the politics of the defense budget. A constant theme is the comparison of past defense policies with those of the present administration.

The authors offer insights on important aspects of the Carter defense policy, provide an assessment of the impact of the president's policies on future U.S. defense posture, and present a conceptual framework for examining both the president's role in defense policymaking and the general concept of national security.

Sam C. Sarkesian is professor and chairman of the Political Science Department, Loyola University of Chicago. He is associate chairman of the Inter-University Seminar on Armed Forces and Society.

Defense Policy and the Presidency: Carter's First Years

edited by Sam C. Sarkesian

LONDON AND NEW YORK

First publishing 1979 by Westview Press, Inc.

Published 2018 by Routledge
52 Vanderbilt Avenue, New York, NY 10017
2 Park Square, Milton Park, Abingdon, Oxon OX14 4RN

Routledge is an imprint of the Taylor & Francis Group, an informa business

Copyright © 1979 Taylor & Francis

All rights reserved. No part of this book may be reprinted or reproduced or utilised in any form or by any electronic, mechanical, or other means, now known or hereafter invented, including photocopying and recording, or in any information storage or retrieval system, without permission in writing from the publishers.

Notice:
Product or corporate names may be trademarks or registered trademarks, and are used only for identification and explanation without intent to infringe.

Library of Congress Catalog Card Number: 78-21353

ISBN 13: 978-0-367-01792-7 (hbk)
ISBN 13: 978-0-367-16779-0 (pbk)

Contents

List of Tables and Figures	xi
Preface	xiii
Acknowledgements	xv
INTRODUCTION	1

Sam C. Sarkesian

National Security Perspectives	2
The Dimensions of Policy	5
The President, Political Actors and National Security Policy	8
The President: Constraints and Limitations	11
Summary	18
The Carter Administration: Prevailing Perspectives on Performance	19

1 CHANGING STRATEGIC ISSUES   28

Thomas A. Fabyanic

Introduction	28
The Strategic Nuclear Dimension	30
Superpower Confrontation	35
The Most Crucial Dimension: Power Projection and Intervention	38
Conclusions	47

2 THE PRESIDENT AND THE NATIONAL SECURITY APPARATUS   53

Vincent Davis

Introduction	53
The Presidential Leadership Style and Impact	61
Vacillating Foreign and Domestic Policies	69
Domestic Policy	72

Lack of Confidence	73
Presidential Reaction and Image Building	77
The Primary National Security Agencies: Internal Politics	82
The U.S.S.R.: Friend or Enemy?	88
Conclusions	96

3 NATIONAL SECURITY ORGANIZATION AND PROCESS IN THE CARTER ADMINISTRATION   111

    Lawrence J. Korb

Introduction	111
The NSC System: 1969-1977	111
NSC System: 1977	115
Strengths and Weaknesses	121
Conclusion	134

4 THE POLICY IMPACTS OF THE CARTER DEFENSE PROGRAM   138

    Lawrence J. Korb

Introduction	138
Size	141
The Carter and Ford Budgets: Dollars and Priorities	142
Distribution	147
Implications	166
Strategic Policy	175
Conventional Policy	190
Conclusion	195

5 INTERVENTION POLICIES OF THE CARTER ADMINISTRATION: POLITICAL AND MILITARY DIMENSIONS   200

    Doris A. Graber

Introduction	200
The Historical Antecedents of Carter's Intervention Policies	202
The Setting for the Intervention Policies of the Carter Administration	207
The Calculus of Intervention	213
The Carter Intervention Policies-- Year One	221
Prospects for the Future	226

6	EUROPE AND THE SUPERPOWERS	236

James A. Linger

Introduction	236
The 1970s: The Nixon-Ford/Kissinger Legacy	236
The Carter Administration's Approach to Defense Policy Formulation and Promulgation	238
The National Security Structure	244
A Balanced Perspective	247
Carter's Defense Policies	248
The European Perception of Carter's Defense Policies	270
Carter's Defense Policies: Impact and Prospects	277

7	THE UNITED STATES, CHINA AND JAPAN	289

George P. Jan

Introduction	289
American Perceptions of China and Japan	290
China's Perception of the Carter Administration	302
Japan's Perception of American Defense Policy	307
Conclusion	313

8	THE PRESIDENCY AND DEFENSE POLICY: QUESTIONS FOR THE FUTURE	319

Sheldon Simon

Introduction	319
Policy Analysis	320
U.S. Security and Military Capability	324
Conclusions	329

A FINAL WORD	330

Sam C. Sarkesian

ABOUT THE AUTHORS	333
INDEX	337

Tables and Figures

Table

3.1	Presidential Review Memoranda (PRMs)	120
3.2	Status of PRMs - March 1978	122
3.3	Presidential Directives and Other Unnumbered Presidential Decisions	127
4.1	The Defense Budget FY 1977-78 in Current and Constant Dollars (in billions of dollars)	140
4.2	Defense and the Economy FY 1978-83	146
4.3	Defense Authority By Budget Title FY 1978-83, The Ford and Carter Proposals (in billions of current dollars)	148
4.4	Major Procurement Programs FY 1978-79 (in millions of current dollars)	151
4.5	Defense Authority by Program FY 1978-83, The Ford and Carter Budgets (in billions of dollars)	154
4.6	Defense Authority by Department FY 1978-83 (in billions of dollars)	158
4.7	Shipbuilding Authority for the Navy FY 1978-83 (in billions of dollars)	161
4.8	Shipbuilding Programs FY 1978-82	163
4.9	Navy Fighter and Attack Procurement FY 1979-83	165
4.10	Army Procurement FY 1975-83 (in millions of dollars)	167
4.11	Defense Budget Totals for FY 1978 and 1979	171
4.12	Projected and Anticipated Actual Expenditures for Defense FY 1978-83 (in billions of current dollars)	174
4.13	Strategic Forces for the U.S. and U.S.S.R. for Selected Years	176
4.14	Characteristics of Manned Bombers	186
4.15	The Original U.S. Fleet Ballistic Missile Program FY 1978-95	188

4.16	Proposed Allocation of Funds for FY 1979 to Major Procurement Programs Related to NATO (in millions of dollars)	192
7.1	American Expectations of Chinese Power	300

Figure

3.1	The National Security Council System in 1976	113
3.2	NSC Structure	116
3.3	NSC System Documents	118
3.4	Organization Proposed for Review of National Strategies and Force Posture (PRM 10)	125
4.1	Defense Budget Authority FY 1955-1978 (in billions of FY 1978 dollars)	140
4.2	Target Coverage in Soviet Union of Air Launched Cruise Missiles	182
7.1	Greater Threat to World Peace--Red China or Russia? - 10 year trend -	301

Preface

At the end of his second year, President Jimmy Carter was facing difficult times at the hands of pollsters. His popularity and people's confidence in his ability to handle the job of President had dramatically decreased since his inauguration. Although such ratings expressed public disenchantment with unemployment, inflation, and the general state of the economy, they also signified concern about the ability of the United States to maintain its power and protect its security in a vastly complicated and easily misunderstood world environment.
These matters as well as an increasing concern about the gap between policy pronouncements and U.S. capabilities prompted several academicians to come together at the Midwest Political Science Association annual meeting, April 20-22nd, 1978, in Chicago, Illinois, to discuss the Carter administration's handling of national security matters. Recognizing that prognostications about national security are always a gamble, the group nevertheless focused on pressing security issues, ranging from the President and his staff to U.S. security policy in Asia. What emerges in this volume is a critical inquiry into national security during the first two years of the Carter administration.
Five of the chapters are revised versions of papers originally presented for the panel on "Defense Policies of the Carter Administration: An Assessment" at the Midwest Political Science Association annual meeting. In addition to these papers, excellent analysis and commentary by the discussants, Sam Huntington, Congressman Edward Derwinski, and Sheldon Simon has been included. To balance the presentation, some of the major points made by the discussants are incorporated into the Introduction, and Sheldon Simon has written a chap-

ter based on his comments as a discussant, providing a counterpoint to the other authors.

Thomas Fabyanic, although not participating in the Midwest meeting, prepared a paper specifically for this volume. His chapter provides a broad view of U.S. strategy, strategic concepts, and the international security environment, setting the stage for the remainder of the volume.

Larry Korb's chapter on "National Security Organization and Process" was originally prepared for the 19th Annual Meeting of the International Studies Association, Washington, D.C., February 22-25, 1978. It is a summation of the national security structure and important national security directives.

A final note: since the preparation of this volume, events may have taken place that date several points in the various chapters. For example, the United States arms embargo on Turkey was lifted in August 1978 by a House vote of 208-205. Linger's paper makes specific reference to the impending debates in Congress on the arms embargo. The fact remains, however, that such events do not change the general thrust and conclusion of the papers and this volume.

Additionally, public opinion is a fragile component in defense policy. Unexpected security developments, dramatic reversals in relationships, and the nature of domestic leadership can easily affect opinion polls of national security performance. Thus, it is possible that weaknesses in American national security policy and the current administration's policy posture may be corrected by events beyond the control of the leadership. To reiterate however, such possibilities do not change our assessment of the first two years of the Carter administration, nor of the general character of the national security policy process and the central role of the President.

Assessing national security policy of any President touches political nerves and sensitivities. Recognizing this, we have attempted to maintain a scholarly objectivity, regardless of personal preferences. Our main concern is a critical assessment of national security and an articulation of our roles as political scientists.

> Sam C. Sarkesian
> Chicago, Illinois
> September 1978

Acknowledgments

I wish to thank the participants of the panel on "Defense Policies of the Carter Administration: An Assessment" presented at the 1978 annual meeting of the Midwest Political Science Association, for their invaluable contributions to the publication of this volume. The participants included Vincent Davis, Congressman Edward Derwinski, Doris Graber, Sam Huntington, George P. Jan, Larry Korb, James Linger, and Sheldon Simon. This combination provided for spirited debate and comprehensive assessment of national security under President Jimmy Carter. I also wish to acknowledge the assistance of Margaret Kranzfelder and Phyllis Oman, both of Loyola University of Chicago, in preparing the manuscript for publication. Additionally, Phyllis Oman provided valuable editorial assistance.

Defense Policy and the Presidency

Introduction
Sam C. Sarkesian

If the results of Watergate signaled the end of the "imperial presidency," then the denouement in Vietnam marked the final end of the post-War period. The Ford presidency, with a legacy of Watergate and Vietnam, was a transition to the Carter presidency, a return to a democratically elected executive, and presumably a more coherent domestic and international policy. The end of the transition period saw Congress reassert itself in foreign affairs and national security policy, to the dismay of the Executive. In the international field, the transition period ended with a more realistic view of the superpowers ability to dictate policy for other nations and of the use of military force to achieve policy goals. Thus, the end of Watergate and Vietnam are related, not only in terms of the effectiveness of the political system and policy process, but also with regard to constraints and limits on the use of power. One showed the limits of presidential power; the other showed the limits of America's ability to impose its will on even a relatively weak foreign power, which denigrated our national security capability. Our concern here is not with the end of the imperial presidency, but with the presidential role in national security in the post-Vietnam Era--an era of new security alignments within a vastly complicated international security environment.

The present administration, by-and-large, has the same basic structures and legal authority in national security as preceding administrations have had. However, the changed security context, the President's use of these structures, and his perceptions of the legal authority, have resulted in a different military posture and a different set of security equations. How the present administration has responded, how these structures have been used and are likely to be used, and what is the likely national security outcome are the subjects of this volume.

In this context, my introduction reviews the major components of the national security process, discusses the limits and constraints upon those involved in the process and the process itself, and provides a framework for the critical assessment of President Jimmy Carter's administration in terms of its policy making and conduct of national security.

NATIONAL SECURITY PERSPECTIVES

While national security may appear self-evident to many, the fact is that confusion exists over its meaning and implementation. Some writers use national security and foreign policy synonymously.[1] Others perceive national security to encompass all of the possible dimensions that have some impact on the security posture of the country, ranging from the challenge of the Symbionese Liberation Army to the threat of Soviet nuclear warfare.[2] Still others use a much narrower, and traditional, definition focusing specifically on international affairs and their military implications.[3]

There is a great deal of literature reflecting these perspectives. It is unnecessary to detail the arguments here, but nevertheless it is helpful to focus briefly on some of the major perspectives as a way of developing our concept of national security.

Most agree that national security is closely associated with the protection of core values from external threat.[4] As Brodie observes:

> According to customary usage, those of our interests are "vital" that we are ready to fight to preserve. For them, in other words, we are prepared to take or threaten some kind of military action, including if necessary--and, one would hope, if sufficiently "vital"--full-scale war. It does not appear that all wars that we or other nations have fought concerned issues of the gravest importance. The obverse is also true: Some international issues or conflicts of real importance are churned over and either resolved or left unresolved without anyone's

thinking to resort to arms over them.
Why? No doubt it is to some extent a
matter of tradition, perhaps going back
to the days of mercantilism when all
foreign trade was conceived to be a kind
of conflict about which one did not use
arms. The element of tradition always
matters greatly. It works just as much
on the opposite front, too, that is, on
the determination of those things that
are presumed to be worth fighting over.[5]

The connection between national security and
national interest seems clear. But the difficulty
of defining national security makes it equally difficult to be precise about national interest. As
Knorr suggests, national security is "...a rather
unsatisfactory label for a field whose boundaries
and chief structural features remain to be defined.
I take 'National Security' to be an abbreviation of
'National Military Security,' and I take this term
to denote a field of study concerned primarily with
the generation of national military power and its
employment in interstate relationships."[6]

These definitional difficulties historically
have had important political implications. Not only
has the presidential role become primary in defining national security, but the President also determines the national interest. To be sure, there are
a number of political actors involved in these matters, but the historical patterns in the American
political system, as well as constitutional practices, point to the primary role of the President.
Thus, with the exception of clearly perceived crises articulated to the American people by a number
of political actors, the President has a wide latitude in determining national interest and national
security.

Examining this question, Brodie concludes:

The persons who at any particular moment
determine what our vital interests are,
and how they should be defended, if menaced,
are naturally the political leaders of the
nation. The responsibility and prerogative
is centered first and foremost--by a wide
margin--in the President, whose authority
in these matters, at least over the short
term, is awesome. Questions as to what
is possible or feasible must take into
account the mood of the whole population;

but the guiding ideas come from that small minority who maintain an interest in foreign affairs, and especially from that portion of the latter who through special intellectual gifts or privilege of position can command the attention of others.[7]

While there is no <u>one</u> definition of national security (and national <u>interest</u>) that is completely satisfactory for studying policy, there are several elements that are essential in any definition. These include concerns for the projection of national power, survival and well-being of the state, and military posture and capabilities. In this context, national security policy is that policy designed to protect the nation from external threat (national interest), to project the nation's power into areas of the world in order to create a favorable environment to the nation's well-being, and to maintain a military posture and capability enabling the nation to carry out these policies. It is appropriate to use the term defense policy (as in the title of this book), since it indicates a specific focus on the military instrument. Thus, national security policy and defense policy are used synonymously here.

On the surface and in the popular imagination, making national security policy may appear to be a rather simple and uncomplicated process. The President determines America's national interest and invokes national security to protect this interest. But as most students of the presidency and national policy are quick to point out, these are complicated matters, perplexing not only to experts on national security, but to elected leaders and decision makers who must translate national security and national interest into meaningful policy goals and programs.

As one observer notes:

> The critical question becomes, then, what are the circumstances that justify deliberate departures from the truth? The most obvious answer is the "national interest," but, historically, such a vague, patriotic rationale has had a way of serving very personal and narrow interests. With the "national interest" thus a matter of subjective definition, it is difficult for leaders even with the best of intentions to disentangle their own advantage from that

of their country.[8]

In sum, the meaning of national security and national interest in no small measure, is determined by the world view and political power of the highest policy makers, particularly the President. While there may be some limitation and constraint regarding the degree of presidential latitude in these matters, the fact is that such limitations and constraints are primarily those associated with the President's own perceptions of the world and the effectiveness of his political leadership. The qualitative difference in the national security policy between one administration and another is attributable to these subjective considerations rather than institutional and constitutional differences. To understand presidential performance in national security policy (defense policy) therefore, it is necessary to develop an understanding of policy studies in general.

THE DIMENSIONS OF POLICY

The study of policy invariably raises the question of focus and perspective.[9] Policy studies include a variety of approaches and disciplinary perspectives. For example, those concerned about policy effectiveness may well focus their attention on what policy accomplishes, i.e., what did our involvement achieve in Vietnam? Or, what impact has school desegregation had on student performance? Others may be concerned with the substance of policy. They are concerned about the rationale and goals of policy, and what resources are needed to achieve these goals. For example, what should be our policy (and the reasons) with respect to the Sino-Soviet split? Finally, the policy process can be examined to assess the institutional arrangements, the role of political actors, and how these interact to determine policy. Thus, in examining the United States role in Vietnam, for example, political actors would be studied to determine their role and effectiveness in shaping America's Vietnam policy.

All of these approaches are reflected in the selections in this volume. But it is the policy process that is of primary concern. This is based on our conviction that examining presidential performance in defense policy must begin with a study of the incumbent's world view, leadership style, and political ability. Additionally, this dimension includes a study of those around the President and the political actors involved in the highest levels of policy making. Analyzing policy making during the Vietnam war, one author concludes, for example, that the policy process is the crucial factor, "...since the way we make and carry out foreign policy appears to have a lot to do with the quality of the policy that is produced and the chances of its succeeding. Of the many lessons that might be learned from Vietnam, this ought to be among the least debatable."[10] Another scholar concludes that in our Vietnam experience "...the most important cause of the policy mishap was the world view of the top decision makers."[11] Additionally, the author notes that the nature of the policy making process had a decided impact on the substance of policy.

In examining the role of various policy-makers, yet another scholar notes:

> These big pictures of the world may be consciously or unconsciously held. But they are indisputably important. They signify very basic assumptions and inclinations: from attitudes about communism and revolutions to preferences for pressure or persuasion; from notions about the efficacy of American military might to feelings about where the fundamental threats to American society lie; from ideas about America's capacity for influence in the world to views on the importance of other people's attitudes toward us. Psychologically, some lean toward deterrence, others toward detente.[12]

In studying national security policy, the authors have linked the intricacies of the process with considerations of policy accomplishments and substance. This is a recognition of not only the close relationships between these perspectives, but also an awareness that the broader range of policy issues cannot be limited solely to one or the other perspective. In this volume therefore, we look at defense policy from a relatively broad dimension, ranging from the defense budget and military intervention to more focused policy issues in Europe and the Far East. In this regard, the defense budget is one of the most important indicators of the nation's national security posture. Analysis of defense programs, trends, and policy rationale provides significant insight into the President's perceptions and the internal politics of the national security process. Thus, throughout the study the primary theme is the performance of the Carter administration. Invariably, the crucial elements in this performance include the structure of the policy process and the power and politics of those involved in it.

The basis for any coherent policy rests fundamentally on the President's understanding and appreciation of at least four national security requisites. First, the national security process must start with some sense of national purpose and national objectives. This is primarily a political decision and must come from the President, for it is he who embodies and projects the national objectives of the country. The manner and style in which these objectives are articulated will, in no small measure, determine the thrust of the nation's national security posture. At a minimum it will establish the boundaries within which national security issues are debated.

Second, the direction of policy and its ultimate goals must seriously reflect an assessment of the intentions and capabilities of potential aggressors. Thus, much of what the President and his staff establish as national security policy reflects their perceptions of such threats. In brief, national objectives, as defined and affected by threat perceptions, shape the perceptions and attitudes of those involved in the policy process. This effect should not be so overwhelming that one recognized threat obscures potential threats in other areas of the world.

Third, national security policy must take into account the fact that there is a long lead time from policy to implementation. For example, the more sophisticated weapons require as much as ten years to develop, some even a generation, before they can make some impact on national security. Moreover, no one can say with any degree of certainty what the final impact of decisions regarding weapons, manpower levels, force posture, and technological breakthrough will be. There must be enough flexibility in national security policy to account for, as much as possible, imponderables that intervene between policy decisions and their final impact.

Finally, the cohesiveness and effectiveness of national security policy is affected by the ability of the President and his staff to develop popular confidence in the administration's performance on a range of domestic issues. The strength of the domestic economy and political system is linked to the overall perception of strength in national security; an effective national security policy in turn builds on domestic strength. A successful administration must have the ability to articulate this strength and linkage.

THE PRESIDENT, POLITICAL ACTORS AND NATIONAL SECURITY POLICY

The national security policy process appears to be a rational organizational approach to decision-making. Such an approach presumes each important part of the process provides reasonable and rational inputs. The process then is supposed to synthesize these inputs into a series of policy alternatives from which the most feasible and effective policy option is selected and implemented. The result, according to this view, is a systematized and rational process that produces outputs integrating the most rational choices produced by the process.

It is clear, however, that while on a legal and organizational level the process appears rational, in reality it is highly political (and at times irrational), reflecting the power and interests of political actors who wish to affect the process for a variety of reasons. In the vital center of this process stands the President. Depending on his leadership style and the effectiveness of his own exercise of power, the President can subdue or at the least minimize the influence of other political actors on the national security policy process. If he is successful, the President can stamp national security with his own style and outlook.

Most political actors, such as Congress and the media, are likely to defer to the President in matters of national security. The courts have made it clear that it is the President who dominates issues of foreign affairs and national security. Although various legislative acts have attempted to restore some congressional power in this area, the fact remains that the President's position as Commander-in-Chief and Chief Executive provides him with both legal and political authority to dominate the fields of national security and foreign policy.

The Nixon administration is illustrative of this point. Under the Nixon presidency, national security became the justification for a variety of activities ordered by the executive office. Ranging from the Cambodian excursion to Watergate, national security was entoned to the point of incredulity. Even in such circumstances, however, few would deny the dominance of the President in the national security policy process.

As most observers of the national security process know, in recent years the formal national security mechanism has been more-or-less subordinated to the role of the President's immediate staff. This may allow the President a more responsive and manageable system, but such a personalized system may severely isolate the process from political actors whose expertise and leadership could provide the President with needed alternative perspectives.

Reflecting on problems experienced by President Johnson during the Vietnam years, two scholars conclude:

> Even granting the most thorough information and the best of intentions, this is a method of policy making whose grave defects were demonstrated throughout the Vietnam war. It limits meaningful debate to a small and highly selected circle within the government. Indeed, as the importance of the issues becomes greater and has more political significance, the circle becomes even smaller. The president chooses the members of this circle and establishes the limits of their debate. Thus, the nature of the debate and the variety of the viewpoints expressed in this circle are of vital importance. But these individuals most certainly share the values and perspectives of the president and identify with his beliefs. They also must feel some personal loyalty and attachment to the man responsible for their very presence in that inner circle. This places an almost impossible burden upon the man within that circle who dissents from the apparent trend of the president's views. Such dissent at some point results in ostracism or even dismissal.[13]

Indeed, the manner in which it is debated within administration circles provides insights into the nature of the national security process.

> National security decision-making is, it is true, less able to brook vehement public dissent because of possible foreign

> misperception of our purposes, but the
> history of military affairs is replete with
> dissent carried on inside, as witness the
> controversy over President Eisenhower's
> "New Look" against which Air Force General
> Hoyt Vandenburgh expressed vigorous dissent.
> ... At no time could dissent be waged as
> it is in the domestic sector today by HEW
> Secretary Joseph Califano or as it was by
> Daniel Patrick Moynihan in the White House.[14]

Janis, in his groupthink theory, also supports the contention that the quality of policy is a direct reflection of the process and who is involved.

> Every cohesive group that is required to
> make policy decisions tends to develop a
> set of policy doctrines, derived from the
> members' subculture, that provides the
> members with a cognitive map for concep-
> tualizing the intentions and reactions of
> opponents, allies, and neutrals.... The
> shared belief that "we are a wise and good
> group" inclines them to use group con-
> currence as a major criterion to judge the
> morality as well as the efficacy of any
> policy under discussion.[15]

Any examination of the policy process must, therefore, include particular attention to the political style of the President, his attitudes and views, and an assessment of the political-psychological dimension of his leadership. Additionally, since the President's immediate staff is, in many respects, an extension of the President's own political style and reflective of his world view, the composition and style of the immediate staff must also be examined. Much of the national security policy process rests on the subjective matters of the interlocking and inter-related relationships between the President and his immediate staff.

In this respect, the perspectives, attitudes, and personal relationships between the Secretary of State, the Secretary of Defense, and the President's National Security Advisor (the Trio), are a major influence on presidential perceptions of national security. Power maneuvers and attempts to dominate policy by one or the other of this Trio are eventually reflected in access to the President and in the direction of national security policy. (This situation was clearly seen during the Kissinger years--the Nixon and Ford administrations.) Indeed, the national security policy process could conceivably be structured to flow from the dominant member of the Trio to the President.

It is also possible for the President to ignore the entire national security structure and his immediate advisors, and turn to trusted friends and associates who are not formally involved in the process. John F. Kennedy's reliance on his brother, Robert, the U.S. Attorney General, was well demonstrated during the Cuban Missile Crisis in 1962. To put it simply, the structure is there to be used, but the President is at liberty to establish virtually any process and involve any individuals in national security as he sees fit. Obviously, there are political costs if such a process excludes political actors who would normally be expected to have a meaningful input. But a strong President may be willing to incur such costs for the sake of a firm hand on national security issues.

THE PRESIDENT: CONSTRAINTS AND LIMITATIONS

The assertions about the paramount role of the President in national security must be qualified by a number of observations. First, while there are distinctions between the national security policy process and the domestic policy process, they are not as clear now as they have been in the past. There are two reasons for this: in the wake of the Vietnam era and Watergate the presumed superiority of the President in national security policy has become suspect. The motivations behind a certain policy and the way in which policy is made have become highly sensitive issues to the Congress and to other political actors. The presumed secrecy (closed system) by which decisions on national security have been made have to a great extent lost their rationale, if for no other reason than fear of the resurgence of an "imperial presidency." Additionally, the basis for national security policy has shifted qualitatively. The clear and concise purposes of national security that were characteristic of the 1950s and 1960s have eroded considerably: the idea of monolithic communism and the superpower confrontations have undergone significant revisions. The United States may be friends with one communist nation while confronting others. At the same time, developing nations, some of whom now sit on an ocean of oil are not politically nor even militarily the pawns they were in the past. The ability of oil rich nations to seriously affect the policy of larger powers was well demonstrated in the oil crisis in 1976. What this also indicates is a much closer relationship between national security, energy sources, and domestic politics.

Second, most Presidents assume office inheriting the preceding incumbent's structures, commitments, and personnel. In this respect, a new President does not have the freedom of action most people might assume. Part of this is a result of the new President's fear and/or reluctance to dramatically change national security early in his administration.

In an assessment of the policy process during the Vietnam era, Gallucci concludes "... the President is not the only actor even when he is the one who finally chooses. His calculations will turn out the way they do, as will his choice, in large part because of the way the bureaucratic-political apparatus has defined the situation and his options, and because interests, besides his own and the nation's, will have advocates that he will not want to ignore. The President, partial creator of the system that serves him, is also constrained by it and may become to some degree the victim of it."[16]

This situation exists because continuity of national security policy goes beyond any one President--a continuity necessitated by the impact American national security policy has on allies, potential aggressors, and the general balance of power in the world. As some have suggested, "Experience suggests that a President's view of the White House national security staff is likely to be conditioned by his assessment of the practices of his predecessors. Each President brings to office his own style of doing business, his own concept of what was wrong with the previous system, and his own view of what is needed."[17]

Third, most Presidents have difficulty in dealing with the national security establishment--particularly the military. The character of military professionalism, the general orientation of the military institution, and the linkage between the military institution and civilian political actors, erodes the President's ability to act as a free agent.

Moreover, it is unlikely that candidates will be elected to the presidency because of their expertise in foreign affairs or national security.

Rather, Presidents are generally elected because of their perceived ability to handle domestic issues or because of their style of leadership. National security remains the prime province of military experts and civilian specialists who tend to develop a legitimacy because of their expertise--an expertise, it might be added, upon which most Presidents depend.

As one observer concludes:

> Presidents find it difficult to develop alternative means to carry secure implementation of decisions in the domain of the military. For example, the President may use special envoys in place of career Foreign Service Officers to carry out delicate negotiations while he can hardly ask a retired businessman to land American forces in Lebanon or to command a nuclear missile-carrying submarine.
>
> Presidents also have great difficulty convincing the military to create new capabilities, which they may need in the future but which might tend to alter the traditional role of a particular branch. The services emphasize the forces which conform to their notion of the essence of their role and resist capabilities which involve interservice cooperation (e.g., airlift), noncombat roles (e.g., advisers), and elite forces (e.g., Green Berets). At least until recently, they have also resisted the maintenance of combat-ready non-nuclear forces.[18]

The military, contrary to the presumed "apolitical" label given them by some scholars, are drawn into the political battle over national security policy. As one scholar observed, the national security process during the Eisenhower period, even with the military legitimacy given to decisions by a General President, was characterized by intense politics.

> The very nature of the appropriations process, then, served to draw even the most reluctant general or admiral into the political arena. Those innovators solidly committed to their particular causes rather than that of the administration

needed little in the way of temptation to spring into the thick of things.[19]

The author also notes that

> Given the nature of the American political system, 'military planning cannot be done, and it is not expected to be done, in a political vacuum.' The governmental process, premised as it is on a decentralization of power and the parcelling out of functions among several institutions, affords groups (both within and without government proper) myriad means of access to the decision-making process.[20]

Fourth, the bureaucracies concerned with the national security policy process resist changes that may affect their own area of responsibility or their budgetary allocations. In fact, there are times when bureaucratic loyalty takes precedence over policy priorities.

> Of central importance to those actors associated with the large bureaucracies of the military service, the Departments of State and Defense, and the intelligence agencies is the maintenance of the stature, role and budgets of their organizations or organizational subunits. Their perspective on matters of foreign policy is strongly influenced by their bureaucratic affiliation. Although some senior actors who help make policy are without such association, they have often already made an investment in a policy by virtue of their previous stands and therefore proceed with a personal interest, if not also a bureaucratic one, to protect.[21]

As Kissinger has stated, "The nightmare of the modern state is the hugeness of the bureaucracy, and the problem is how to get coherence and design in it."[22]

The power of the bureaucracy in national security is well summarized in the following passage:

> It is the bureaucracy which could neutralize an explicit order by President Kennedy that our obsolete and provocative Jupiter missiles be removed from Turkey, simply by

not implementing the order. It is a bureaucracy which could at the same time pursue delicate negotiations with North Vietnam and unleash bombing attacks on Hanoi which destroyed any chance of the negotiations succeeding. It is a bureaucracy which could locate a blockade around Cuba in October 1962, not where the President wanted it in order to minimize the danger of rash Soviet response, but where the Navy found it most consistent with standard blockade procedures and the military problems as the Navy saw them. It is a bureaucracy which can provide unbalanced or incomplete information, continue outmoded policies through its own inertial momentum, and treat the needs of particular offices and bureaus as if they were sacred national interests.[23]

The President and other political actors in the national security policy process are to a degree captives of the bureaucracy. The ability of the bureaucracy to frustrate national security policy is further reinforced if bureaucratic political actors are able to forge political alliances with other political actors outside the executive office. Theodore White's famous description of the "iron triangle" is particularly appropriate.[24] To frustrate such alliances and establish a degree of control over the bureaucracy, the President needs to establish a consensus within the bureaucracy--a consensus that will allow the President to establish his national security policy and implement it as he intended it to be implemented. Thus, the President must attempt to minimize the effect of political actors outside of the executive office while establishing a policy direction that appears coherent and effective. This is primarily a matter of leadership rather than managerial talents.

Fifth, Congress has taken a more active role in the national security process, both through the politics of the defense budget and through its own attempt to reassert itself in the process. For example, the House and Senate Budget Committees (The Congressional Budget and Impoundment Control Act of 1974), have provided Congress with a structure for serious examination of the budget and have developed a capability to prepare their own version of the budget. Most importantly, the Congress has developed a capability to present its own views on defense policies. Part of this increased capability is the result of an increase in staff and its expertise. All of these developments do not provide Congress with a staff equal to the President's, but they have strengthened Congress' hand in dealing with the presidential national security establishment.

Allison and Szanton observe:

> ...the fundamental reason for the changing relation of the Congress to the executive in foreign policy is the changed context of that policy. Our relations with other countries are no longer dominated by the terms of alliances, the duration of base rights, or the breadth of security guarantees; they are also shaped by issues arising from the tightening economic and physical interdependence among nations. Those issues affect prices, jobs, and the condition of daily life; they are the stuff of domestic politics. It is this fact that makes congressional activism inevitable.[25]

To conclude, most Presidents appear to consciously or unconsciously opt for a trusted staff of advisors to play a primary role in the conduct of national security policy. For a variety of reasons, ranging from fear of media leaks to the distrust of political actors, Presidents generally feel more comfortable with a select group of advisors-- limited in number, and owing their loyalty to the President. This is especially true in the national security process. One major fear is that the involvement of a wider range of political actors-- even those whose normal duties may require involvement in the national security policy process may generate internal conflict and political fallout leading to inconsistency and vacillation in policy. The proper posture appears to be one of balance between the various political actors and their priorities. This provides the President with a variety of policy alternatives to choose from. Such a view is well expressed in the following passage:

> The problem is not to eliminate restraint-- for reasonable limitations on power are a necessary part of the democratic system-- but rather to efficiently balance restraint and imperative, pro and con, civil and military, foreign and domestic, and a host

of other multifaceted priorities. In the end, the national security structure should provide that blending of its constituent elements, that fluidity and flexibility, best suited to the effective development and implementation of policy. It should properly integrate responsible individuals and institutions, orchestrate their views and knowledge, and coordinate their action in support of mutually designed objectives. And finally, if it is to be successful, it must offer what Senator Henry M. Jackson has described as "a clear sense of direction and coherence of policy at the top of government."[26]

In any case, compared to the "open" domestic policy process, national security is a "closed" process. While both processes may be within the boundaries of a democratic system, the way problems are defined, policies are articulated, and dissent is expressed differs.

Briefly then, the President is at the center of the national security policy process. This is generally true with respect to the general policy process, yet it is particularly characteristic of national security. The closed nature of the process, the limited number of political actors involved outside of the executive structure, the limited knowledge of the general public on such matters, and the tradition of deference to the President on national security, reinforces the President's dominant role. Nevertheless, there are a number of countervailing forces that few Presidents can ignore if they are to retain their political effectiveness. Equally important, the potential of national security issues becoming perceived crises necessitating a popular consensus, limits the extent to which the President can venture into national security areas without some consensus among major political actors, including friendly foreign nations.

Finally, most Americans expect a certain ethical and moral content to national security policy. This in turn is reflected in fundamental premises regarding governmental processes, accountability, responsibility, and democratic values. Theoretically, the democratic process is supposed to invite inputs from a variety of political actors and be responsive to the values and expectations of the political system. This democratic environment, in itself, establishes constraints on the nature of the security policy process and the degree to which national interests may be pursued.

SUMMARY

In summary, there are a variety of political actors involved in all phases of the policy process, at all levels of the American political system. Yet, all political actors are not involved with the same degree of intensity on all issues at any given time. Moreover, values, goals, and the power of political actors differ widely. The domestic policy process is vulnerable to the influence of political actors who may be involved for different reasons, seeking different goals.

The highly specialized character of national security matters and the limitations on the political actors involved makes the national security process relatively isolated and monolithic compared to the general policy process. The relative lack of public involvement and the clearly dominant position of the President, his immediate staff, and the Department of Defense makes the national security process relatively immune from critical inquiry or from the serious influence of other political actors. While the public has knowledge of the general imperatives of national security (e.g., the need for a strong military and the need to protect our vital interests), they can hardly know about complex matters associated with such items as weapons capabilities, research and development, and enemy capabilities and intentions. Thus the process associated with national security tends to be focused upon a handful of political actors removed from the general scrutiny of the public. Moreover, there are serious limits on alternative inputs to the national security process since the major actors are the President and his immediate staff. There is no question that in comparison with the domestic policy process in the American political system, the national security process encourages, develops, and perpetuates an elitist system.

A policy process in which a very small number of political actors determine the boundaries of debate and define the extent of inputs is susceptible to abuse, distortion, misjudgment, and narrow intellectual insights. The magnitude of the errors depends upon the President and his leadership style. There are many who fear centralization and the fact that such a system is susceptible to idiosyncracies of one man.

There are other dangers, however.

> Without a multitude of conflicting organizational interests and centers of power, it is difficult to see how the vigor and variety of dialogue and dissent at lower echelons can be sustained. Inevitably, the centering of so much authority in an office of the special assistant for national security affairs will have a depressing effect upon independence of thought and initiative at other levels of the system. What is clearly required is organizational strength at the bottom as well as the top, if executive deliberations are to retain any vitality.[27]

THE CARTER ADMINISTRATION: PREVAILING PERSPECTIVES ON PERFORMANCE

The following chapters of this book concern the performance of the Carter administration. Nevertheless, it is helpful to review the major prevailing views on President Carter and his conduct of national security policy. These assessments must be viewed in the context of our general framework, which regards the President as the dominant political actor in a national security environment characterized by various, but limited, constraints. Additionally, we should recall that policy progresses through various phases, and hence it is possible that differing assessments may emerge as different phases of the policy process are being examined.

Discounting the existing attitudes of loyalists and detractors, whether they are on the "right" or the "left," there is a middle group of political actors in the United States who view the national security policy process in pragmatic terms. The policy process and the sense of policy direction and cohesiveness are important criteria by which such political actors judge presidential performance.

Although President Carter came into office with a clear consensus and high expectations, a deep sense of disappointment and even anger has developed at the perceived direction or lack thereof in national security polity and at its apparent inconsistency. Equally important, there is some sense that the national security process itself has evolved into an incoherent and highly "political" system. So far no one appears to be speaking in the name of national security or articulating national purposes in a meaningful way.

There are also those who argue that the redirection of national security policy is a difficult matter. It should be expected that in the initial years of the Carter administration some sense of ambiguity would develop--at least until a restructuring and reorganization of the system and the process has been completed. Supporters of President Carter's policy point to the success of human rights policy, the "peace" image of the United States, and an even-handed approach in the Middle East and Africa. According to this view, the Carter administration has indeed developed a more realistic and coherent policy in these areas than preceding administrations. The argument goes on to point out that Carter's policies have restored American moral prominence in the international field, and that the same is true in national security policy.

At the conclusion of President Carter's two years in office, however, the critics of his national security policy appear to be the more pronounced and articulate. Criticism comes not only from anti-Carter sources but also from other political actors whose initial expectations of the Carter administration were positive. In any case, much of the negative opinion and criticism of Carter is based on assessments that national security policy is contradictory, vacillating, and fragmented.

After the first year of the Carter administration, one scholar concluded that American foreign policy (and presumably national security) has accomplished litte.

> With mixed returns of his first year, the President may become a born-again diplomat. Following a baptism by fire in many areas and on many issues, he may approach international problems in a more thoughtful and experienced manner. The heady optimism of a White House wrapped in euphoria seems to be waning. A "sadder but wiser" President --to borrow a phrase from the sweet-talking Music Man--can now face a second year with lessons learned, disappointments overcome, and sustained high hopes for the future.[28]

Henry Kissinger's observations over fifteen years ago appear particularly relevant.

> The attitudes of our high officials and their method of arriving at decisions inevitably distorts the essence of policy. Effective policy depends not only on the skill of individual moves, but even more importantly on their relationship to each other. It requires a sense of proportion and a sense of style. As long as our high officials lack a framework of purpose, each problem becomes a special case. But the more fragmented the approach to policy becomes, the more difficult it is to act consistently and purposefully.
>
> ...our top policymakers often lack the assurance of the conceptual framework to impose a sense of direction on their administrative staffs. Their unfamiliarity with their subject matter reinforces the already powerful tendency to think that a compromise among administrative proposals is the same thing as a policy.[29]

The views of foreign countries both allies and potential enemies, support the negative views of presidential performance. They perceive an increasing inability of the United States to influence world affairs. Moreover, many argue that the United States has decreased its capability to respond in meaningful ways to perceived threats around the world, including Europe. Some critics also conclude that the apparent unstructured national security process of the Carter administration has not only weakened the U.S. position in the world by producing policy that reflects the weakness of the process, but also that the President's own role in the process reflects weak leadership, producing rhetoric and a "retreat" of American influence. In the words of a respected foreign newspaper:

> The way President Carter reached his decision on the neutron bomb gives rise to serious misgivings. After urging the bomb's acceptance on initially hesitant allies, he chose the moment of their acquiescence to announce postponement of production, thus openly leaving them in a lurch. Carter hopes to use his abstention

from the bomb as a lever to extract concessions from Moscow, but Brezhnev has made it perfectly clear that the Russians are not prepared to give anything in return, beyond themselves desisting from building a similar weapon. As far as Moscow is concerned, the White House actions have merely confirmed the existing image of a wavering president from whom further advantages can be wrung provided the tough Soviet stand is maintained. Carter's attempts to be all things to all men has disconcerted his supporters and strengthened the determination of his opponents.[30]

Another observer commenting on President Carter's human rights policy concludes:

A more far-reaching crisis of credibility and capability confronts the nation's human rights policy. The Administration has staked much of its political reputation on promotion of human rights. And it has said that those fundamental freedoms include all rights set forth in the Universal Declaration and that they apply at home and abroad. However, a look at the Administration's record on human rights, the challenges ahead, and the areas for different emphasis gives pause. In sum, the future of U.S. policy on human rights lies in the response to the larger question that launched the Republic: What price principle?[31]

According to some, this observation on human rights policy applies as well to national security policy.

Another indication regarding the assessment of Carter's approach to the presidency that is particularly relevant to national security is a scholar's argument regarding Jimmy Carter's political-psychological strength. Most are familiar with James Barber's categorization of Presidents into passive-positive, active-positive, passive-negative, and active-negative; with active-positive characterized by "a conviction of capability, investment without immersion, a sense of the future as possible, a repertoire of habits, the communication of excitement."[32] Barber has categorized Jimmy Carter as active-positive.[33] As several scholars suggest, however:

The first several months of President Carter's administration do suggest a discrepancy between the image projected during the campaign and performance in the White House. So although Barber predicted an active role for Mr. Carter in the White House, some reactions to the administration thus far perceive a passiveness in the President; and that possibility is discernible in a stylistic tendency which conforms to a distinct trend in compositional preferences of other Presidents identified by Barber as passives.[34]

Yet, the first sign of a more coherent and forceful security policy may develop out of the Carter administration's response in mid-1978 to the Soviet-Cuban support of rebels in Zaire. One journalist concluded that the administration's tough response, after months of apparent vacillation, was forced upon the administration. "When put to the test, Carter could not stand the appearance of himself as a feeble leader. Change the southern drawl for a fuzzy German accent and Carter could have sounded like Kissinger."[35] Additionally, in the Summer of 1978 there were some expectations that the SALT II negotiations and the response of the Carter administration to the Soviet trial of dissidents Shcharansky and Ginzburg would signal a clear direction and firmness in U.S. policy that is a harbinger of the national security policy thrust.

The fact remains that at the end of 1978 even Jimmy Carter's most sympathetic supporters were reluctantly concluding that there was something wrong in the national security area. The weight of opinion seemed to be that the national security policies lacked initiative, were primarily reactive, and reflected the administration's inability to ascertain a clear focus and purpose. It may be too early to predict the long-range national security impact of the Carter Presidency, but the first years have created some major misgivings about presidential performance in national security, and indeed the entire national security establishment. The true import may not reveal itself for a number of years. In the meantime, it is clear that the present administration has not developed the confidence of the American people nor of many friends and allies in the area of national security. This in itself may create a long-range negative impact.

In the final analysis, the real test of the

democratic national security policy process is its ability to balance a variety of priorities, to orchestrate the inputs of responsible political actors, and to "coordinate their action in support of mutually designed objectives." The instruments of national security policy are directly responsible to the President and it is he that directs policy, determines the scope of debate, and develops the necessary image and symbol of a "clear sense of direction and coherence of policy at the top of government."

The following chapters will examine a range of defense policy issues to determine the validity of prevailing views on the President and national security. Presidential performance will be assessed in terms of policy coherency and direction in the context of broad national objectives directly related to national security. In this context, we need to recall the various policy perspectives, the general distinctions separating domestic from national security policy, the imperatives of national security, the attitudes and internal politics of the immediate presidential staff, and above all, the character and effectiveness of the presidential leadership.

NOTES

1. John H. Esterline and Robert B. Black, Inside Foreign Policy (Palo Alto, Calif.: Mayfield Publishing Co., 1975). See also I.M. Destler, Presidents, Bureaucrats and Foreign Policy: The Politics of Organizational Reform (Princeton, New Jersey: Princeton University Press, 1972), p. 5.

2. Phillip S. Kronenberg, "Interorganizational Politics and National Security: An Approach to Inquiry," in Frank N. Trager and Phillip S. Kronenberg (eds.), National Security and American Society: Theory, Process, and Policy (Lawrence, Kansas: University of Kansas Press, 1973), pp. 17-34.

3. Klaus Knorr, "National Security Studies: Scope and Structure of the Field," in Trager and Kronenberg, Ibid., pp. 5-34.

4. See for example, Eugene J. Rosi (ed.), American Defense and Detente: Readings in National Security Policy (New York: Dodd, Mead and Co., 1975), p. 3.

5. Bernard Brodie, War and Politics (New York: Macmillan Publishing Co., Inc., 1973), p. 342.

6. Knorr, pp. 5-6.

7. Brodie, pp. 358-359.

8. Thomas Halper, Foreign Policy Crises: Appearance and Reality in Decision Making (Columbus, Ohio: Charles E. Merrill Publishing Co., 1971), p. 18.

9. For an excellent treatment of the various policy approaches see Thomas R. Dye, Understanding Public Policy (Englewood Cliffs, New Jersey: Prentice-Hall, 1975), Second Edition: especially Chapters 1 and 2; Chapter 11 is on Defense Policy.

10. Robert L. Gallucci, Neither Peace Nor Honor: The Politics of American Military Policy in Viet-Nam (Baltimore: The Johns Hopkins University Press, 1975), p. 156.

11. Erwin C. Hargrove, The Power of the Modern Presidency (New York: Alfred A. Knopf and Co., 1974), pp. 148-151.

12. Thomas L. Hughes, "The Fate of Facts in a World of Men: Foreign Policy and Intelligence-Making," Headline Series, December, 1976, Number 233, published by the Foreign Policy Association, p. 18.

13. Herbert Y. Schandler, The Unmaking of a President: Lyndon Johnson and Vietnam (Princeton, New Jersey: Princeton University Press, 1977), pp. 329-330.

14. Thomas F. Roeser, "Comparison Between National Security and the General Policy Process," (Unpublished paper), March 8, 1977, p. 2.

15. Irving L. Janis, Victims of Groupthink (Boston: Houghton Mifflin Co., 1972), p. 204.

16. Gallucci, p. 136.

17. Keith C. Clark and Laurence J. Legere (eds.), The President and the Management of National Security (New York: Frederick A. Praeger, 1969), p. 55.

18. Morton H. Halperin, *National Security Policy-Making: Analyses, Cases, and Proposals* (Lexington, Mass.: Lexington Books, 1975), p. 145.

19. Richard A. Aliano, *American Defense Policy from Eisenhower to Kennedy: The Politics of Changing Military Requirements, 1957-1961* (Athens, Ohio: Ohio University Press, 1975), p. 273.

20. *Ibid.*, p. 13.

21. Gallucci, p. 138.

22. As quoted in Destler, p. 3.

23. *Ibid.*, p. 3.

24. Theodore White, *The Making of the President, 1972* (New York: Bantam, 1973), pp. 71-72.

25. Graham Allison and Peter Szanton, "Organizing for the Decade Ahead," in Henry Owen and Charles L. Schultze (eds.), *Setting National Priorities: The Next Ten Years* (Washington, D.C.: The Brookings Institution, 1976), p. 242.

26. Stanley L. Falk and Theodore W. Bauer, *The National Security Structure* (Washington, D.C.: Industrial College of the Armed Forces, 1972), Revised Edition, p. 6.

27. Francis E. Rourke, *Bureaucracy and Foreign Policy* (Baltimore: The Johns Hopkins University Press, 1972), p. 74.

28. Kenneth L. Adelman, "The Runner Stumbles: Carter's Foreign Policy in the Year One," in *Policy Review*, Winter, 1978, No. 3, p. 115.

29. Henry A. Kissinger, *The Necessity for Choice* (New York: Harper and Row Publishers, Inc., 1961), pp. 342, 345, and 346.

30. From *The Neue Zurcher Zeitung* as quoted in *Swiss Review of World Affairs*, Vol. XXVIII, No. 2, May, 1978, p. 31.

31. Sandra Vogelgesang, "What Price Principle? - U.S. Policy on Human Rights" in *Foreign Affairs*, July, 1978, p. 841.

32. James Barber, <u>The Presidential Character: Predicting Performance in the White House</u> (Englewood Cliffs, N.J.: Prentice-Hall, 1977), pp. 210-211, Second Edition.

33. <u>Ibid.</u>, pp. 534-539.

34. Ronald H. Carpenter and William J. Jordan, "Style and Discourse as a Predictor of Political Personality or Mr. Carter and Other Twentieth Century Presidents: Testing the Barber Paradigm," in <u>Presidential Studies Quarterly</u>, Vol. VIII, No. 1, Winter, 1978, Center for the Study of the Presidency, Janice Jacobsen and Kathleen Dewitt (Acting Editors), pp. 72 and 75. See also Louis Harris, "Harris Survey: Confidence is Carter's Problem," in <u>Chicago Tribune</u>, July 6, 1978, Section 3, page 4. It is interesting to note that of 1,523 adults surveyed nationwide, a majority of 51-to-35 percent feel that Jimmy Carter "does not inspire confidence as a President should." Yet, by a large majority of 83-to-9 percent, feel that the President "with all the problems he has, he is trying his best to do a good job."

35. John Maclean, "Why Carter is Blasting Soviets," in <u>Chicago Tribune</u>, June 4, 1978, Perspective, p. 1.

1
Changing Strategic Issues
Thomas A. Fabyanic

INTRODUCTION

Defense policy is the result of a complex interaction of domestic and international issues which cut across the spectrum of political, economic, and military affairs. The policy is formulated within a conceptual framework which derives primarily from institutional and individual perceptions found among the elected and appointed members of the executive leadership, bureaucratic groups including the military services, and Congressional Committees charged with specific dimensions of national security. Given the diverse interests of these groups, defense policy is formed by an evolutionary process characterized by debate and compromise, both of which can reflect varying degrees of misinformation, misperception, and parochial interests. The result, therefore, usually is a policy that is somewhat **less than precise, lacking in innovation, and without** a clear sense of purpose.[1]

Ideally, defense policy would establish a rational and feasible course of action to include both the objectives or aims of the policy and the means to attain them. But neither the ends nor

---

Disclaimer: The views contained herein are those of the author and not to be construed as representing the views, policy, or position of the Department of Defense, the United States Air Force, or any other governmental agency.
Author's Note: The author is indebted to Dr. Paul H.B. Godwin, Air University, for his assistance during the initial exploration of the analytical framework used in this chapter and for his subsequent critique of the draft.

means are subject to precise definition, since the former usually relate to a condition that is somewhat abstract and the latter to capabilities that, for the most part, are not easily quantified. In broad terms, the objective is always national security, a condition for which the definition must remain flexible once one goes beyond the notion of self-defense. Means vary, but usually they include various elements of national power, such as politico-economic or politico-military influence. However, given the fundamental alterations of power relationships that are occurring within the international system, it is now reasonably clear that the means formerly used by the Great Powers to attain national security objectives are becoming less efficacious.[2] As a result, the interrelationship between the aims of defense policy and the traditional means used to attain them has become an issue of overriding importance. In no area is this alteration more pronounced than in the use of military force as a means to attain the ends of defense policy.

The fundamental strategic issues, therefore, appear to be the interrelationships that exist between military force capability as a means of national power and the ends or aims of defense policy. Increasingly, analyses of these issues are made more complex due to the changing nature of deterrence as a central strategic concept. In the less complex bi-polar world of the recent past, deterrence based largely upon adversarial relationships functioned reasonably well. But in the emerging international system, characterized by nascent multipolarity and power diffusion, the adversarial orientation of deterrence may require a refocusing which takes into account the new perceptions held by aligned and nonaligned nation-state actors. Stated differently, the emerging task may be to continue adversarial deterrence, while simultaneously providing increased assurance to our allies and maintaining, at a minimum, the <u>status quo</u> with nonaligned nations. Given the current trends in the variables which are part of the strategic nuclear equation, existing concerns about conventional force capability, and developments which raise fundamental questions about the efficacy of power projection and intervention in the Third World, the ability to deter adversaries while concurrently assuring favorable perceptions by allies and nonaligned nation-states appears to be a formidable task indeed.

THE STRATEGIC NUCLEAR DIMENSION

The central strategic notion of the post-World War II period is that of deterrence, and it is instructive to note that technological influences are largely responsible for contemporary applications of the deterrence theory. Prior to the availability of nuclear weapons, a failure of deterrence most likely would result in a classical military struggle between the protagonists. That is, the immediate military objective of both sides would be the destruction of the opposing force, after which an attempt would be made to secure territorial, political, and economic objectives. But with the pre-World War II development of the strategic bomber, air-minded military strategists began to suggest that a decisive victory could be achieved by destroying the industrial means and political will of the adversary through a selective strategic bombing campaign which, for the most part, would bypass opposing military forces.[3] In the immediate post-World War II period, possession by the United States of the nuclear weapon and a proven means of delivery provided a degree of credibility to the notion of decisive victory through the use of strategic attack. Moreover, this strategic advantage by the United States made it possible to articulate a policy of Massive Retaliation, a policy that remained credible only so long as the United States held a unilateral advantage. Eventual development of a credible strategic nuclear capability by the Soviet Union, however, made Massive Retaliation a nonviable policy and restored the classical strategic situation by forcing the United States to deal with an opposing strategic force. Moreover, the conditions which forced a major modification of the strategic policy of the United States also led to a fundamental change in the concept of deterrence by adding a new characteristic of quasi-permanent competition in the strategic force balance.

Competitive Balance

For the most part, this characteristic of competitive balance is an outgrowth of the roughly equal technological competence which has been demonstrated by both sides in their strategic nuclear capabilities. A major consequence of this competitive balance has been the relatively minor but nonetheless frequent alteration of stated United States strategic nuclear policy since the demise of Massive Retaliation. There followed, in rather quick succession, the policies of Graduated Deterrence, Flexible Response, and Assured Destruction-Damage Limiting. Throughout the decade of the 1960s, these policies possessed operational rationality due to some measure of strategic offensive superiority by the United States. Eventually, however, the Soviet Union gradually matched and then exceeded the United States in certain static measurements of strategic nuclear capability. As often occurs in the force-counter-force equation that applies to all military force assessments, Soviet technological advances had altered the strategic relationship to such an extent that the United States found it necessary to reassess both its policy and force structure in order to retain a sense of strategic balance and hence the credibility of deterrence.[4]

The emerging United States strategic nuclear policy appeared to be an admixture of the previous Assured Destruction and Flexible Response policies. Then Secretary of Defense James R. Schlesinger made this clear in 1974 when he stated that "in order to protect American cities . . . we shall rely into the wartime period upon reserving our 'assured destruction' force and persuading . . . any potential foe not to attack cities." The other dimension of the Schlesinger policy established the need for flexibility in the strategic nuclear response options available to the National Command Authorities.[5] This latter modification in strategic nuclear policy reflected an attempt by the United States to use the technological advantage it possessed at the time to offset Soviet advances and to satisfy the credibility dimension of deterrence.

The criteria required to operationalize the flexibility aspect of the modified policy clearly identified the need for a technological edge. First, the United States needed to maintain a condition of essential equivalence, which Schlesinger defined as no major asymmetries in throwweight, accuracy, yield-to-weight ratios, and reliability. Second, the United States required a highly survivable force for targeting against the economic base of the Soviet Union. Third, a retaliatory force was needed, with some hard-target counterforce kill capability, that "could implement a variety of limited preplanned options and react rapidly to retargeting orders so as to deter any range of further attacks that a potential enemy might contemplate."[6]

The last of these criteria stood out as the

most important, since it implied United States acceptance of the classical strategic notion that one must plan to engage the opposing force once hostilities occur. Due to the element of competitive balance inherent in the strategic nuclear force structure development of both sides and the acceptance of classical strategic concepts by Soviet theoreticians,[7] it is reasonable to assume that the planned destruction of the opposing strategic force structure also became a logical objective for the Soviet Union. Both sides, therefore, appear to be engaged in continuous competition to improve their respective strategic force structure, the net result of which may be the mutual vulnerability of the silo-based intercontinental ballistic missile (ICBM). Should this occur, the consequences could be profound.

Technological Considerations

The essential technological factor is the reduction of circular error probability (CEP) of silo-launched ICBM systems. Given the formula of $K = Yield^{2/3}/CEP^2$, circular error probability becomes the critical dimension of offensive force capability. Existing trends would seem to suggest that the element of competitive balance is operative, since the CEP of silo-launched ICBMs held by both sides appears to be approaching zero.[8] This is of particular significance for the United States due to the relatively large ICBM throwweight advantage possessed by the Soviets. Basically, the formula $K = Y^{2/3}/CEP^2$ demonstrates that a 50% reduction in CEP equates to an eight-fold increase in yield. Thus, comparable accuracies would seemingly place the United States at some disadvantage, assuming a high order of overall Soviet system reliability.

Alternatives for the United States

Given the possible threat to the survivability of the silo-based ICBM, more obvious response options for the United States would be to (1) maintain the silo-based ICBM while improving its survivability through technological means and modifying the conditions under which it may be launched; (2) provide mobility to the land-based ICBM; (3) rely primarily on the retaliatory capability of a strategic dyad consisting of sea-launched ICBMs and air breathing weapons, such as manned bombers and cruise missiles; (4) or, perhaps, some combination of the above.

Regrettably, none of the foregoing may be particularly attractive, either from the standpoint of perceived war-fighting capability or the larger and more significant dimension of strategic nuclear deterrence. Stated briefly, the option to improve the survivability of the silo-based ICBM through hardening offers little advantage, since major improvements in hardening can be overcome by relatively slight increases in accuracy by the attacker.[9] The possibility of assuring survivability against a disarming first-strike by proclaiming launch tactics which would permit launch on warning or launch under attack appears to be out of the question for a number of reasons: first, it might lead to accidental war because only minutes are available to assess warning signals which could be false alarms; second, it leaves the National Command Authorities little option except a massive response to what in fact may be an accidental or unauthorized attack; third, and finally, it weakens the credibility of deterrence because those who understand American values would question the assumption that the United States would launch a nuclear strike without confirmation of an attack.[10] Likewise, the switch to a mobile configuration of land-based ICBMs would raise serious questions of verification, land availability, and costs.[11] There are equally realistic concerns about a dyad of sea-launched ICBMs and air breathing systems. The former, although it may appear to be the least vulnerable strategic system at present, does not offer the command and control efficiencies or the accuracy of the land-based ICBM and air breathing systems.[12] Air-launched cruise missiles (ALCM) appear to offer much potential in that their estimated accuracy is superior to the existing accuracy of the land-based ICBM,[13] their subsonic speeds do not raise the issue of first-strike capability, and large numbers can be launched from either stand-off or penetrating heavy bomber carriers. Nevertheless, they remain subject to formidable defensive systems and, like the mobile land-based ICBM, pose verification problems. Presently, an attractive mix includes three elements. First, the use of airborne carriers that do not penetrate enemy air-space to launch some cruise missiles. Second, the use of heavy bombers penetrating enemy air-space to launch cruise missiles. Third, concurrent attacks by penetrating heavy bombers.[14] This approach may serve as a complimentary third leg of the triad, but its credibility as part of a dyad consisting of the sea-launched ICBM would satisfy the adversarial deterrence requirement only if the Soviet Union followed suit.[15]

Although it may appear that these options and the choices they offer are of strategic significance, they in fact are merely tangential to the major issue of strategic consequence--the relationship of force structure to the attainment of national security objectives. The fundamental objective is to deter nuclear war, and force structures must be designed and employment strategies formulated with that end in mind. As has been the case during the entire history of the strategic nuclear balance, if the Soviets perceive that United States strategic forces provide a powerful and credible retaliatory capability for inflicting a decisive level of destruction on those elements of the Soviet Union that its leaders consider vital to the existence of Soviet society, it is logical to conclude that the Soviets will be deterred.

The "technical" vulnerability of the silo-based ICBM does not render it useless by any realistic means of measurement. The Soviet Union could not ignore the silo-based ICBM force, regardless of perceived vulnerability, and would be required to allocate a sizable percentage of Soviet capability against it. Moreover, the best Soviet efforts against the United States silo-based ICBM would not result in the elimination or total destruction of United States ICBMs, any calculations pertaining to its vulnerability notwithstanding. Practical operational limitations that apply to any military force employment and the conditions peculiar to nuclear weapons, such as fratricide, would suggest that technical vulnerability of the silo-based ICBM and its actual destruction are vastly different propositions.

Thus it appears that vulnerability of the silo-based ICBM need not alter the credibility of the deterrent nuclear force or disrupt existing superpower perceptions about the consequences of a nuclear exchange. In other words, we can continue to expect that nuclear war will be deterred. That is not to say, however, that technical vulnerability of the United States silo-based ICBM will not alter Soviet perceptions of relative superiority during conditions generally referred to as a crisis situation involving other nation-state actors.

SUPERPOWER CONFRONTATION

Aside from the question of deterring nuclear war, one must logically ask what effect the possible vulnerability of United States silo-based ICBMs will have on superpower confrontation focused on strategic issues in Europe, the Middle East, Africa, or East Asia. More specifically, if the Soviets appear, in the near future, to hold some measure of quantitative or qualitative nuclear superiority, is it possible that they may be tempted to exploit their perceived advantage in a regional crisis?

Unfortunately, the historical record does not make clear the extent to which some measure of perceived nuclear superiority can confer advantage in this type of crisis situation. For example, it can be argued that in the 1962 Cuban Missile Crisis, the Soviets were forced to acquiesce due to the preponderant strategic nuclear superiority of the United States and the threat by the President to employ it. On the other hand, it should be recognized that the Soviets attempted to place offensive missiles in Cuba despite the very obvious fact that the United States possessed an overwhelming degree of nuclear superiority. Thus it would seem that the value of superiority depends upon how meaningful it appears, at the time, to the decision maker and how that superiority is perceived by the other side.[16]

The overwhelming nuclear superiority possessed by the United States at the time of the Cuban Missile Crisis is, of course, gone. And what must be guarded against is drawing incorrect inferences in possible future crises, similar to the Cuban experience, wherein the United States may not appear to be successful. In such situations, the full range of operational conditions must become part of any analysis. For example, perhaps the Soviet decision to back down in the Cuban Missile Crisis is explained less by the existence of United States nuclear superiority at the time and more by the inability of the Soviets to logistically support the operation due to the distances involved and the relative lack of Soviet naval power in the Caribbean. Likewise, the Soviet threat to intervene in the Arab-Israeli War a decade later, by which time it had gained rough nuclear equivalence, may be explained best by the ability of the Soviets to project military power into an area not too distant from the Soviet border. Similarly, if one wishes to explain the confident nature of the decision by the United States in 1972 to blockade North Vietnamese harbors despite the presence of Soviet ships at anchor, one must look beyond the existence of rough strategic parity. What these situations might suggest is that the strategic nuclear balance is becoming quite separate and distinct from other types of crises, and that the existing competitive state of the balance and the marginal nature of any improvements may not be a transferable asset during regional confrontations.[17] Thus, any suggestion that one should make qualitative or quantitative improvements in the strategic nuclear balance to gain advantage in a regional crisis involving the superpowers should be subjected to a most rigorous analysis.

Essential Equivalence

One of the essential requirements for the United States is to assure that its nuclear force structure does not appear to be inferior to the perceived capability of Soviet nuclear force. Current American policy includes this criterion as part of a revised definition of essential equivalence. As stated earlier, the United States defined essential equivalence in 1974 as the absence of major asymmetries. However, possible recognition that the nonadversarial dimension of deterrence is of growing importance seems to have led to a new definition of essential equivalence. The current interpretation calls for the maintenance of conditions such that:

> Soviet strategic nuclear forces do not become usable instruments of political leverage, diplomatic coercion, or military advantage; nuclear stability, especially in a crisis, is maintained; any advantages in force characteristics enjoyed by the Soviets are offset by U.S. advantages in other characteristics; and the U.S. posture is not in fact, and is not seen as, inferior in performance to the strategic nuclear forces of the Soviet Union.[18]

This expanded definition of essential equivalence is obviously of greater political than military significance. It reminds one of President John F. Kennedy's comments after the Cuban Missile Crisis, that Soviet missiles in Cuba would not have altered the existing strategic nuclear balance of power. Nevertheless, he said, "It would have politically changed the balance of power. It would have appeared to, and appearances contribute to reality."[19] In today's international system, characterized by emerging multipolarity and power diffusion, such an assessment seems particularly appropriate. Moreover, what the late President said in terms of nuclear force deployments also applies with equal validity to force structure changes resulting from technological advances.

Allies and American Credibility

But, as has been suggested, one should not confuse the net effect that superpower force structure changes might have on their respective perceptions, with those perceptions that might be gleaned by allies and nonaligned nations from the same force structure changes. The nonnuclear allies of the United States are dependent upon the notion of extended deterrence for their security, and any technologically induced alteration of their perceptions of American nuclear perceptions vis-a-vis the Soviet Union could be quite damaging to the fundamental nature of the strategic nuclear balance. A sense of uncertainty or possible insecurity by nonnuclear allies raises the issue of nuclear proliferation in which the relevant factor is not technological competence but one of threat assessment. Should a number of American allies perceive that the United States strategic force structure lacks credibility against a common threat, then one must expect those allies to consider other defensive means at their disposal including the acquisition of some limited nuclear strike capability. Given the incalculable nature of nuclear power diffusion, it appears imperative, therefore, that one should not make any force structure changes that could possibly lead in that direction. The condition of superpower competitive nuclear balance, as perceived by the superpowers, requires both a real and imagined sense of parity between the two, but inherent in such a condition is the risk that nonnuclear allies may view this sense of strategic balance as strategic impotence. This new, Janus-like nature of current deterrence theory would suggest that, regardless of difficulty, one should develop a nuclear strategy and design a strategic nuclear force structure to deter nuclear war, while simultaneously assuring that such strategies and designs also give one's allies and those not allied the correct message.

THE MOST CRUCIAL DIMENSION: POWER PROJECTION AND INTERVENTION

The requirement to structure deterrent forces for contingents short of a major East-West crisis is perhaps the most challenging conventional strategic issue at present. These contingencies could occur in several areas where the United States logically can identify distinct vital interests, areas such as the Persian Gulf, the Middle East, and the Far East. After having identified its national security objectives in these and perhaps other similar areas, the task for the United States then would be to assure the formulation of military force structures theoretically sufficient to deter conventional conflict in these peripheral areas while concurrently maintaining an appropriate level of favorable perceptions with allies and those nations not aligned. The task is particularly complex because of the uncertainties about the deterrent effect of such forces, concerns about traditional United States power projection capabilities, and general limitations that presently seem to apply to military intervention as a concept.

Power Projection and Intervention

Briefly, one can define power projection as means whereby a nation employs appropriate levels of military force over some distance to advance political objectives:

> ...by supporting friends and clients, by coercing enemies, by neutralizing similar activities by other naval powers, by exerting a more diffuse influence in politically ambiguous situations in which even one's own objection may be uncertain, or merely by advertising one's . . . power or "showing the flag."[20]

By contrast, intervention usually is defined as the use of limited armed force in the internal affairs of another nation for the "defense of some concept of ideal political order as conceived by the intervener."[21] Traditionally, the United States has used its naval surface forces to project power, but increasingly, both land-based and carrier-based airpower is used as the means. Intervention, on the other hand, usually requires some form of ground combat force which can be deployed and inserted by either surface ships or aircraft.

Naval Forces

The structuring of naval forces to advance political objectives is particularly difficult at present for a number of reasons, perhaps the most important of which is the uncertainties that exist about the dominant military operational conditions under which naval forces may operate. The threat posed to naval surface forces by a combination of effective reconnaissance systems, surface and subsurface systems armed with precision guided weapons, and land-based aircraft with stand-off attack capability, is most formidable. As a consequence, the design of United States naval force structures and weapon systems have tended to focus more on means or capability against another naval force rather than the political objective or aim of naval force employment. Indeed, for a number of years the United States has tended to assess its naval force structure needs on a "worldwide war at sea with the Soviet Union, concurrent with a NATO war,"[22] rather than the force structure needed for power projection or intervention. As a result, a qualitatively superior United States force may exist when the need appears to be shifting to a force with quantitative advantage.[23] One might assume that a force structure designed for a war at sea with the Soviet Union could be employed effectively for the power projection or intervention roles, but such an assumption would ignore the trade-offs that occur in quantity and quality in force structure design. Sophisticated qualitative capability requires enormous budget expenditures, and consequently, force structures designed for effective employment in high threat environments are produced in relatively limited numbers. A quantitatively limited force structure may not pose a problem for power projection or intervention, provided the contingencies occur but one at a time; simultaneous contingencies, however, may overextend the force.

A crucial dimension for consideration in the design of naval force structures for power projection or intervention is the threat that one expects to face. If it can be demonstrated that the expected Soviet seapower challenge to American power projection or intervention capabilities might be roughly comparable to those existing in a "worldwide war at sea," then a high order of quality would appear essential for the emerging United States force structure. But, if the Soviet threat is limited in those contingencies wherein United States power projection or intervention may occur, then American force structure design might more profitably reflect the quantitative over the qualitative dimension.

It can be demonstrated that the Soviet Navy has grown in size and effectiveness in recent years, and it is possible that high naval-shipbuilding rates will continue. Moreover, it is likely that Soviet combat seapower will be improved in various ways, such as continued construction of the 40,000 ton <u>Kiev</u> class antisubmarine warfare (ASW) carrier,* which is equipped with relatively short ranged vertical take-off and landing (VTOL) aircraft, and acquisition of a naval version of the Backfire bomber, equipped with an air-to-surface missile, which is expected to reach an operating strength of about 90-100 in the next few years.[24]

It does not automatically follow, however, that these and other capability improvements are detriments to American power projection and intervention capabilities. Serious deficiencies, such as limited underway replenishment capability and lack of ordnance reload capability suggest that the Soviet Navy might be at a disadvantage in a conflict with the United States Navy in those areas where additional Soviet support could not be provided by land-based air forces.[25] Moreover, the preponderance of evidence seems to suggest that the majority of Soviet improvement efforts are directly related to the requirements for strategic nuclear deterrence and, to a lesser extent, are designed to assure open sea lines of communication to the Far East in the event of Sino-Soviet war.[26] In addition to these war related tasks, the Soviet Navy apparently is charged with the peacetime mission of "countering imperialist aggression," the objective of which is to challenge United States intervention in situations involving "progressive states" and "national liberation movements." But the political commit-

---

*The Soviets define this vessel as an ASW "cruiser," but its flight deck configuration and operational capabilities would classify it as an aircraft carrier.

ment of the Soviets to this latter peacetime mission seems to be low, or at least uncertain, given the obvious importance attached to the wartime mission of strategic nuclear deterrence.27

By contrast, the United States traditionally has employed its naval forces in power projection or intervention roles, but it appears that the results have been less than optimum when contrasted with the use of other types of armed force. In the post-World War II period, United States naval forces have participated in more than 80 percent of all incidents involving the use of force, but analysis suggests that such forces were least successful in terms of securing a favorable outcome for the United States.28 Moreover, the more recent acquisition of sophisticated precision guided munitions by lower developed states provides those states with some capability "to defend themselves against external intervention and, in several cases, to prevent use of their coastal seas."29 These technologically advanced surface-to-surface systems have been provided by the Soviet Union, France, and other powers, but given the adage that "missiles don't know their mums," this growing diffusion of military capabilities raises further questions about the effective use of naval forces for power projection or intervention in hostile situations.

Nevertheless, if it can be assumed that United States naval forces can be reoriented for greater efficiencies in the power projection and intervention roles on the basis of limited Soviet naval challenges, then the question returns to the issue of perceptions. A powerful United States Navy, designed to fight a "worldwide war at sea with the Soviet Union" would most likely create strong impressions for any and all observers, and any reduction of that force capability must be weighed carefully in terms of adversarial and allied perceptions. If the Soviet Navy is not assigned a primary operational mission of denying American access in certain geographical areas or preventing American power projection or intervention, then it is difficult to conclude that any reduction of United States capability would materially alter Soviet perceptions. On the other hand, if American allies and nonaligned nation states presume that the Soviets commit part of their force structure to the denial of United States use of the sea lanes of communication and the prevention of power projection by the United States, then any meaningful reduction in United States capability could have serious consequences.

Air Power

To a certain extent, the use of airpower for power projection and intervention raises some of the same force structure questions that apply to naval forces used in a similar manner. For the most part, the elements of airpower used for power projection or intervention are those that would be used in direct combat with the Warsaw Pact in a NATO war. Given the highly sophisticated nature of such a war, the quantitative and qualitative factors mentioned earlier apply, that is, there may exist a qualitatively superior force structure for a NATO war, but one that reflects definite quantitative limits for power projection or intervention. Moreover, the extent to which a qualitatively superior air force capability is necessary or desirable for power projection or intervention is a most appropriate question. Once again, the need for qualitative superiority is a function of the expected threat, and in this regard the Soviet threat appears less than obvious.

Although the evidence does not suggest that the Soviet air forces have been forward deployed to the same extent as the Soviet Navy, the Soviet Union's strategic airlift capability is a matter of concern when one considers power projection or intervention contingencies. The strategic airlift capability demonstrated by the Soviets in the Arab-Israeli War of 1973 and their deployment of Cuban forces to Africa more recently are impressive, and they reflect a substantial improvement in Soviet airlift capability over the past decade.[30]

Nevertheless, it appears that certain dimensions of United States strategic airlift capability are unmatched by the Soviets. The range and cargo carrying capacity of Soviet strategic aircraft are far less than their American counterparts, and even the latest Soviet strategic lift aircraft, the IL 76, is not as capable as the C-5A of the United States Air Force.[31] The United States not only has the ability to deploy ground combat forces via strategic airlift, but it has demonstrated the capability to deploy air combat strike forces from the United States to Europe, the Far East, and the Middle East during crisis situations; moreover, the United States routinely accomplishes similar deployments of combat air units on a scheduled basis. The Soviet Union, by contrast, apparently has not deployed air combat units in conjunction with its strategic airlift efforts, nor does its force structure seem to possess any significant capability of that nature.[32]

Notwithstanding this apparent superior dimension of United States strategic airlift and force deployment capability, it must be recognized that the force has its operational limits. As is the case with naval forces used for power projection or intervention, should more than one contingency occur at a time, the strategic airlift forces could find themselves stretched very thin indeed. Moreover, power projection and intervention by air is not without attendant problems.

Deployments of forces by air over any great distances usually require the use of forward basing for staging and refueling. But the availability of such bases should not be taken for granted, since in some cases they might not exist or may be denied.[33] Moreover, long-range deployments by air do not permit the vast amounts of cargo that can be deployed by sea, and extended deployments of virtually any moderately-sized force would require eventual resupply by surface craft.

On balance, however, the United States would appear to have the edge in terms of conventional force deployment by air for the purpose of power projection or intervention, and planned improvements in strategic airlift capability would suggest that the United States advantage can be maintained. Currently, the United States is capable of augmenting forces in NATO Europe with slightly more than one division and 40 tactical fighter squadrons within a 10-day period, but the goal for 1983 is "five divisions and 60 tactical fighter squadrons in the same amount of time."[34] Of necessity, some of that deployment would be accomplished by airlift to meet the 10-day requirement. Granted, this enhanced airlift is needed to add credibility to the NATO conventional deterrent, particularly in view of the recent Soviet buildup in Central Europe. Yet, on the other hand, it must be recognized that strategic airlift deployment capability need not be restricted to NATO augmentation. Any enhancement of strategic airlift capability for use in support of NATO Europe is also an improvement in United States airlift capability to the Persian Gulf, the Middle East, the Far East, and elsewhere, a point not likely to be missed by the Soviet Union and others as well.

Effectiveness of Deterrence Strategy

But the existence of some power projection forces and their ability to serve in a deterrent role are entirely different issues. In a theoretical sense, the overall assumptions inherent in the deterrence concept does suggest that deterrence is possible at the level of conflict where power projection or intervention forces are used. The existence and capability of such forces simply must contribute to the process that alters the political calculus of the potential adversary in such a way that the perceived risks appear to exceed the possible benefits. The question then becomes one of focus, that is, whom does the United States wish to deter at this level of conflict? Given the hypothesis presented earlier, that the Soviets place a lower priority on power projection or intervention, perhaps the thrust of a United States deterrent capability should be directed less at the Soviets and more at their allies and surrogates. This suggests, of course, that the Soviets are faced with the problem of exercising control over their allies and at times are reluctant partners in certain regional confrontations. Indeed, some evidence does exist to support this argument. For example, prior to the Sino-Soviet split, the Soviets gave indications to the People's Republic of China on two different occasions that the Soviets would not support attempts to remove the Chinese Nationalists from the off-shore islands of Quemoy and Matsu.[35] Although the Soviets were successful in these instances, there are other situations wherein it appears that the Soviets were unable to restrain an ally. Prior to the Arab-Israeli War of 1973, for example, the evidence suggests that the Soviets attempted to discourage the Egyptians by denying the latter's persistent request for additional military equipment. The Soviets perhaps became involved, therefore, only after their ally had initiated hostilities, at which time the Soviets had little choice.[36]

It may well be, therefore, that the general lack of favorable deterrent outcomes for the United States at those levels where power projection forces are employed may stem primarily from the inability of the United States to identify who must be deterred. If there exists little or no need to deter the Soviets at this level, then no effort in this direction seems warranted. If, however, there are nation-state actors that should be deterred to assure some measure of order in the international system, then it might be prudent for the United States to design some of its conventional force structure specifically for the purpose of deterrence and, should they not deter, their possible employment.

Indeed, there is empirical evidence to demonstrate that armed force can be effectively employed as a political instrument for relatively modest and comparatively short-term gains.[37] However, legal proscriptions pertaining to the use of American military forces outside of the continental United States place severe time restrictions on force employment before congressional approval must be obtained. This would suggest the necessity of effective power projection and intervention capability to conduct a controlled, discrete, and swift employment phase of operations in order to achieve a desired political outcome.

Political Objectives and Military Capability

Of crucial importance in such operations would be the political objectives, for they must be within the military capabilities of the force. The classical employment of armed force in power projection or intervention roles either has been to effect a change or modification in behavior through coercion or to provide support for the actions of a given state, and thus far the record tends to suggest that favorable outcomes are more likely in the latter case. Moreover, the evidence seems to suggest that "favorable outcomes" usually are little more than the buying of time, during which the political process could assert itself.[38]

But the traditional patterns of military force employment for power projection or intervention may be changing, as they have for strategic nuclear forces whose greatest utility remains in their nonuse. Those nation-states with which the United States may find itself involved in the Persian Gulf, Middle East, and elsewhere, are not the relatively weak and largely defenseless nations that composed the Third World sector of the international system in the recent past, but rather they are reasonably wealthy, developing states with substantial and growing military capability. In many instances certain measures of their military capability are the qualitative equal to the sophisticated weapons in the arsenals of the superpowers.

Given the changing nature of arms transfers in regions such as the Middle East, where the United States is becoming a major supplier to both sides, future hostilities there would likely result in a clash of arms less representative of Soviet weapon systems, and a conflict more closely mirroring the United States weapons inventory. Under such circumstances (and Soviet intervention notwithstanding), it undoubtedly would be in the best interest of the United States to possess military forces which could intervene swiftly for the primary purpose of controlling, deescalating, or terminating the conflict. Indeed, it is entirely possible that, aside from the long-term consequences of another Middle East War, the destructiveness and intensity of modern combat might leave both sides militarily denuded, without the means of legitimate self-defense or, perhaps, the resources to acquire them.

The nature of a new Middle East conflict, or one similar to it, might therefore suggest that it is in the best interest of the United States Armed Forces to concentrate less on the traditional power projection and intervention roles and more on the emerging nature of these military employment tasks. The notion offered here is that military concepts of employment and the design of force structures for use in power projection or intervention might well possess more functional utility if their primary mission became one of escalation control or conflict termination.

Current service doctrine, however, pays scant attention to such nontraditional employment concepts. The United States Navy, although it does not possess a specific, written doctrine of employment, states that its primary functions are sea control and power projection and thus apparently ignores the possibility of nontraditional use of its force. The latest doctrinal expression of the United States Army, likewise, stresses the traditional concept of fighting to win the land battle and does not suggest the notions of deescalation or conflict termination. Only the United States Air Force, in its basic doctrine, states that one of the fundamental objectives of military force is to "resolve conflict . . . (and to) quickly and effectively end hostilities. . . ."[39] This general lack of conceptual employment expression would suggest that little actual capability is available for the nontraditional roles, since existing force structures are designed for employment concepts that are compatible with the expressed doctrine.

Thus it would appear that one of the most pressing issues relating to conventional forces is the question of force employment objectives. If conventional forces are to be used in the traditional power projection and intervention roles, then existing employment concepts may suffice with only minor alterations to reflect technological changes in force capability. If, however, the future modes of employment are to reflect the notions of deescalation and conflict termination, then both the concepts of employment and the supporting force structure might need to undergo radical transformation.

CONCLUSIONS

The concept of strategic nuclear deterrence appears to have undergone somewhat of an evolutionary change in that it now functions in an environment best characterized as a competitive strategic balance between the superpowers. This competitive balance, based for the most part on fundamental technological equivalence, may soon lead to a condition in which at least some of the strategic nuclear offensive systems are mutually vulnerable. Such a condition would clearly distinguish between the deterrent and warfighting functions of strategic nuclear systems and would bolster the former at the superpower level. However, the vulnerability of strategic nuclear systems raises an equally important question of perceptions held by nonnuclear allies. They must not view the new competitive strategic balance as mutual impotence, and strategic nuclear force structures must be designed with that end in mind. Otherwise, the possibility exists that the most serious future threat to the superpowers may not be each other, but it may be their respective nonnuclear allies, should such allies be tempted to seek independent strategic nuclear capabilities.

More realistically, the most pressing strategic issues seems to be the possibility of East-West confrontations in the peripheral areas. The articulated policy in this regard is of crucial importance, since existing trends seem to suggest that these are the most likely contingencies. The dangers, however, are multiple. It appears that either the concept of deterrence that applies elsewhere is operative at the margins, or that it is tested more frequently at the margins; thus, it may well be that force structure capability for power projection or intervention must in fact exist if it is perceived that United States interests would require their use. The assumption that those force structures designed for highly sophisticated East-West confrontations in the central areas are equally well suited for employment in power projection or intervention roles must undergo rigorous analysis. And, moreover, it would appear imprudent to assume that existing military employment concepts are appropriate for future power projection or intervention roles.

Thus the primary need appears to be one of strategic direction. Concepts such as deterrence and coercive diplomacy are not easily assimilated by military professionals charged with the responsibility to operationalize such concepts. Should power projection or intervention become the dominant dimension of military force employment in the immediate future, then it would be essential to understand how the political aims of power projection or intervention might differ from conventional force employment concepts. Otherwise, the force structures intended to deter at the conventional level in NATO Europe are those most likely to be employed for the purposes of power projection or intervention, and it is not certain that the objectives in the latter case would be consistent with the inherent capability of the force.

NOTES

1. Samuel P. Huntington, The Common Defense (New York: Columbia University Press, 1961), p. 123.

2. Robert L. Pfaltzgraff, Jr., "Emerging Major Power Relationships," Air University Review 28 (March-April 1977), pp. 7-15; Stanley Kaufmann, "The Acceptability of Military Force" in Force in Modern Societies: Its Place in International Politics, Adelphi Paper No. 102 (London: International Institute for Strategic Studies, 1973), pp. 4-7; David C. Gompert, "Constraints of Military Power: Lessons of the Past Decade," in The Diffusion of Power: I: Proliferation of Force, Adelphi Paper No. 133 (London: International Institute for Strategic Studies, 1976), pp. 1-13.

3. See for example, Major General Haywood S. Hansell, Jr., USAF (Retired), The Air War Plan That

Defeated Hitler (Atlanta: Higgins-McArthur/Longino and Porter, Inc., 1972). These views notwithstanding, it appears that defeat of the opposing force remained an essential element for military success in World War II. See for example, Noble Frankland, "The Combined Bomber Offensive: Classical and Revolutionary, Combined and Divided, Planned and Fortuitous," Command and Commanders in Modern Military History (Washington: Government Printing Office, n.d.), pp. 253-267.

4. U.S. Department of Defense, Annual Defense Department Report: FY 1975, pp. 3-5.

5. Ibid., pp. 4-5.

6. U.S. Department of Defense, Annual Defense Department Report: FY 1976 and FY 1977, pp. 1-13.

7. V. D. Sokolovskiy, Soviet Military Strategy, trans. Harriet Fast Scott (New York: Crane, Russak and Company, Inc., 1975), pp. 276-290.

8. Colin S. Gray, The Future of Land-Based Missiles, Adelphi Paper No. 140 (London: International Institute for Strategic Studies, 1977), pp. 4-5 and 32-33; Clarence A. Robinson, Jr., "Soviets Boost ICBM Accuracy," Aviation Week and Space Technology, 3 April 1978, pp. 14-15; David G. Hoag, "Strategic Ballistic Missile Guidance--A Story of Even Greater Accuracy," Aeronautics and Astronautics, May 1978, pp. 28-39.

9. Gray, pp. 17-18.

10. U.S., Congress, Senate, Committee on Armed Services, Authorization for Military Procurement, Research and Development, Fiscal Year 1971, and Reserve Strength, Hearings, Part 3, 91st Cong., 2d sess, 1971, pp. 2278-2282.

11. U.S. Department of Defense, Annual Report: Fiscal Year 1979, p. 107.

12. Gray, pp. 9-10; Hoag, pp. 32-33.

13. Gray, p. 32.

14. Annual Report, Fiscal Year 1979, p. 114.

15. For further discussion see Jacquelyn K. Davis,

"End of the Strategic Triad?" *Strategic Review* 6 (Winter 1978), pp. 36-44.

16. For further discussion see Glenn H. Snyder and Paul Diesing, *Conflict Among Nations* (Princeton: Princeton University Press, 1977), pp. 459-462.

17. Hannes Adomeit, *Soviet Risk-Taking and Crisis Behavior: From Confrontation to Coexistence?* Adelphi Paper No. 101 (London: International Institute for Strategic Studies, 1973), pp. 34-37.

18. *Annual Report, Fiscal Year 1979*, pp. 5-6, 56-57.

19. Quoted in Snyder and Deising, p. 461.

20. Hedley Bull, "Sea Power and Political Influence," in *Power at Sea, I, The New Environment*, Adelphi Paper No. 122 (London: International Institute for Strategic Studies, 1976), p. 5.

21. Urs Schwarz, "Great Power Intervention in the Modern World," *Problems of Modern Strategy* (New York: Praeger, 1970), pp. 176-177.

22. *Annual Report, Fiscal Year 1979*, p. 164.

23. James A. Nathan and James K. Oliver, "The Evolution of International Order and the Future of the American Naval Presence Mission," *Naval War College Review* 30 (Fall 1977), pp. 45-46.

24. Worth H. Bagley, *Sea Power and Western Security: The Next Decade*, Adelphi Paper No. 139 (London: International Institute for Strategic Studies, 1977), pp. 35-36.

25. U.S., Congress, Congressional Budget Office, *U.S. Projection Forces: Requirements, Scenarios, and Options* (Washington: Government Printing Office, 1978), p. 57.

26. Michael MccGwire, "Changing Naval Operations and Military Intervention," *The Limits of Military Intervention* (Beverly Hills: Sage Publications, Inc., 1977), p. 170; Eric Morris, *The Russian Navy* (New York: Stern and Day, 1977), p. 126.

27. MccGwire, pp. 171-172.

28. Barry M. Blechman and Stephen S. Kaplan, <u>The Use of the Armed Forces as a Political Instrument</u> (Executive Summary) (Washington: The Brookings Institution, n.d.), pp. 11-12.

29. MccGwire, p. 159.

30. <u>Annual Report, Fiscal Year 1979</u>, p. 75. There is some evidence to suggest that the Soviets have airlifted approximately 60,000 tons of military hardware to Africa over a 7-month period ending May 1978. (<u>Foreign Report</u> 7 June 1978, pp. 1-3) By contrast, the United States Air Force during the 1973 Arab-Israeli War airlifted, over much greater distances, approximately 22,000 tons in one month; moreover, the United States Air Force never committed more than 24 percent of its aircraft on any given day. (Comptroller General of the United States, <u>Airlift Operations of the Military Airlift Command during the 1973 Middle East War</u> (Washington: Government Printing Office, 1974), pp. 8, 16).

31. John W.R. Taylor, ed., <u>Jane's All the World's Aircraft</u> (London: 1977/78), pp. 338-339, 435-436.

32. There is evidence that Soviet pilots and aircraft flew air defense missions to protect Cairo in 1970, but it is not certain that Soviet units were involved. See Kenneth R. Whiting, <u>The Development of the Soviet Armed Forces, 1917-1977</u> (Maxwell Air Force Base, Alabama: Air University, 1977), p. 108.

33. <u>Annual Report, Fiscal Year 1979</u>, p. 230.

34. <u>Ibid.</u>, p. 7.

35. Paul H.B. Godwin, <u>Doctrine, Strategy Ethic: The Modernization of the Chinese People's Liberation Army</u> (Maxwell Air Force Base, Alabama, 1977), p. 31.

36. Galia Golan, <u>Yom Kippur and After</u> (London: Cambridge University Press, 1977), pp. 44-56, 63-73.

37. Blechman, pp. 8, 14-15.

38. <u>Ibid.</u>, p. 7-8.

39. Draft Air Force Manual 1-1, <u>Functions and Basic Doctrine of the United States Air Force</u> (Washington, 1978), pp. 1-6.

2
The President and the National Security Apparatus

Vincent Davis

INTRODUCTION

One of the first problems in examining roles, structures, processes and bureaucratic behaviors within that part of the U.S. government engaged in making foreign policy and defense policy is that little is known about these bureaucracies (notice the plural "bureaucracies") or anybody else's bureaucracies. Why is this? Why don't we know more, particularly about our own U.S. bureaucracies?

There are doubtless several explanations. For one thing, bureaucracies are not easy to study. They generally don't like to be studied. Of course very few individuals and groups like to be studied by behavioral scientists--perhaps this is Behavioral Science Law No. 1. Therefore, the cost of studying bureaucracies is fairly high, and scholars are not often able to find the money or to commit the time required--at least, the money and time required to do it right. Research blind alleys are especially acute problems in research on bureaucracies, and most scholars prefer not to begin work without considerable assurance of research "success." If military officers have a bias in favor of "military victory," then scholars have a bias in favor of "research victory," which initially requires being very well funded before starting. Also, it is not always easy to publish studies on bureaucracies, especially since the early 1960s when the new fashion for computer-assisted research at macro-systems levels made it very unfashionable to do case-study work at the nitty-gritty level of bureaucracies.

One can observe another curious set of circumstances that may help to explain why we know as little as we do about bureaucracies, if we look at some of the history of scholarly research in the foreign policy and defense policy subfields of the international politics field in the United States since World War II. We can divide the research scholarship in these related policy subfields into two general categories.

First, is the "looking at them" research, which focuses on some one or more foreign nations, often those nations that have come to be regarded as enemies, and sometimes in the context of us-them interactions, but very seldom including much attention to the internal bureaucratic decision-making activities of either us or them in relation to policy outputs. As a shorthand expression, this is labelled "strategy" research, for it is ordinarily substantive in nature and appears almost always aimed at influencing U.S. national strategies and policies.

Second, is the "looking at us" research, which is a scholarly effort to unravel the mysteries of our bureaucratic decision-making processes, presumptively as a device for understanding why resulting policies are what they are, and often as a slightly disguised device for suggesting that a change in structures and/or processes would result in "better" policies. Unfortunately, the crucial link between specific structures and/or processes on the one hand, and specific policy outputs on the other hand, is almost never spelled out--at least, not in any persuasive fashion.

Other dimensions of this situation become apparent if we examine the four major U.S. presidential elections since World War II which included a switch in party control of the White House: 1952, 1960, 1968 and 1976. In each case, great dissatisfaction with foreign and military policies seemed to be a major, if not the major, issue accounting for the switch. The interesting point is that in each of these four time periods surrounding or immediately before these four national elections, there was an upsurge in scholarly research on bureaucratic decision-making for foreign and defense policies. However, over the long periods between these major national elections, the "looking at them" or the "looking at them-us" interactions, strategic focus seemed to dominate academic work in these policy subfields. Scholar-strategists such as Herman Kahn and Henry Kissinger, for example, seemed to emerge in that between-elections period in the mid-1950s.

"Looking at Us" Syndrome

The kinds of literature that were published around the 1952, 1960, 1968 and 1976 election periods reflected a "looking at us" focus. As Eisenhower was getting elected and inaugurated while promising to go to Korea to end the war in the period 1952-53, Richard C. Snyder and his colleagues H.W. Bruck and Burton Sapin were producing "the granddaddy" of our post-World War II literature utilizing the "looking at us" bureaucratic focus. This work resulted in the famous Snyder-Bruck-Sapin monograph eventually published in 1954.[1]

Around 1960-61, as Kahn and Kissinger and their fellow strategists had become the new superstar scholars for their work in the mid-1950s while the Snyder-Bruck-Sapin monograph was gathering dust, there was again a sudden upsurge in the "looking at us" bureaucratic decision-making literature. For example, Richard Neustadt's acclaimed <u>Presidential Power</u> was published in January 1961 just in time to become the so-called "bible" of the new Kennedy administration.[2] Also, in 1961, Samuel Huntington published <u>The Common Defense</u>[3] and Paul Hammond produced <u>Organizing for Defense</u>.[4] The Jackson Subcommittee research papers, many of which were written by prominent scholars, emerged from the U.S. Senate during this same period, with a focus primarily on these same questions of government organization for foreign and defense policymaking. Demetrios "Jim" Caraley initiated research leading to his later book <u>The Politics of Military Unification</u>,[5] and I was starting my own research on the Navy's bureaucracies which led to later books.[6] Finally, Morton Halperin at the same time was writing his doctoral dissertation analyzing the way in which the U.S. governmental bureaucracies in the foreign and defense policy fields had evolved their ideas about limited war in the earlier period of hostilities in Korea.[7]

The evolution of Halperin's work provides a good example of how quickly the "looking at us" emphasis on bureaucratic decision-making tends to shift back to the prevailing stress on "looking at them" strategy research following the major presidential election periods noted here. Halperin's 1963 book on limited war, although incorporating some of his 1960-61 work on decision-making, focused more on strategic issues than on bureaucratic matters. Halperin's shift away from bureaucratic studies to his new emphasis on strategy studies was complete as of his China and the Bomb, Contemporary Military Strategy,[8] his essay (with co-author Tang Tsou) "United States Policy Toward the Offshore Islands,"[9] and in Public Policy yearbook. Halperin capped this emphasis with his Defense Strategies for the Seventies.[10] But then, several years after Halperin had completed his White House service with his erstwhile friend and colleague Henry Kissinger, he came full circle in his own work and wrote Bureaucratic Politics and Foreign Policy.[11]

In the mid-1960s after the flurry of books on bureaucratic organizational and decision-making matters around the 1960 election period, Thomas C. Schelling's The Strategy of Conflict, although published in 1960 [12] did not gain much attention until the middle of that decade when it became probably the most respected and talked about book among foreign policy and military policy scholars. Thus, by the mid-decade Schelling, and also once again, Kissinger, were the super stars from Harvard while Huntington was momentarily reduced to being admired in a place like the University of Chicago where sociologist Morris Janowitz was the leader of a little group called the Inter-University Seminar on Armed Forces and Society.

By 1968-69, as the White House was once again changing hands from one party to the other, accompanied by great public dissatisfaction over foreign and military policy matters, a new upsurge of scholarly research on bureaucratic decision-making in such policy areas was developing. Raymond Tanter, always theretofore a dedicated practitioner of research at macro-systems levels based on computerized data considered doing a case study looking at the international bureaucratic factors in foreign policy decision-making.[13] Charles F. Hermann, a talented younger scholar coming into the limelight at that time, sought to develop simulation models based on bureaucratic decision-making in foreign policy and military policy crises.[14] Robert J. Art was producing his book on the TFX decision,[15] and Lawrence Korb was starting his research on the Joint Chiefs of Staff,[16] while Harvey Sapolsky was writing his case study on the development of Polaris.[17]

Perhaps the most acclaimed of the new younger scholars in academic life who were writing on bureaucratic decision-making in the context of foreign policy and defense policy during the 1968-69 major presidential election period was Graham Allison. He designed three conceptual models from five cases of bureaucratic decision-making (although primarily the case of the Cuban missile crisis of 1962), and published all of this research in a doctoral dissertation, a paper for the 1968 annual convention of the American Political Science Association, a monographic publication from the RAND Corporation, an article entitled "Conceptual Models and the Cuban Missile Crisis," a book, and later in an essay that he co-authored with Morton Halperin for a special book-type supplement to World Politics,[18] as well as perhaps in some other places that have escaped my attention.

Younger scholars were not the only ones demonstrating the upsurge of research and writing on organizational and bureaucratic issues in the context of foreign and defense policies during the 1968-69 presidential election and transition period. Stanley Hoffmann entered the lists,[19] and I was summoned back to work on matters of this kind.[20]

The 1971-73 presidential election period did not include a transition because it did not bring a switch in party control of the White House, but it did certainly feature a spirited contest that occasioned high hopes in many scholarly circles for such a switch. Accordingly, among those who held those hopes, and perhaps among others who had hoped for some changes in structures and processes even in case of the re-election of the incumbent, there was again a bull market for research and writing on bureaucratic decision-making and organizational matters in the context of foreign and defense policies.[21]

The 1976-77 presidential election and transition period served as the next occasion for an outburst of publications on bureaucratic decision-making and related organizational matters in the context of foreign and defense policies. Most of these derived in one way or another from papers prepared in connection with the work of the Commission on the Organization of the Government for the Conduct of Foreign Policy--more generally known as the Murphy Commission because it was chaired by former Ambassador Robert D. Murphy.[22] Perhaps the Commission by-product that attracted the most attention--in part because it made an effort to be the most comprehensive--was the full-length book by Graham Allison and Peter Szanton, Remaking Foreign Policy: The Organizational Connection.[23]

Conclusions

What can be concluded from this brief review of the intellectual history of a sector of the U.S. scholarly enterprise since World War II? For one thing, and tangentially, it seems to take one political party about eight years to make such a mess of foreign and defense policies that the people turn to the other party in desperation.[24] Second, and more relevantly here, the scholars who work this corner of the academic vineyard seldom stray very far from the daily headlines--partly, if not entirely, because it is the public concern reflected in the news that creates support resources and publications outlets for this kind of work.

Third, this historical review suggests that scholars in the "looking at us" category who focus on bureaucratic decision-making and related organizational issues in the context of foreign and defense policies are no less eager than those in the "looking at them" category of strategic analysts to join the U.S. government in positions of some note and distinction. At least, it can be observed that many of those mentioned here have accepted such positions, or have been reliably reported at various times to have been enthusiastically interested in such opportunities.

Fourth, these scholars--like most Americans--have a limited concern about bureaucracy and decision-making, about structures and processes, as long as things ssem to be going reasonably well in U.S. foreign relations, but become very concerned about these organizational questions primarily when things do not seem to be going all that well.

Fifth, and related to this fourth point, these scholars--again like many if not most Americans--seem to feel that policy problems are the consequence of defective structures and processes and other organizational deficiencies, not so much the consequence of inadequate people. So, during those major times of presidential elections and transitions, at roughly eight year intervals for most of the period following World War II, many Americans, including many scholars, have joined in looking at structures, processes, and bureaucratic questions in general in proposing organizational reforms. However, if and when policy seems to be going pretty well again, or if and when a new administration has settled down and there appears to be no possibility for significant reforms until another major presidential election period, these proposals for organizational reforms are shelved and we turn to other policy preoccupations--usually back to the "looking at them" emphasis.

Sixth, and most importantly, most scholars have never come anywhere close to doing what Allison and Szanton suggested in the subtitle of their 1976 book that they did. They called it The Organizational Connection, but this is what scholars have not established. We do not have the foggiest notion what might be some systematic causal relationships between process machinery on the one hand, and policy output on the other. Most tend to assume that there is some kind of basic key relationship between the sausage grinder and the sausage, but we have never empirically demonstrated it.

We do know a few minor things. For example, we sort of know, from Allison's work, some of the fairly probable implications of a rigid use of his Models I, II, and III, except that we hardly ever find one of these rigidly and purely used. Perhaps the most important thing that scholars rediscovered in Allison's work is that answers depend largely on the questions asked. We know for example what a military innovator is likely to look like, if one emerges, but are unable to say exactly under what circumstances one is likely to emerge in the first place, or how likely he is to be successful if he does emerge.[25]

In the main, our bureaucratic and decision-making studies have failed systematically to classify and utilize situational variables and issue-specific variables. The only situational variable that has received significant attention is the crisis situation, but this has not got us very far for two reasons. First, there are extraordinarily gross distinctions between a crisis and everything else which is thus residually regarded as a non-crisis. Second, much if not most of what happens in foreign policy and military policy is in the non-crisis context.

Our models are far too gross. Almost all of them are verbal models. None is precisely and elegantly subject to mathematical manipulation. We lack possibilities for empirical testing with the use of control groups, or at least we have not yet invented any such situations. We write as if all bureaucracies are mainly the same--a homogeneous set of entities. Our apparent belief is something like, "If you've seen one bureaucracy, you've seen 'em all." But there are in Washington, just within the foreign policy and defense policy community, many bureaucracies, widely varying in size, in budgets, in missions, in needs and requirements, in linkages to other entities in Washington, in linkages to grassroots America, in history, and in tribal characteristics. There are also ad hoc alliances that cut across the formal bureaucracies, but we know next to nothing about why and how these form and operate and dissolve and sometimes form again, how they are led, how they communicate internally, and how they relate to the formal established bureaucracies across which they cut. Much of this is terra incognita to us, unmapped, uncharted, unconceptualized.

In defense of our ignorance--in explanation of how little we have accomplished within that small subsector of academic life which specializes in the study of bureaucratic politics, decision-making, and other organizational matters in the context of foreign and defense policies--we can say again that part of our problem is the lack of continuous sustained interest and support except during those major presidential election and transition periods at roughly eight-year intervals. But, finally, I think, our problem--as I have implied in earlier comments here--is that we have failed to produce the kinds of theoretical guidelines that might subsume criteria for quality controls. In the ultimate judgment, nobody--not even scholars--really cares about structures and processes, as long as the policy outcome is thought to be desirable. But this kind of judgment on policy outcomes is entirely and completely normative, resting on each person's judgment of what is "good" and what is "bad" in the world. Furthermore, it is a judgment that changes for succeeding generations as values change and evolve.

In the long run, more in the manner of an anthropologist than a political scientist, I think we can say that strongly institutionalized patterns within a bureaucracy that has survived for a long time--such as, the U.S. Army or the U.S. Navy, in existence for more than 200 years--will help to determine certain outcomes such as innovation, partly because these patterns will determine how easy or difficult it may be to forge intra-organizational political alliances in favor of changes. But, in the short run, I think we can say very little in the nature of a statement such as: If we use Organizational Structure and Process x, we will get a policy outcome that we will like much better (on whatever criteria one may prefer to suggest-- cost efficiency, for example) than if we use Organizational Structure and Process y.

The main thing that seems to happen, in the short run, if we switch from Organizational S&P x to Organizational S&P y, is to make it somewhat easier or harder for specific individual actors to assert themselves. But the basic determining variable here becomes the characteristics of the individual actors, rather than x or y. Furthermore, it's my observation, again in the short run, that the individual actors with intelligence, drive, determination, and a skill for operating effectively within an organizational environment will push to the fore in any such environment and will emerge in the leadership roles regardless of formal titles or ranks or positions. This is closely analogous to another of my observations, as a teacher, that the truly talented students will emerge with the best records regardless of the kind of testing techniques or evaluative procedures that an instructor devises.

All of these pages accordingly also constitute a warning that the generalizations about the Carter administration in the remainder of this paper are to be taken as highly tentative, highly impressionistic, and perhaps premature. Nevertheless, these observations do constitute an attempt to integrate the views of knowledgeable sources and my own experience around the foreign and defense policy bureaucracies in Washington. Even so it is difficult to address the question of importance of process vis-a-vis substance or the impact of structural/ procedural changes on policy output.

THE PRESIDENTIAL LEADERSHIP STYLE AND IMPACT

The one most important actor to study and to emphasize in trying to understand U.S. foreign and defense policy is the President of the United States. In recent years the Congress has attempted to assert a stronger role for itself, with some but limited success. New forms of expression for public opinion are allowing specialized sets of citizens as well as the public at large (not merely the U.S. public, one should quickly add) to make stronger inputs to the policy-making process. For one thing, a wide variety of frequent opinion polls are carefully studied by most political figures. But, notwithstanding the changing nature and roles of the Congress, and the enhanced opportunities for inputs from people who are not inside the decision-making community, the U.S. Constitution and the very nature of foreign policy put the President in the all-important central position.26

The Carter Personality

Most observers understand this crucial central role of the President, and therefore most observers have been trying to figure out the nature of Jimmy Carter since he emerged as a leading candidate for the White House. The one word that most writers have seemed to use most frequently in describing this man is enigmatic. For example, the Wall Street Journal reported in September 1977: "All of us ... still have a lot to learn about the man who has transfixed Washington, the enigmatic Jimmy Carter."27 The Parade Sunday supplement newspaper magazine in November 1977 featured a cover story by syndicated columnist Jack Anderson under the title: "What is Jimmy Carter Really Like?" The opening sentence read: "The most publicized man in America, Jimmy Carter, still remains a mystery to millions of people."28 In April, 1978, longtime foreign correspondent Robert A. Haeger wrote in U.S. News & World Report magazine that European allies of the United States remained "puzzled" and expressed "mystification" about Carter.29

Based on my own experience in Washington in the summers of 1977 and 1978, in a combination of research and consultant-type duties, sometimes in close connection with staff activities of the National Security Council in the White House and Executive Office Building complex, sometimes in Executive Branch agencies elsewhere around town, and sometimes for Legislative Branch personnel on Capitol Hill, followed by fairly frequent follow-up contacts throughout the 1977-78 academic year, and reinforced by extensive commentaries published by respected journalists in many media, enigmatic is not the one word that comes most readily to my mind when I think of President Carter and his immediate entourage. Rather, the one word is amateurish.

James Reston reached essentially the same conclusion in his editorial column in the New York Times except that he used the more tactful term inexperienced.30 Michael J. Robinson, in his

"Learning by Doing" in Presidential Studies Quarterly, said basically the same thing. It has been a commonplace observation.

All of this is readily understandable. Mr. Carter, 53 years old as of early October of 1977, has spent less than a dozen of those years in political life, and most of his staffers have spent considerably less time in government and politics. This contrasts to all other U.S. Presidents since World War II, who were in one or another form of public service for virtually their entire adult lives. The President, one must remember, understood all of this very well, and advertised it as a virtue in his 1976 campaign. He was running as the outsider against the "old pros" in the political "establishment." Carter and his associates believed that the traditional ways of getting things done in the federal government were "bad." But he and his people have been unable to agree on--and to obtain a wide consensus on--a new set of groundrules. This factor, I think, accounts for at least some of the continuing confusion and uncertainty in Carter's Washington as of the middle of summer 1978. For all of this and more, he has been exposed to a steadily stronger drumbeat of criticism from an even wider array and range of sources.

In some respects, the situation is not as unique as current commentators might have suggested. Americans were typically rough critics of Presidents throughout the 19th century. We did not think of them as poor beleaguered souls who needed our sympathy, nor did we deferentially treat them as if they were crowned heads of royal families. Little that President Carter has attempted, and virtually none of the circumstances in which he has attempted it, are wholly unprecedented in the history of the American presidency. Almost all Presidents have promised and perhaps genuinely attempted to deliver more "good things"--such as prosperity at home, peace internationally, and strong security against external threats. Almost all Presidents have promised and perhaps genuinely attempted to prevent or at least to minimize "bad things"--such as inefficient government, a swollen bureaucracy, higher taxes, hard times, and war. Some Presidents have used moralizing tones to lecture if not also hector their fellow Americans. Numerous Presidents have encountered unruly obstreperous Congresses. Many Presidents have experienced divided counsel, sometimes divided loyalties, and often contentious personal rivalries among and between their closest aides and advisors. None of these things is new. What may be relatively new, perhaps even unprecedented, in the case of the Carter administration, is a President who has promised so much, and at least initiated so much, with so little relevant experience and knowledge of national government and national problems as well as international affairs, with such a mixed bag of aides and advisors, in the face of so many massive and intractable problems at home and abroad.

Presidential Appointment Process

The President's amateurish inexperience was most immediately evident in the appointments process, and this in turn complicated and aggravated all of his subsequent problems. In the first place, he knew relatively few people personally, and therefore had to place heavy reliance on advice from strangers. Notwithstanding all of the press reports in late 1976 and early 1977 about an allegedly thorough and comprehensive talent search to find the very best people to staff the new administration, the process moved very slowly, and many key positions remained either unfilled or else filled by Ford administration holdovers for a year and more after Jimmy Carter's inauguration. This resulted in inordinate delays in dealing with some policy issues, and in curious anomalies in other areas. For example, the policy on Reserve and Guard forces that was incorporated in President Carter's first defense budget, presented to Congress in early 1978 for FY'79, was based on a recommendation from Defense Secretary Harold Brown which he had routinely received from the Assistant Secretary of Defense for Manpower and Reserve Affairs William Brehm--who in turn was a Ford administration holdover who gave Secretary Brown precisely the same recommendation on this matter that Brehm and former Defense Secretary Donald Rumsfeld had packaged for President Ford's final defense budget. Not until the spring of 1978 was Harold W. Chase (a longtime professor of public law and public administration at the University of Minnesota, as well as a major general in the U.S. Marine Corps Reserve) appointed to serve as Deputy Assistant Secretary of Defense for Reserve Affairs.

More serious than delays in filling some jobs, however, was the uneven procedure followed in filling those for whom appointees were found relatively early. Criteria were seldom obvious or, if evident, were difficult to accept. In the debacle in finding a person to become the Director of Central Intelligence, for example, a number of newspaper editorials in various papers around the nation stated in effect: We do not know whether Theodore Sorenson or Admiral Stansfield Turner would be the best man for this position, but the men are so starkly different in backgrounds and perspectives that it's hard to understand what criteria were utilized in picking either one. That was in the spring of 1977. One year later, in the spring of 1978, Carter made the critically important appointment of the man to become the new Chairman of the Joint Chiefs of Staff: Air Force General David C. Jones. The <u>New York Times</u> suggested that one important factor in selecting General Jones was the President's pleasure in being able to discuss religion with this military officer, and that Carter had in fact included General Jones in presidential "prayer breakfasts" at the White House.[32] In looking at the sources of appointees, we can deduct a mix of personal, political and technical.

    First, as one source of appointees, Carter was drawn to some new acquaintances because of the feeling of close personal affinity based on shared values not directly relevant to the jobs in question. Second, the President (at least in the beginning) turned to many people whom he had known in some context in his native Georgia. The <u>Washington Monthly</u> reported "There are now 51 Georgians on the White House staff and 18 more at OMB."[33] Third, Carter turned to people with whom he had enjoyed some contact, no matter how limited, such as many he had come to know to some extent in the meetings of the Trilateral Commission, and his old Naval Academy classmate Stansfield Turner (although he had not known Turner at the Academy, and had met him on only a few occasions while Carter was Governor of Georgia). Fourth, Carter appointed some people urged on him by leaders of various Democratic Party groups and factions--a traditional technique for unifying a party behind its new representative in the White House after a divisive election. President Carter apparently relied most heavily on Vice President Mondale in this context, and many "Mondale people" sprinkle the Carter administration. Fifth, in keeping with his pledge to move back toward strong "cabinet government," including considerable autonomy for cabinet officers, Carter allowed many cabinet people to recruit their own key subordinates. As a result, some cabinet officers rejected appointees urged on them by the White House; this was particularly true for Defense Secretary Harold Brown who rejected at least two people whose appointments to high Defense positions had already been announced in the press, although these two salvaged attractive positions on the NSC staff and preferred to say that they had turned down Secretary Brown rather than the other way around. Sixth, some holdovers from the Ford era were invited to remain indefinitely, particularly in areas of technical specialization, such as Navy Captain Gary Sick who remained as one of the two key Middle East specialists on the NSC staff.[34]

Top presidential appointees drawn from widely diverse sources are not an unusual situation and would not be debilitating for the Carter administration if the President were capable of welding them into a unified team. Jimmy Carter had not revealed this capability as of mid-summer 1978, however, for reasons based partly on some of his own characteristics, and for other reasons deriving from major policy disputes crashing around him like mountainous tidal waves.

Carter's Decision-Making Style

One of his characteristics had been a tendency to immerse himself in reading massively detailed documents while in isolation from staffers for prolonged periods. He prefers receiving information and recommendations in these written forms rather than in face-to-face briefings and discussions. In the face-to-face situations, several knowledgeable sources reported that he often provides little or no feedback comments or even indicative gestures or facial expressions, such that staffers feel deprived of instructive interaction.[35] Decisions have often been made by the President in a mechanical style that he likes, checking "yes" or "no" boxes on long lists of written options prepared for him by key aides. These and other important aspects of Carter's decision-making style were comprehensively covered by noted reporter Hedrick Smith.[36]

More importantly, a second characteristic of Carter's style was revealed in this same Hedrick

Smith profile, summarized in the subheading under the title: "At the end of President Carter's first year, it is clear that he has chosen to rush into decision-making at the cost of projecting a clear vision of the American future." The critical question here is whether Carter in fact has any such vision. The previously mentioned Perry article in the Wall Street Journal, based on interviews with almost everybody who had ever known the President, reported that the following query was addressed to all interviewees: "Does he have any vision?" The reply: "Almost without exception, the answer is no."[37]

A third Carter characteristic is a tendency to work closely with only a very few people on his immediate staff and treating these intimates with great loyalty. This was evident enough when Bert Lance, Hamilton Jordan and others seriously injured the President's authority and integrity but were treated most gently. But, even more generally, Carter appeared very reluctant to "knock heads" or to apply punitive pressures against any wayward appointees or congressional adversaries. To the extent that he was aware of actions by such people which could damage him politically, he was nevertheless remarkably tolerant and permissive.[38]

Perspectives on U.S. - U.S.S.R. Relationship

The problems associated with the extraordinarily mixed bag of aides, advisors, and key appointees, in conjunction with the three characteristics of Carter himself noted above, have become all the more serious in view of the one most fundamental and momentous issue confronting him and all others associated with foreign policy and defense policy for the United States. This issue, quite starkly, is to what extent the Soviet Union is the enemy of the United States, and how serious is the threat that the USSR might pose to U.S. security?

This same question was of fundamental importance in the years immediately after World War II. After raging debate within Truman's cabinet and in many other quarters from late 1945 until the fall of 1946, for about a year, the decision was gradually reached that--yes--the USSR was the prime enemy of the United States and did pose a serious threat. Although Truman did not state this decision in public to the American people until March 1948, U.S. foreign and defense policies for a quarter of a century following World War II were premised on this basic tenet. Given the preoccupation with the Vietnam War in the later 1960s, and some signs of a warming thaw in American-Soviet relations, the question of the Soviet Union along the friend-enemy continuum in American thinking was put in abeyance. Concepts such as peaceful coexistence and detente, along with some evidence to support them, caused a continuation of a moratorium on the basic question into the mid-1970s. As of the beginning of the Carter administration, however, this dominant old question once again was pushed to the forefront (although not always immediately visible in the forefront, because of an occasional rhetorical smokescreen) of debate. Morton Kondracke, in an article entitled "Is There a Present Danger?" summarized some of the key dimensions of this most basic of all basic questions at the outset of the Carter administration's tenure.[39] The fate of this administration--and without sounding excessively melodramatic, the fate of the nation and indeed the world--could well hinge on how Carter ultimately answers the question.

The results have not been reassuring, primarily because the question had not been squarely faced. If it had been faced, it was then answered in many contradictory and incompatible ways at different points over remarkably short spans of time. It is precisely because of this circumstance that Carter was increasingly accused of "vacillation" and "indecisiveness", if not worse in the first 18 months of his White House residency. The heat began to build with a major cover story in Time magazine under the title "Carter's Foreign Policy: Jimmy in the Lion's Den."[40] Earlier, on stylistic issues, U.S. News & World Report under the title "Foreign Policy by Committee--Can It Really Work?" raised procedural issues, but by the fall of that year the doubts and debates focused on the alleged mishandling of substantive problems.[41] Jack Anderson and Les Whitten, in their syndicated column for August 19, 1977, were reinforcing the argument that the President tended to immerse himself in trivia and minutiae at the expense of American long-range goals, which was a point also raised in the U.S. News & World Report ("...allies and foes are wondering who's in charge of Carter diplomacy--and what American goals really are.")[42] An article, evaluating the President's first nine months in office, appeared on the front page of the New York Times which declared that growing numbers of leading politicians and government executives were raising serious questions about Carter's "competence."[43] A Harris Poll widely reported in the final week of November 1977 indicated that 57% of the public were also questioning the President's "competence."

VACILLATING FOREIGN AND DEFENSE POLICIES

In the field of foreign policy and defense policy, the clear evidence has pointed to a bewildering array of zigs and zags on almost every significant issue. Often even the speeches and the rhetoric have been inconsistent but, where some thread of continuity could be seen in verbal declarations, the talk was often at substantial--sometimes diametric--variance with the actions. Sometimes it appeared to be merely bungled planning, as in the case of the major presidential trip abroad that was announced early in the fall of 1977, then soon thereafter was postponed on the grounds that Carter could not leave the country until the Congress could enact his energy bill, and then was eventually rescheduled (although omitting several key countries that had been on the original itinerary) notwithstanding that no progress had been achieved on the energy bill and a major coal strike was pending. But bungled planning was a minor matter in comparison to far more serious difficulties on substantive policy issues of great significance. Joseph Fromm, for almost 30 years the chief of European correspondents for U.S. News & World Report but by summer 1977 back at Washington headquarters as the No. 2 person in charge of that magazine (with the title deputy editor), said in a report that the Soviets no less than the Americans were "baffled" by Carter's foreign policy.[44] Fromm suggested that, over the first 15 months of the Carter tenure, this foreign policy had moved through three phases particularly with regard to the USSR. The first phase was "uncompromising in condemning human rights violations in Russia, pressing for drastic reductions in nuclear arsenals and expressing determination to challenge Russia in the Horn of Africa." The second phase was marked by a sharp shift almost in the opposite direction, emphasizing "conciliation and cooperation with the Kremlin." Now in the spring of 1978, said Fromm, Carter's détente policy was entering a third phase that "reflects growing concern inside the administration about Soviet behavior and controversy over what to do about it."

Two articles in the New Republic expressed amazement over recent zig-zags in Carter's foreign and defense policy statements and actions. In the first of these pieces, by highly respected and long-time White House correspondent John Osborne, the story reported on the role of Zbigniew Brzezinski, Samuel P. Huntington and Secretary Harold Brown in "toughening up" the President's by now famous Wake Forest speech in Winston-Salem on March 17, 1978. But, reflecting back on the Notre Dame speech on May 22, 1977, and even earlier campaign speeches by Carter, John Osborne concluded: "The record testifies that the speech represents yet another shift in the Carter rhetoric of foreign and defense policy and little if anything more."[45] Morton Kondracke, author of the second of these pieces, reinforced the same point by noting that the President's well-publicized visit to a substantial U.S. naval force steaming in the Atlantic Ocean off the Carolina coast, during which an array of dazzling naval weaponry was displayed at considerable cost, came on the afternoon before the President's Wake Forest speech.[46] The two events together--the naval display, and the speech--seemed to signal a very stern message to the Kremlin. But then, Kondracke noted, the Navy budget will be sharply cut in the recommendations recently sent to Congress by Carter, thus undermining whatever message of tough resolve that the President might have wanted Moscow to perceive. Similarly, Kondracke reported, Brzezinski was saying that progress on SALT II might well hinge on a reduction of Soviet involvement in the Horn of Africa while Carter was telling syndicated and prominent columnists that he wanted to press ahead on SALT II without mentioning Africa or any other coupled problems.

Morton Kondracke, writing again in the New Republic, observed that there is "a growing feeling in this country that the US is weak and getting dangerously weaker.[47] It is reflected in public opinion polls, in high intellectual discourse about nuclear strategy and in a new respect being accorded to panicky time-is-running-out pronouncements that previously were dismissed as so much new missile-gappery. This infectious perception of US weakness has spread widely in Congress." Kondracke ably summarized Carter's role in creating this new perception of American military weakness among Americans. He noted for example:

President Carter must restore confidence in the country's military and political strength. But repeatedly he has done exactly the opposite. He has created a strong impression that he lacks any geopolitical vision or strategic sense, any understanding of how moves in one part of the globe affect events and judgments in other parts. He appears to have come to office with a set of vague themes in his head for making the world good--"human rights," "disarmament," "nuclear proliferation," "North-South dialogue"--but without any notion of how to put them into effect, or how they might affect the East-West power balance. He has been forced to back down and shift course repeatedly, creating doubts about his resolve and judgment.

Carter has shown himself to be as poor a tactician and negotiator as he is a strategist. He decided to pull US ground forces out of South Korea without obtaining any quid pro quo from North Korea. He has pursued rapprochement with Cuba without achieving any Cuban restraint in Africa. He decided against building the B-1 bomber without asking the Soviet Union to limit production of its Backfire. Not only does he toss away bargaining chips in negotiation; often, he seems to start playing poker by showing everyone his hand, as he has done again and again in the Middle East.

The neutron bomb question was one issue that provoked new waves of doubt and anxiety about President Carter's competence, both at home and abroad. James Reston did his best to put a good face on the President's actions and decisions, offering a variety of reasons to support him at that point in time. But, the day before, the New York Times used its lead editorial space to mount one of its harshest attacks against the President under the headline "The Mishandled Bomb."[48] The editorial writer zeroed in on both the procedural and substantive aspects of the presidential action on this issue in the prior week. Subsequently, Hedrick Smith reporting from Washington and Flora Lewis reporting from Europe candidly stated that Carter's performance on the neutron bomb issue had deepened the already serious reservations about his leadership abilities both within the United States and abroad.49

DOMESTIC POLICY

At least as serious as the steadily growing crisis of confidence in President Carter's leadership on foreign policy and military policy issues in the spring of 1978 was a similar crisis of faith and trust in his capacity to deal effectively with a gathering storm of economic issues both domestic and international. Indeed, the domestic and the international economic problems were closely linked, and both together were closely linked to issues on such defense policy questions as military spending. There was very little if any evidence to suggest that Carter understood the nature of the linkages, but there was ample evidence supporting the perception of approaching economic disasters. Although economic news rarely makes the front pages, reports with these themes increasingly appeared "up front" in The New York Times and all other major U.S. newspapers from the fall of 1977 into the mid-summer of 1978. The New York Times deployed its highly respected corps of economic journalists--Leonard Silk, Clyde Farnsworth, and Ann Crittenden in the lead--featuring a relatively major story by at least one of these people in almost every daily and weekend edition for months as the dollar continued to slide in world markets. Farnsworth, attempting to explain "Why U.S. Economic Policy Is At Loose Ends," utilized many of the same comments offered by critics of Carter's foreign and defense policies.50 Here are key excerpts from Farnsworth's analysis:

> Only 10 weeks after a volley of Presidential messages that were to set the Administration's broad strategy for the year ahead, the White House has been jarred by economic misjudgments and reverses .... it raises questions about the Carter economic team and its effectiveness.
>
> Mr. Carter is also faulted for his inability, or unwillingness, to knock heads. He "waffles," as Senator Edmund Muskie...said recently. ... One reason the Administration always seems to be reacting to crises

> rather than anticipating them and heading them off is that the White House (economic) staff is stretched thin.
>
> Other conflicts affect the formation of policy. The President has his economic and his political counselors, and the two camps do not see things in the same light. ...
>
> Mr. Carter holds out the best of both worlds--a low inflation economy, fully employed. But his critics say the indecisiveness of his policies again opens the possibility of the worst of both. ... Mr. Carter says he recognizes the Government's role in the economy. But he has yet to grasp the nettle.

Needless to say, although virtually all major U.S. newspapers and newsmagazines gave full play-- often in front-page reports and cover stories--to the linked national and international economic storms brewing from the fall of 1977 through the summer of 1978, including heavy coverage of the Western economic summit meeting that Carter attended in Bonn during the third week of July (immediately followed by more domestic and international bad news for the dollar), considerable disagreement existed as to desired remedies. The distribution of economic pain is always one of the most challenging issues that can face any political leader. Nevertheless, there was no disagreement that all economic sectors would have ample pain to share in the absence of effective remedies, whatever those prescriptions turned out to be.

LACK OF CONFIDENCE

Public Opinion

Reflections of President Carter's weaknesses were visible almost everywhere in the first half of 1978. As Hedrick Smith noted "...doubts about his leadership and his basic thrust of policy... crop up in virtually every opinion poll."[51] One such poll, reported in U.S. News & World Report showed that more than 65% of the public believed the President's performance in office, in general, to be in some degree worse than they had expected for him.[52] The same magazine, in a cover story entitled "Carter's 18 Months: What Went Wrong?", noted that Carter was receiving lower poll ratings at that stage of tenure than any president since Harry Truman in 1946.[53] Moreover, Carter's decline was steady, whereas his predecessors had ordinarily enjoyed at least one or two significant upturns. The May/June 1978 issue of Public Opinion magazine charted four major polls (Gallup, Harris, CBS/NYT, and NBC/AP) and produced the same conclusion, although printing a commentary by Harvard Associate Professor of Government Gary R. Orren pointing out potentially misleading elements in the techniques used by all of the major commercial polling organizations. Still, Public Opinion's innovative 20-page center section, entitled "Opinion Roundup," aggregated polls on many major public policy and social questions in its May/June issue, and the only findings that might have cheered Carter were Gallup and Harris figures from March-April trial heats showing that the President could still have defeated Gerald Ford and Ronald Reagan--although in a close call over Reagan.[54]

The Congress

Whatever Carter's standing among the general public in the spring and summer of 1978, and it was obviously declining to significantly low levels by all measures and indicators, impressions suggested that his stature was even lower among his fellow workers in the federal government. U.S. News & World Report summarized the President's relationships with Capitol Hill in its "Washington Whispers" column, "Jimmy Carter's stature with a defiant Congress, never very high, has hit a new low. The way lawmakers tell it, the President is so vacillating that they feel free to ignore the White House..."[55]

This overall reputation of the Carter administration with the Congress in general grew more acute with respect to foreign policy issues, particularly in the Senate. Secretary of State Vance returned from a Moscow trip in mid-April assuring the Senate of improving relationships between the United States and the USSR, but James Reston reported something less than an enthusiastic reception. He wrote, "...the Senate is clearly not satisfied with Mr. Vance's vague assurances that the 'atmosphere' is better ... In short, the Senate is skeptical not only of the Soviets but of the Carter administration these days. It wants substance and not atmospherics this time."56

On the other hand, the problem that was causing the most anxiety for the Senators when Reston provided that summary in April was Soviet-backed Cuban penetrations in Africa but, a month later when President Carter in fact did try to take a substantive policy initiative in the form of increased aid and support for African countries possibly threatened by the Soviet-Cuban actions, he drew sharp fire from the Senate. This provoked an angry outburst from the President in a May 25 news conference at the Blackstone Hotel in Chicago, who charged: "There's a trend in Congress that is building up that puts too much constraint on a President to deal with rapidly changing circumstances." Terence Smith reported that the President planned to fight any further congressional limits on his powers to give U.S. aid where he thought it needed,57 and Richard Burt in the same newspaper provided further analysis of the growing controversy in Washington over the limits on presidential power to give aid in confrontation with the limits on congressional power to restrain a President.58 The specific occasion was a Senate that a month earlier had wanted the President to "do something" about Soviet-Cuban actions in Africa, but by late May had suddenly grown fearful of "another Vietnam" if the United States became involved at all. Beyond the specific occasion, however, was the more general and pervasive fact that, whatever President Carter did or did not do, he would be unable to make his leadership prevail on Capitol Hill.

By July, the President's problems with Congress grew even more serious. In what began to look like "open season" on Carter, widespread press reports indicated that relatively few Democratic Party members of the House and also Democratic Senators up for re-election in November 1978 desired the President's campaign assistance, on the grounds that his help was likely to do them more harm than good. Almost every daily newspaper in the nation carried stories on July 28 or 29 about the sudden emergence of major problems for the chief executive with two key Democrats from Massachusetts; Senator Edward M. Kennedy (needless to add, a possible presidential candidate in 1980) denounced the President because of the White House proposal on a national health insurance program, and Speaker of the House Thomas P. O'Neill was "stunned" that President Carter had supported the ouster of O'Neill's close friend Robert T. Griffin as the No. 2 official at the General Services Administration.

The Executive Branch

Turning from the President and the legislative branch to the President and his own executive branch, instances of clear defiance were much less obvious (for obvious reasons), but illustrations of disarray caused by a perceived weakness of presidential leadership were abundant in other forms. My own impressions verified the general conclusions on this point which were reported throughout the media with increasing frequency and vigor during the first half of 1978. On several trips to Washington during the 1977-78 academic year, and again for over a month in the Washington area during the summer of 1978, I talked to a wide variety of relatively senior to very senior civilian and military officials, some of them careerists and some of them political appointees, in major departments and agencies. I found them almost unanimous in the conclusion that the nation was virtually leaderless. Pessimism was deep. Faith and trust in presidential leadership was at a lower point than I had personally ever seen it before, in 20 years of rather frequent and intensive research interviewing and consulting around the Washington area. Even at the depths of the Johnson presidency in the summer of 1968, and at the nadir of the Nixon presidency in the summer of 1974, there was more respect for and confidence in White House authority than I was able to observe in the summer of 1978. The sense of drift, foreboding and gloom was widespread, and was uncorrelated with the policy preferences of any particular individual with whom I happened to talk. By late July there was a little bit of new good cheer in the Department of State because of a feeling that Secretary Vance had gradually won some major policy battles against Brzezinski in the White House (more on this below), but even that cheer was not sufficient to offset larger anxieties stemming from the overall sense of being leaderless at the top.

President Carter for a long time appeared to be relatively indifferent to the growing anxieties about his leadership on all sides. But, as early as October 1977, Press Secretary Jody Powell began suggesting that there were some flaws in the Carter operation. A few changes were made in the senior staff, and a few minor staff reorganizations were implemented over the winter, but the President himself still did not seem overly concerned. Finally, however, according to James Reston, the very close vote on the Panama Canal treaties "has forced a reappraisal by Mr. Carter of his methods, his Cabinet, his White House staff, and his priorities."[59] One forum in which this reappraisal immediately began to occur was a presidential meeting with his senior staff and some cabinet members at Camp David over the weekend of April 15-16. The Camp David weekend stimulated substantial press speculation that it would prove to be a major turning point in the Carter administration in terms of organizational style and procedures. Terence Smith reported that the main results--which the White House made a determined effort to conceal, thus further heightening media speculations--were decisions for a further tightening and centralization of staff procedures, in effect substantially retreating from the President's original commitment to decentralized "cabinet government," and a tough-sounding presidential order designed to shut off the epidemic of high-level "leaks" from the White House and cabinet members.[60]

PRESIDENTIAL REACTION AND IMAGE BUILDING

About a month later in mid-May, the President decided to try another technique to solve his problem of eroding stature when he named his friend Gerald Rafshoon, an advertising and public relations specialist, to a senior White House staff position as an assistant to the President. Martin Tolchin reported that Rafshoon's mission was "to develop long-range programs to carry the President's message to the American people."[61] The general press reaction indicated that this was another mistake by Carter, because he assumed that his problems had to do with his "image" and that these could be solved by cosmetic improvements in communications with the public. Charles Peters reported that the President in mid-May was more and more strident in his assumption that a main problem was White House "leaks," implying that Mr. Carter increasingly resembled former President Nixon in this kind of paranoia.[62]

By summertime 1978, Carter's reputation in all quarters was still on a slippery slope downward. Low morale and grumbling was becoming more pronounced within the White House staff itself, facing more size and money cuts, as reported by Vernon A. Guidry, Jr., in the Washington Star.[63] Furthermore, the staff appeared to be split on almost every significant issue, ranging from American policy on a comprehensive nuclear test ban to domestic policies regarding support for special-interest groups which traditionally supported the Democratic Party (Vice President Mondale led a faction pushing for more money and new programs to support such groups. Hamilton Jordan and Jody Powell led the opposition).[64] These disagreements created internal tensions and aroused suspicions which detracted from any sense of policy coherency. Additionally trying to coordinate staff actions in such an environment was next to impossible.

Presidential paranoia apparently was one factor leading Carter to make increasing use of members of his personal family for diplomatic missions, as if he had come to believe that these were the only people whom he could trust. This trend was reported in U.S. News & World Report.[65] A week earlier the same magazine suggested one of the recurring causes of presidential anger:

> The President is growing frustrated and angered by the appearance of disarray in his administration's foreign policy. Arousing Carter's ire: ... telephone calls from officials of the National Security Council to key senators, suggesting they pressure the President to take a tougher line on the Soviet Union.
>
> One result of the President's fury was a barrage of telephone calls by top White House aides to agencies involved in moves to counter Soviet violations of human rights. The message sent: "The President wants your people to shut up."[66]

Meanwhile, the factionalism and disarray sometimes included petty vicious back-biting (if not back-stabbing) within the official family. The Washington Post reported one particular striking example of this tendency, and indeed printed this same item twice in the column as if to give it more emphasis. "At a going away party for Fred Hitz, who is leaving the Department of Energy for the Central Intelligence Agency, Energy Secretary James R. Schlesinger stood up, looked at Hitz, and said:

'He's the only mammal in town who's swimming toward a sinking ship.' Schlesinger himself left that vessel in 1973."[67]

This kind of episode left little to the imagination in speculating on the possibilities for harmonious working relationships between former CIA Director Schlesinger and incumbent Director Stansfield Turner within the higher reaches of the official Carter family. Although Turner was a remarkably forgiving sort of man who did not tend to carry grudges, one can guess that it would be a little hard to maintain your equanimity when a fellow cabinet officer had accused you of allowing your agency ship to sink--particularly if you are an admiral trained to think that allowing your ship to sink is not a terribly commendable idea. At the very least, Schlesinger--who was fired from an earlier cabinet job largely because of a tendency to lecture everybody in town including the President for whom he then worked--might have chosen a more felicitous metaphor. But Schlesinger seemed as unlikely as anyone else in the Carter administration to give serious consideration to changing any of his ways.

Whatever the widely heralded Camp David meetings of mid-April had been designed to achieve, there were few if any substantial changes evident in Washington by mid-summer, and the "real world" was again beginning to intrude upon the President. Ambassador Andrew Young's remarks about political prisoners in the United States appeared to have been a genuine embarrassment for the President. Once again, the journalist who came closest to summarizing my own impressions of the Carter administration, in this case as of mid-summer 1978, was the distinguished senior White House correspondent for the New Republic, John Osborne. He noted:

> (In order to understand) how Jimmy Carter conducts his presidency and how he and his White House assistants perform under pressure, ... a definition of the pressure in discussion here is necessary. It is cumulative, the sum of many different pressures. In essence, though, it takes a single and special and peculiar form. It arises from a creeping sense of inadequacy--not a sense at the White House that the President and his assistants are inadequate, but a sense among them that

they are perceived elsewhere and by others to be inadequate. The consequence has been a series of extreme, despairing, sometimes panicky statements and actions that have been self-defeating because they have enhanced rather than diminished the impression of inadequacy. Recent behavior at the White House suggests that the place is pervaded by a fear, unspoken but discernible in observed events and attitudes, that the perception of inadequacy has gone too far and sunk too deeply into the public mind to be arrested and turned around.[68]

The President and his key people were suddenly beginning to behave occasionally in the summer of '78 as if they had glanced at a mirror and got a horrifying glimpse of themselves as "lame ducks," even as they began rather desperately to stave off that contingency. U.S. News & World Report reported that plans were already set for Hamilton Jordan to depart the White House staff in 1979 to head Carter's re-election campaign, with Robert Strauss leaving with Jordan to head a "citizens-for-Carter" movement designed to attract the support of businessmen and independents.[69] John C. White, Carter's own chairman of the Democratic National Committee, was already predicting that the President would be challenged (although not successfully) for the Democratic Party nomination in 1980. Political scientist Michael J. Robinson published an intriguing and partially persuasive theory about how to get a presidential party nomination (unintentionally agreeing, one might assume, with John White on a few key points).[70] Robinson's piece even went so far as to name the most likely GOP candidate. More importantly, career and politically appointed bureaucrats all over Washington as of mid-summer 1978 were in many cases persuaded that Carter was already a "lame duck," which often resulted in two quite different kinds of behavior. For the politically appointed bureaucrats--those whom Charles Peters aptly described in the Washington Monthly as having entered government "out of a passion not to accomplish in the public interest but to add to their string of credits...executives who care far less about doing good than they do about looking good" --the feeling of being part of a "lame duck" administration led to a kind of "to hell with it--let's have a good time" attitude.[71] Some, such as perhaps Secretary Joseph Califano at the Department of HEW, however, saw it as a chance to fight for their favorite causes without effective political constraints from the White House. Califano seemed far more interested in his anti-smoking crusade than in staving off the very real threat that the "E" would be removed from HEW if a new cabinet-level Department of Education were legislated--quite uncharacteristic of a bureaucrat, to see a large piece of his turf possibly being taken away without devoting total energies to avoiding such a disaster. Meanwhile, the career bureaucrats--the civil servants--were apparently not much concerned that Carter's proposed reforms of the civil service would ever be enacted, and some of them happily began sidestepping their political bosses on the assumption that the 1980 New Hampshire primary was only a bit more than 18 months away when it would be confirmed that Carter and all of his administration people were "lame ducks." For career bureaucrats, avoiding the effective control of political bosses for a mere 18 months is an easy short stroke.

The President, and, one could add, Mrs. Carter, were apparently able to retreat into their sublime sense of divine destiny whenever pressures from ordinary mortals became too severe and depressing. Sally Quinn writing in the Washington Post quoted a former senior staff member in the Carter White House as having told her: "They're both very naive... They (President and Mrs. Carter) believe that they're right with God. And if what they're doing is right, everything will work out for the best. But the problem is that things don't work out that way in the real world."[72]

U.S. News & World Report tried to sum up all of Carter's problems in a cover story under the title, "Carter's 18 Months: What Went Wrong?"[73] Time in its own cover-corner story got a little closer to the heart of the matter in its title phrasing, "A Problem of How to Lead: Dissatisfaction is the Washington Mood."[74] But the best summary of the situation came in a short final paragraph in Hugh Sidey's column in the Washington Star. He wrote, "There is no great vision hung up on the far horizon, no trumpet call, no banner beneath which to rally. There is not even a slogan on which to hang the mind or to say softly when one needs a quick index of American purpose. Washington right now is nothing so much as a thousand or maybe a million people talking at once--few of them on the same wavelength."[75]

THE PRIMARY NATIONAL SECURITY AGENCIES: INTERNAL POLITICS

If faltering presidential leadership was the dominant impression that one gained in almost all circumstances when observing the Washington scene throughout 1978, one possible ray of hope could conceivably have been to find that foreign policy and defense policy matters were in strong sure hands at lower levels, visibly taking up the slack in the key agencies and departments. While some bright spots, and some determined conscientious officials, could be discerned here and there, the overall scene within the key agencies and departments was not much, if any more encouraging, than the scene at the top in the White House.

The National Security Council

The National Security Council (NSC) hardly exists as such. There was a recommendation to the President in the spring of 1978, as reported in several media sources, that he substitute a meeting of the National Security Council every other week in lieu of the weekly cabinet meetings. As far as can be determined, that recommendation--like most of those emerging out of the publicized Camp David meetings in mid-April--was never implemented. The President continued to schedule fairly regular weekly meetings with various little groups of foreign and defense policy advisors such as Secretaries Vance and Brown, Brzezinski, and CIA Director Turner, somewhat in the manner of President Johnson's famed "Tuesday Lunch" meetings, but these were not the same as full regular meetings of the National Security Council. In this respect, Carter had FDR's instincts for listening to a wide variety of advisers, and the Kennedy-Johnson instincts for avoiding highly regularized organizational procedures--but without the abilities of any of those three predecessors in the White House for making informal organizational styles serve his interests and needs.

Zbigniew Brzezinski did in fact carry out Carter's promise to cut the size of the National Security Council Staff, headed by Brzezinski. A total of 40 to 50 professionals work on this staff, depending on precisely whom is counted. Adding in the secretaries, typists, file clerks, and other miscellaneous personnel, the overall size of the NSC staff under Brzezinski was trimmed to just under 100 people, compared to an overall total of about 125 in the last days of the Kissinger-Scowcroft NSC staff operation immediately prior to President Carter's inauguration. This in turn was down from a maximum of more than 150 working on the NSC staff during the heyday of the Nixon-Ford-Kissinger years according to some estimates. Thus, the organization was streamlined to some extent, although remaining far larger than the largest figure during the pre-Nixon years: estimates of from four to eight in the Truman Administration, from eight to twelve in the Eisenhower years, from about twelve up to maybe 16 in the Kennedy period, and from 16 to 20 or maybe 25 in the Johnson era of the Vietnam War. (It is never easy to know exactly whom to count when adding up the people working on the NSC staff--some are borrowed from other agencies and do not appear on the NSC roster or payroll.)

If Brzezinski succeeded in turning around the growth curve of the staff that skyrocketed in the Nixon-Ford-Kissinger years, he also apparently succeeded in reversing the tense morale situation among staffers that resulted from Kissinger's vicious temper and general ruthlessness toward all subordinates. Removing the complex committee structure through which Kissinger had dominated all aspects of NSC staff operations, ordinarily by personally chairing all committees of any significance or allowing a trusted puppet to handle this task in some cases, Brzezinski with the President's encouragement substituted a simple and flexible system involving mainly two committees--although he did follow the Kissinger pattern in making sure that he chaired whatever it made any difference for him to chair. He attempted to implement the kind of informal "collegial" style that ideally exists among professorial colleagues within a departmental faculty on a university campus, and I have it on what I take to be good authority that he was quite successful in this. A friendly open atmosphere was said to prevail, and Brzezinski made an effort to get NSC staffers personally into the President's office to participate in discussions on all relevant and appropriate occasions. NSC staffers who served under the old regime and then in the Brzezinski model were particularly kind in their remarks about Brzezinski, in comparison to Kissinger's heavy authoritarian hand. Clearly a rival of Kissinger throughout virtually their entire and closely parallel careers in academic life and government, Brzezinski was acutely aware of the criticisms that had gradually mounted against "Super-K." and Brzezinski apparently attempted to avert similar criticisms against himself by using Kissinger as his negative model.[76]

One indicator of Brzezinski's openness, in comparison to Kissinger at a parallel point in his early years running the NSC staff from the White House, was to be found in the fact that far more information about the structure and procedures of Brzezinski's operation was made available. Because of the availability of this descriptive and to some extent analytical information elsewhere, no effort will be made to provide it here.[77]

The Department of State

A number of persons within the U.S. Department of State--ranging from those close to the Secretary, to some distance away--were unanimous in reporting the same kind of morale boost in that building under Cyrus Vance that was similarly reported to me by NSC staffers under Brzezinski. Open, friendly, constructive work had been initiated. The professionals once again felt the possibility of making useful contributions to some part of U.S. foreign policy, even if well qualified observers continued accurately to report the remaining symptoms of serious illness that had plagued the Department of State at least since Sumner Welles effectively displaced Cordell Hull as the man in charge on the eve of World War II.[78] But, thus far, the bottom line as of mid-1978 was that Secretary Vance had earned high marks from his "troops" as a great improvement over Kissinger in almost all respects.

The Department of Defense

The picture conveyed by personal sources in many places in the U.S. Department of Defense was substantially more mixed. Secretary Harold Brown was respected as an experienced bureaucratic warrior with a great deal of technical knowledge in some areas relevant to defense policy, and as a man determined to protect the DOD interests in bureaucratic wars around town--as he saw those interests.

The rub came in that the military professionals--
and many of the civilian professionals--were concerned as of the winter of 1977-78 whether they
would be allowed to have much input in determining
departmental interests. If Brown seemed a bit
paranoid about possible threats to his authority
from other people around Washington, he seemed
equally anxious about possible threats to his supremacy from everyone outside of his immediate staff
and a few handpicked puppets around the Pentagon.

The professional military officers began to
call him "Son of McNamara" when he distributed a
memorandum on October 26, 1977, calling for "improvements in the PPB system" but very much resembling McNamara's successful attempts 15 to 16
years earlier to eliminate professional military
input at all significant stages in the policy-
making process. That trend began to be reversed
to some extent in the final year or two under McNamara, and to a larger extent in the following
tenure of Secretary Laird, but the professional
officers began worrying in 1977 that a re-reversal
was occurring. Brown's plan to study JCS organizational structures and procedures aggravated this
perception. Clearly, the JCS had remained a weak
and defective mechanism over its entire history of
30+ years, because two sets of individuals--the
Secretaries of Defense above the JCS, and the individual armed services below the JCS--never wanted
the JCS to become significantly powerful in its own
right. Nevertheless, any threat to the JCS from
the Secretary of Defense had always been perceived
by the services, ironically, as a threat to their
own military professionalism. A JCS mechanism remaining in the status quo ante was what the individual services preferred, because it was captive
to their interests without threatening their interests, and served occasionally as a useful agent
at the White House, with the Secretary of Defense,
and elsewhere.[79]

The Intelligence Community

The situation in the so-called intelligence
community was also mixed as of the summer 1978.
After almost a year of hashing and rehashing Presidential Review Memorandum 11, which was the NSC
staff working paper designed to bring into existence a revamped U.S. intelligence system, a truce
of sorts was finally reached among enough of the
interested parties that President Carter felt able

to issue in late January of 1978 his Executive Order No. 12036, superseding President Ford's Executive Order No. 11905 of February 18, 1976. Carter's directive was intended to create a greater degree of centralization in the overall system by giving the Director of Central Intelligence somewhat more authority and responsibility, particularly in designing and managing the budgets for all components in the system, and to some extent in designing and managing the assigned collection tasks for all components, while having enhanced authority over the analytical people who put all the pieces together and say what they are supposed to mean. All of this was reported at some length in major stories in the mass media. But the overwhelming question was how all of this would work out in practice. Among other things, S. 2525 was a major piece of legislation (263 pages long) introduced by the Senate Select Committee on Intelligence on February 9, 1978, based largely on the massive work of this group during 1976-77 when it was informally known as the Church Committee (for its chairman, Senator Frank Church at that time). Hearings on this gigantic legislative proposal began only in April 1978, and nobody was bold enough to hazard a prediction when--if ever--a finally revised version might eventually pass the Congress and be forwarded to the President. If that ever happened, or even if it did not, Senate and House actions and sentiments could have a strong influence on the implementation of Executive Order No. 12036.

The comments in this part of this paper on the NSC staff, the Department of State, the Department of Defense, and the U.S. intelligence system by no means cover all of the key governmental players in making American foreign and defense policies. The references to the Senate Select Committee immediately above can serve as a reminder about another increasingly important set of people--the key staffers for a number of individual House and Senate members as well as for a number of House and Senate committees in the Congress.[80] But space and time do not allow a further examination of these players. It is useful however to review interactions among and between the political actors already discussed.

Interdepartmental Relations

The official "party line" heard around Washington from various sources was that interdepartmental relations were relatively cordial as of springtime 1978, but the major case study on the issue of U.S. policy toward Soviet/Cuban activities in Africa in the late spring and summer revealed massive disagreements and major tensions among key participants, particularly along "hawk" and "dove" lines as organizationally based factions emerged on the fundamental question of how to perceive and behave toward the Soviet Union. Vice President Mondale and some of the so-called "Mondale people," many of whom should more accurately have been called the "McGovern people" or the "McCarthy people" because they supported those presidential candidates in 1972 and 1968 respectively, were probably among the 1978 doves. These included David Aaron in his role as Deputy Director of the NSC staff (immediately under Brzezinski), and Richard Holbrooke, Anthony Lake and Richard Moose working generally at the Assistant Secretary level in the Department of State, plus certainly Ambassador Andrew Young and his deputy Ambassador Donald McHenry at the United Nations. Chief dove, needless to add, was Paul Warnke as Director of the Arms Control and Disarmament Agency. Brzezinski was certainly a clearcut hawk almost all of the time, but it was harder to pinpoint the identifications of his NSC staffers. Brown at Defense was also hard to categorize, because he seemed more interested in protecting his own stakes and turf than in protecting the nation. Vance at State and Turner at the CIA tried as hard as possible to be "objective"--but not always successfully in the eyes of others.

Players were fragmented and factionalized on issues other than perceptions of the USSR. One of the most divisive issues was the reorganization of the U.S. intelligence system, and the ill will generated in that ongoing dispute could be expected to color intrabureaucratic perceptions and postures on a variety of other matters. Admiral Stansfield Turner, believing that he had a clear initial mandate from the President to take charge of the overall intelligence system in his position as Director of Central Intelligence, proceeded to do that starting in the early spring of 1977 just after taking office. He was quickly perceived by Brown at Defense, however, as a serious threat, because Defense controlled something well in excess of 90% of U.S. total intelligence assets; thus, any centralizing under Turner was almost certain to mean some losses for Defense, and Brown was never one to surrender turf graciously. Moreover, on that one, he had the full weight of professional military opinion behind him. Vance at State, with relatively little to lose and perhaps something to gain if the overall intelligence product could be improved and made available to him (Defense had always been reluctant to share what it gathered), often sided with Turner additionally because logic and the President seemed behind the Admiral. Brzezinski was a different story, however. With relatively little actually to manage in terms of people and budgets outside of his reduced and streamlined NSC staff, and knowing something about the old "knowledge is power" adage, he made a major effort at one point in 1977 to reshuffle the U.S. intelligence system so that he could manage it from the White House. He did in fact contrive to get something of a finger into the managerial pie, as a result of the new regime described by Executive Order No. 12036.

In this light, it is relatively easy to forecast that a running gun battle on a three-cornered field, with Brown and Turner and Brzezinski at the corners, will continue into the indefinite future in the Carter administration as to who will have precisely how much power over what parts and stages of the intelligence system and process. This battle can and probably will relate to battles over substantive policy issues from time to time as Brzezinski, Brown and Turner color themselves different shades of hawk depending on the issues in hand. An alert and perceptive reader might have had suspicions that some of this had already occurred in 1977 and early 1978 as major "turfing" disputes erupted throughout the Carter administration including but not confined to foreign and defense policy bureaucracies. A major front-page story in the New York Times, written by a team of reporters, analyzed some of these intrabureaucratic struggles for money and authority within the Carter administration.[81] According to this analysis, critics were calling these bureaucratic wars merely more evidence of weak presidential leadership, some scholars were saying that these were routine and expectable events in government, and President Carter was saying that they were not only expectable but a positively good thing because they represented a healthy form of "bureaucratic democracy."

THE U.S.S.R.: FRIEND OR ENEMY?

Most if not all of the apparent confusions and

vacillations in President Carter's foreign and defense policies stemmed from the administration's apparent inability to decide on the threat from the U.S.S.R. and what the relationship should be between it and the United States. Indeed, much of the interdepartmental "infighting" is also a reflection on disagreements regarding the threat posed by the Soviet Union. With no clear answer to this question, there could be no clear answers to any other foreign policy questions, almost all of which were secondary to this primary issue.

Part of the difficulty in answering the question, certainly, was that the evidence was mixed, and Americans do not like mixed evidence. Speaking at a special conference, I commented briefly on this American tendency.

> This (predicted) transition from the old to the new model (of the international system) will require a little bit of schizophrenia on the part of all of us. We will have to maintain some conventional securities against nations, as if they were enemies, while working with some of those same nations as if they were friends in solving some critical new problems. Americans who seem to have a relatively low tolerance for ambiguity and prefer to think in black and white terms may find it especially troublesome to look at another nation as both a feared adversary and a cooperative partner.[82]

Thomas L. Hughes addressed himself to essentially the same problem, except that what I called "ambiguities" he called "contradictions," and he seemed to think that President Carter should have done a better job in "the management of contradictions."[83]

In any case, Carter did not manage contradictions any better than he managed anything else. U.S. News & World Report's Deputy Editor Joseph Fromm, as noted earlier, wrote that Carter's foreign policy toward the USSR had moved through three vacillating stages: initially harsh and demanding, then friendly and conciliatory, and finally just confused but no longer assuming that either harsh or friendly American gestures would automatically produce the desired results.[84]

The U.S. - African Predicament

This third stage--the "confusion" stage--progressed into the "rampant confusion" stage in the summer of 1978, and most notably with regard to efforts by the Carter administration to decide what to do (if anything) about the Soviet-backed Cuban involvements in Africa. The bewildering array of zigs and zags, flips and flops, became even more bewildering--almost unbelievable. As noted previously, Carter's Wake Forest speech was widely heralded in the press as marking the triumph of Zbigniew Brzezinski and the "hawks" around Mr. Carter who wanted the President to take a new tough line with the USSR. But there was substantial evidence pointing in the other direction; that it was not necessarily true that the President was taking a new tough line with the USSR; and that in fact the Wake Forest speech may have been merely sound and fury signifying very little except that some advisors told him that it might be useful with certain domestic and foreign audiences if he made a tough-sounding speech. Even at this writing, it is still hard to say exactly what the Wake Forest speech meant or symbolized, with some contending that it was a tough new Carter line, and some saying that it was merely rhetoric for whatever his reasons might have been.

Vance versus Brzezinski on Africa

Starting with the Wake Forest speech in mid-March, continuing through April and May and June, highlighted again by the President's early June speech in Annapolis, there was a period of more than three months when Carter steadily escalated a drumbeat of verbal assaults against the USSR for its actions in Africa. Brzezinski was widely heralded in the media as the architect of this new hard line, and he seemed to be enjoying every minute of the attention that he was getting. The anxiety of American "liberals" concerning the increasingly repressive Soviet treatment of dissidents made it difficult for them, ordinarily strong in their criticisms of hard-line policies, to resist the strident aggressiveness of the "hawks" under Brzezinski's banner--moreover, "hawks" who seemed to be carrying the day with the President. But, behind the scenes, and largely unreported in the press, a different line of reasoning was reaching the President from Secretary of State Vance, supported by Vice President Mondale, and ably assisted by the "recycled Vietnam doves" in high positions in the Department of State--most notably Assistant Secretary of State for Africa Richard Moose, Director of the Policy Planning Staff Anthony Lake, and several others probably including Special Assistant to the Secretary George H. Mitchell (a young career Foreign Service Officer of considerable talent, and not one of the "recycled Vietnam doves" serving in political appointments, but an African specialist). This group's "inside man" in the White House was David Aaron, Vice President Mondale's longtime protege serving immediately under Brzezinski as Deputy Director of the National Security Council Staff. Indeed, Aaron had led Moose and Lake on a special assignment for Secretary Vance to Ethiopia and elsewhere in Africa earlier in the spring to attempt to resolve issues of Soviet/Cuban penetrations and involvements there. Also playing key roles for Secretary Vance in the effort to turn around the Brzezinski-led hard-line faction were Ambassador Andrew Young at the United Nations and, even more importantly, Young's deputy also serving with the rank and title of ambassador, Donald F. McHenry. Finally, serving as the Secretary's key "man in the field" in this effort was Ambassador to Nigeria Donald B. Easum, longtime distinguished career Foreign Service Officer who had previously occupied the position of Assistant Secretary of State for Africa during a period in 1974 when Secretary Kissinger was momentarily interested in improving U.S. relations with Africa.

The chief goal of this Vance-led group was to look at the African situation in its own terms rather than as an extension of worldwide Soviet-American competition and rivalry. Whereas the Brzezinski-led "hawks" wanted to mount a substantial effort to support and prop up the Mobutu regime in Zaire in the wake of the atrocity-ridden invasion of Zaire's Shaba province by Katangese irregulars from Angola, further prodding the President's macho instincts by telling him that his authority was being challenged both by the Soviet leaders and by out-of-line Senators, the Vance faction contended that there was ultimately no way to save Mobutu without losing a lot of Carter's credibility on the "human rights" issue--given that Mobutu was not exactly a paragon of democratic values. Further, the Vance group contended that, with a bit of skillful diplomacy, the authorities in Angola might be pried away from Soviet domination.

The first hint that the Vance faction might be winning against the Brzezinski faction appeared in an inside story in the Washington Star by Henry S. Bradsher--a chief foreign policy specialist for that newspaper. One day later, on June 22, Bradsher had his story on the front page, and it was much bigger news. Several excerpts from Bradsher's account are worthy of inclusion here:

> A month ago the Carter administration was exploring the idea of increasing aid to Angolan insurgents. Now it is trying to cut off the main aid channel through Zaire.
>
> This switch in approaches is contained in an effort to work out an agreement between Angola and Zaire that would halt interference in each other's affairs across their central African border.
>
> The deputy U.S. ambassador to the United Nations, Donald McHenry,...will try to convince the government of President Agostinho Neto that it is in Angola's interest to resolve problems on both borders.
>
> When the Shaba invasion began, administration officials began exploring the possibility of retaliating against Angola and increasing the problems of its Cuban backers by increasing U.S. aid to UNITA. National Security Adviser Brzezinski was reportedly behind this reaction.
>
> It was squelched by congressional leaders who opposed any change in 1975 legislation to prevent CIA involvement in the Angolan civil war. Agostinho Neto won that war...[85]

The Washington Post also wheeled into action with a front-page story on the fast-breaking events, utilizing reporters Walter Pincus and Robert Kaiser to provide details on Ambassador McHenry's mission to Angola.[86] On June 25 the same newspaper carried a blow-by-blow chronology of the events, written by senior military and diplomatic correspondent Don Oberdorfer with assistance from Pincus and Kaiser.[87]

They noted that CIA Director Stansfield Turner had been used by the President to attempt to persuade Senator Dick Clark, Democrat of Iowa, and one of the chief Senate skeptics, that in fact the Cubans had been heavily involved and that the Cubans had been supported substantially by the Russians. Turner appeared to have been a victim of Carter's political efforts to do whatever he thought that he had to do in order to salvage the Brzezinski policy, until the Vance group finally succeeded in persuading the President that Brzezinski's recommendations were bound to fail on almost every count.

Charles Bartlett commented on the story from another dimension. "The Carter hardline policies have triggered lots of emotion, probably more here (in Washington) than in Moscow. The danger is less that they will precipitate new tensions with the Soviet Union than that they will divide the Carter policymakers into an open break (among themselves). The risk is that the President will look as if he is presiding over a two-headed administration."[88] The lead editorial in the Washington Star on that same day was headlined, "When huff comes to puff," and tried to put a good face on the policy switch by saying, "We would like to look at the bright side and say the apparent contradictions are no more than the calculated ambiguities appropriate to a flexible diplomacy."[89] But the editorial writer knew that this apology would not stand up, and concluded with the anxiety that--however appropriate the Carter-Brzezinski hardline talk might have been as a recognition of the problem of "Soviet expansion" in Africa "via the Cuban surrogate"--verbal recognition was "not the same thing as effectively countering that expansion."

Joseph Kraft's column in the Washington Post focused on "Vance's role":

> Out of the swirling mists of bureaucratic war there has emerged a clear victor in the struggle for preeminence in foreign policy. Secretary of State Cyrus Vance-- not the widely publicized national security adviser, Zbigniew Brzezinski--has come out on top.
>
> Still it remains a question whether Vance can assert himself for long as the undisputed master of foreign policy under President Carter. For it is not clear that he has the personal qualities to be a

strong secretary of state.

One reason Vance is so little prone to take charge lies in his post-Vietnam experience. As a leading--perhaps the leading--lawyer in New York, he lived at the center of an establishment that had lost confidence. He came to believe in a certain American guilt--for the condition of the blacks, for the plight of the Palestinians and, of course, for aggressive (U.S.) actions all over the Third World.[90]

The New York Times featured a highly laudatory personality profile on Ambassador Donald McHenry by Kathleen Teltsch, thus making it clear in this and other ways that it was pleased with the emergence of the Vance-led group.[91] But, as always with the Carter administration, events were never as clear as they might have seemed. U.S. News & World Report stated that Carter had ordered Brzezinski and Ambassador Young to "lie low" while the President and Secretary Vance assumed responsibility for making all future major statements on foreign policy issues.[92] At about the same time, however, Henry Bradsher writing in the Washington Star was not wholly convinced that Brzezinski had gone into eclipse; the story was headlined "Who Sets Foreign Policy, Vance or Brzezinski?"[93] Don Oberdorfer, following the pro-Vance editorial line of his paper the Washington Post, wrote a very laudatory front-page story under the headline "Vance Presents a 'Positive' U.S. Foreign Policy"--but yet did not quite answer the question in Bradsher's headline.[94] U.S. News & World Report dramatized the question under the headline "Tug of War over Foreign Policy," and featuring a cover cartoon with Vance, Brzezinski and Young trying to wrestle the President for his attention as Carter himself tried to hang on to a global map.[95] In its July 3 issue, this same magazine reported, "Conflict between Zbigniew Brzezinski's National Security Council staff and Cyrus Vance's State Department has grown so tense that it is now rated as worse than when Henry Kissinger at the White House was feuding with Secretary of State William Rogers..."[96]

By June 23, just as most of the pundits were agreeing that Vance and his policies had won over Brzezinski and his policies, Carter again confused

the issue by making a speech in Fort Worth that the
Washington Star publicized with a banner headline,
"'Not Going to Let Soviets Push Us Around'--Carter
Defends Brzezinski, Talks Tough on Foreign Policy."[97] The President "talked tough" again on July
12 in Geneva, harshly accusing the USSR of violating the 1975 Helsinki human rights accords in the
trials of Soviet dissidents Shcharansky, Ginsburg
and others. This story was widely reported in the
U.S. press on July 13, and Marvin Stone, writing in
U.S. News & World Report--among other prominent
journalists saying the same thing--urged the President to continue applying the heat to the USSR on
this issue.[98] The lead story in the same issue of
the same magazine, however, sounded none too confident about what Carter was likely to do, but confident that he would in fact continue to be tested
by the USSR, as evidenced by the story's headline,
"Carter's next test: A hostile Kremlin--repressive
at home, expanding abroad--creates the biggest headache yet for the President."[99]

  Carter in the first evening prime-time televi-
sion news conference of his presidency, sounded
highly conciliatory toward the USSR. James Gerstenzang, in a widely published report, stated,
"President Carter's off-again, on-again feud with
the Soviet Union is off again. ... Carter, whose
spokesman announced only one day earlier that he
was imposing trade reprisals against the Russians,
reported that 'we would like even to enhance trade
with the Soviet Union.' ... The President's comments on the Soviet Union were the latest in a
series he had made to define the U.S.-Soviet relationship."[100] The press conference on the evening
of July 20 therefore clarified nothing.

Summary and Conclusions

  What can one conclude from observing Mr. Carter's efforts over roughly the first half of 1978
in attempting to define the Soviet-American relationship? First, he certainly did not like to be
perceived as weak and vacillating by anybody, within the United States or abroad, and had tended to
try to solve this problem by a new image-building
program headed by Gerald Rafshoon while he himself
continued to flood the market with statements on
the subject. These statements had only made the
problem worse. Unless one believed that consistently confusing and ambiguous words and deeds,
statements and actions, were always a useful ploy

in foreign and defense policies, it was hard to explain--much less justify--whatever it was that Carter was doing. It was true that Secretary Vance and his group, with substantial assistance from a group of Senators, had successfully forestalled further U.S. military involvement in Africa in June, but it was not clear that the President was necessarily happy about this, and it was not clear that Brzezinski had gone down for a final ten-count in the boxing match with Vance. On the contrary, heading into the final months of 1978, that fight continued, and very little was clear. Jeffrey Antevil reported, "...Vance has been gaining in stature, and apparently in self-confidence, in the past few weeks. A couple of months ago, the harder line of White House national security adviser Zbigniew Brzezinski seemed to be in the ascendancy. But since then, Vance has clearly established himself as the President's top foreign policy adviser."[101] My own opinion is that this may be true, but on the other hand it may not be true. As the sportscasters sometimes say, "Don't go away, sports fans--this game is not over yet." The stakes of the game, however, are enormous, not merely a contest between rival bureaucrats and bureaucracies in Washington, but a struggle over competing policy visions for the benefit of a President who--by all accounts and all of the available evidence--has no vision of his own.

CONCLUSIONS

President Carter is in fact a weak leader, and may have been permanently injured beyond the possibility for full recovery by all of the apparent zigzags in foreign and defense policy matters thus far. He reads a lot, absorbing many details, but he understands very little, particularly in foreign policy and defense policy matters. At the same time, he has a sublime kind of self-assurance in his knowledge and his abilities, which he perceives to be far greater than almost anybody else will ever again perceive them to be. This terrifying sense of being right is not much mitigated by an inclination to think that he may in fact be wrong from time to time. If and when he thinks that he has been wrong, it will be because some perceived inner voice, not the voices of others, will have told him so.

For these reasons, it really does not much matter, in terms of overall grand policy decisions, that bureaucratic wars will erupt and flare up and occasionally rage from time to time among and between and within the various components of the foreign and defense policies apparatus. The President will want and will study the structured information and recommendations provided to him by the components of this apparatus, but he will eventually hear whatever he wants to hear from whatever sources--and his wants in these matters will be determined by a complex personal value structure not easy to pinpoint and describe. He will thus notice the bureaucratic wars, but he will not be overly concerned by these matters because he will not perceive that they have that much significance for him either in terms of his policy preference or his own political future. Therefore, he will intervene to dampen down bureaucratic wars in his family only if the noise and furor become a nuisance, and not because of governmental reasons--only to remove an annoyance, not an impediment.

All of the above also implies that Carter will be more concerned with making policy than with monitoring its implementation. He will discover only too late, if ever, that many of his policies will have been undermined by bureaucratic warriors to whom he paid too little attention.

If he has a vision, it is an engineer's vision of efficiency in government, and one important bottom line will be a balanced budget. The major report in the Wall Street Journal in September 1977, cited at a number of earlier points herein, said as much.102 For this kind of reason, and not because he also made an issue of these matters in his 1976 campaign promises, he will indeed continue struggling to hold down the size of the federal budget, the federal debt, and the federal bureaucracy. A McNamara-style "body count" showing a smaller number of people in federal service at the end of his presidency than at the beginning would surely be pleasing to him, regardless of any other unpleasant consequences associated with such a reduction.

Carter will be particularly attracted to cutting down the defense budget, because it is an attractively large target, and because--notwithstanding his Naval Academy education--he has little or no understanding of the diplomatic or hostile uses of armed forces in any case. Lawrence J. Korb, in a briefing for the press in Washington on "Changing Defense Priorities: The FY 1979-83 Defense Program" held on February 1, 1978, said the following things about the President's defense budget:103

> The Carter administration gives less priority to defense than any post-World War II administration. For the first time since FY 1950, defense outlays will fall below 5% of GNP as of FY 1981. The figure was 10%, for example, in 1967, and Secretary McNamara was bragging about that.104 The FY 1979 defense budget is at best level in constant dollars, and would be a declining budget if the Congress should cut the presidential request by more than 1.8%.
>
> The emphasis will be on fighting a short intensive war in Europe, with a bit more money for the Army and a bit less for the Air Force and Navy, but enough less particularly for the Navy that its capabilities will be severely reduced as of FY 1983-- indeed, so reduced that even the Army is worrying on it, because the Army needs the Navy to take it wherever the Army could be asked to fight overseas.105

Carter will undertake even unilateral disarmament measures in the nuclear weapons category, blocking new weapons developments and slowing down or halting the procurement of more older weapons, if the SALT negotiations should fail--although he will be prepared to make almost any concession so that SALT negotiations do not fail. Many in Congress will be alarmed, and will threaten and attempt to take many actions and sanctions against Carter, but they will ultimately fail because when public opinion is ultimately confronted with the costs either in inflation or new higher explicit taxes required to support the new military items desired by some in Congress, the public will opt against the military items. In short, in the face of a growing taxpayers' revolt nationwide, and the increasing public anxieties about inflation, butter will win over guns. Many instinctive hawks will choke on the butter, but butter it will be.106

A favorite and traditional American solution will try to disguise some unpleasant consequences. In contrast to the advice of Theodore Roosevelt, President Carter and many Americans of bellicose inclinations will speak stickly while carrying a big soft. Rhetoric will heat up as capabilities cool down. But it will be only rhetoric. The New Republic's distinguished longtime White House correspondent John Osborne was right when he reported that Carter's tough-talking Wake Forest speech of March 17 raised "a question whether the defense speech represents the 'shift in emphasis in American foreign policy' that an angry Moscow response said it did."107 Osborne continued, "The gaps between Carter's fiscal 1979-80 defense budget projections and the scope of responsibility defined at Winston-Salem (i.e., the Wake Forest speech) raise the same question." Osborne answered the question, quite correctly in my judgment. He concluded, "The record testifies that the speech represents yet another shift in the Carter rhetoric of foreign and defense policy and little if anything more." In short, the tough talk was all fluff and bluff. The reality is a weaker and weaker United States, in terms of military capabilities and--for that matter, at least in the spring of 1978--in economic capabilities too.

Jimmy Carter, therefore, is not really a 1970s Democrat. Rather, he is a 1920s and 1930s isolationist Republican. He and Herbert Hoover would have got along very nicely--many of the same moral feelings, many of the same instincts of engineers, and many of the same blind spots and incapabilities. But the Republican whom Carter most nearly resembles is the late Senator William E. Borah. Carter too would have favored something like friendlier relations with the USSR, the collection of war debts, the avoidance of intervention in Latin America, the support for disarmament and the Kellogg-Briand Pact.

NOTES

1. Richard C. Snyder, H.W. Bruck and Burton Sapin, Decision-making as an Approach to the Study of International Politics (Princeton, N.J.: Series No. 3 in the Foreign Policy Analysis Project, Princeton University, 1954).

2. Richard M. Neustadt, Presidential Power: The Politics of Leadership (New York: John Wiley & Sons, Inc., 1961).

3. Samuel P. Huntington, The Common Defense:

Strategic Programs in National Politics (New York: Columbia University Press, 1961). A book edited by Huntington and appearing one year later, Changing Patterns of Military Politics (New York: The Free Press of Glencoe, 1962), was an even more clearcut study of structural and procedural questions in the context of bureaucratic defense politics.

4. Paul Y. Hammond, Organizing for Defense: The American Military Establishment in the Twentieth Century (Princeton, N.J.: Princeton University Press, 1961).

5. Demetrios Caraley, The Politics of Military Unification: A Study of Conflict and the Policy Process (New York: Columbia University Press, 1965).

6. For example, Vincent Davis, The Admirals Lobby (Chapel Hill: University of North Carolina Press, 1967).

7. Morton H. Halperin, Limited War in the Nuclear Age (New York: John Wiley & Sons, Inc., 1963). This was originally published in May 1962 as Occasional Paper No. 3 from Harvard University's Center for International Affairs, and attracted widespread attention both for its emphasis on the way in which U.S. governmental bureaucracies reacted to an unanticipated kind of situation--limited war--but also for its emphasis on the policy implications of the situation itself.

8. Morton Halperin, China and the Bomb (New York: Frederick A. Praeger, 1965), Contemporary Military Strategy (Boston: Little, Brown and Company, Inc., 1967) and Technical Progress Report No. 309 (China Lake, Cal.: U.S. Naval Ordinance Test Station, February 1, 1963).

9. Morton Halperin and Tang Tsou, "United States Policy Toward the Offshore Islands," Public Policy (Cambridge, Mass.: Harvard Center for International Affairs, 1966).

10. Morton Halperin, Defense Strategies for the Seventies (Boston: Little, Brown and Company, Inc., 1971).

11. Morton Halperin, Bureaucratic Policies and

Foreign Policy (Washington, D.C.: Brookings Institution, 1974).

12. Thomas Schelling, The Strategy of Conflict (Cambridge, Mass.: Harvard University Press, 1960).

13. Discussion with Tanter. Some of Tanter's thinking at that time was evident in an essay called "Research Access to Relevant Government Data and Policymakers," included in an informal publication that I edited, under Vincent Davis, New Research on American Foreign Policy: A Conference Transcript (Denver: Graduate School of International Studies, May 3-4, 1968), pp. 83-89. Further evolution was evident in Raymond Tanter and Richard H. Ullman, (eds.), Theory and Policy in International Relations (Princeton, N.J.: Princeton University Press, 1972); especially see pp. 7-39.

14. Charles F. Hermann, Crises in Foreign Policy: A Simulation Analysis (Indianapolis: The Bobbs-Merrill Co., Inc., 1969).

15. Robert J. Art, The TFX Decision: McNamara and the Military (Boston: Little, Brown and Company, Inc., 1968).

16. Lawrence J. Korb's many papers were ultimately pulled together and presented as chapters in his book, The Joint Chiefs of Staff: The First Twenty-Five Years (Bloomington: Indiana University Press, 1976).

17. Harvey M. Sapolsky's work was first produced in a highly limited and informal version from the Office of Naval Research and then as a book, The Polaris System Development: Bureaucratic and Programmatic Success in Government (Cambridge, Massachusetts: Harvard University Press, 1972).

18. Graham Allison, Essence of Decision: Explaining the Cuban Missile Crisis (Boston: Little, Brown and Company, Inc., 1971); the Allison-Halperin essay, "Bureaucratic Politics: A Paradigm and Some Policy Implications," was in Tanter and Ullman (eds.), pp. 40-79, and originally published in World Politics, special issue, 1971. See also, Graham Allison, "Conceptual Models and the Cuban Missile Crisis," American Political Science Review,

September, 1969, Vol. LXII, No. 3, pp. 689-718.

19. Stanley Hoffmann, Gulliver's Travels, or the Setting of American Foreign Policy (New York: McGraw-Hill, 1968). Only the middle part of this book dealt with societal and governmental aspects of U.S. foreign policy; the rest of it analyzed the international scene (i.e., the "looking at them" approach).

20. I wrote, by invitation, a 105-page draft study of the Department of Defense as part of a White House project funded by the Ford Foundation, housed at the Institute for Defense Analyses, and assigned to review the key agencies involved in making U.S. defense policies. A shortened version appeared as Chapter VI in the two-volume IDA Report R-150, The National Security Process (Washington, D.C.: IDA, November 1968). It also appeared in the commercial form of this report, Laurence J. Legere and Keith C. Clark, eds., The President and the Management of National Security (New York: Frederick A. Praeger, 1969). Finally, it appeared under Vincent Davis, "The Office of the Secretary of Defense and the U.S. Department of Defense," in James N. Rosenau, Vincent Davis, and Maurice A. East, eds., The Analysis of International Politics (New York: The Free Press, 1972), pp. 345-370.

21. In addition to Allison's previously noted Essence of Decision, the following are some examples:
John F. Campbell, The Foreign Affairs Fudge Factory (New York: Basic Books, 1971);
I.M. Destler, Presidents, Bureaucrats, and Foreign Policy (Princeton, N.J.: Princeton University Press, 1972);
Stephen A. Krasner, "Are Bureaucracies Important?" in Foreign Policy, Summer 1972;
Robert L. Rothstein, Planning, Prediction and Policy Making in Foreign Affairs: Theory and Practice (Boston: Little, Brown and Company, Inc., 1972);
Charles Yost, The Conduct and Misconduct of Foreign Affairs (New York: Random House, 1972).

22. The Report of the Commission on the Organization of the Government for the Conduct of Foreign Policy, 278 pp., dated June 1975, is (or was) available at $2.75 under Stock No. 022-000-00108-6

from the U.S. Government Printing Office.

23. Graham Allison and Peter Szanton, <u>Remaking Foreign Policy: The Organizational Connection</u> (New York: Basic Books, 1976). Szanton became the director of that component of the governmental reorganization group in the Office of Management and Budget in the Carter administration charged with reviewing and recommending possible reorganizations in the foreign affairs agencies, and--as will probably surprise no one--Allison became his chief outside consultant.

24. Tom Wicker, in <u>The New York Times</u>, October 18, 1977, p. 37, speculated that problems confronting a U.S. President are becoming so intractable that any President is likely to lose public support quickly, thus leading the United States into an era of one-term Presidents.

25. Vincent Davis, <u>The Politics of Innovation: Patterns in Navy Cases</u> (Denver: Graduate School of International Studies Monograph Series in World Affairs, 1967).

26. <u>Foreign Policy and the State Department</u>, a 19-page pamphlet issued by the State Department (Department of State Publication 8869 in Department and Foreign Service Series 154, from the Office of Media Services, Bureau of Public Affairs), addressed this issue of presidential primacy and the role of Congress in an interesting and cautious manner; see pp. 4-5. This pamphlet was released in September 1976, but is the most recent of its kind.

27. Bylined James M. Perry, but based on interviews by virtually the whole staff of that newspaper with almost everybody who ever knew Jimmy Carter, <u>Wall Street Journal</u>, September 23, 1977, p. 1.

28. Jack Anderson, <u>Parade</u> magazine, November 13, 1977, p. 9.

29. Robert A. Haeger, "Carter and NATO: Allied Leaders Size Him Up," <u>U.S. News & World Report</u>, April 3, 1978, pp. 35-36. For an even stronger report on this subject, see Flora Lewis, "NATO Officials Uneasy Over Carter Administration's Foreign Policy," <u>The New York Times</u>, April 1, 1978, p. 5.

30. James Reston, editorial column, The New York Times, September 25, 1977.

31. Michael J. Robinson, "Learning by Doing," Presidential Studies Quarterly, Spring-Summer, 1977, (Guest Editorial).

32. Bernard Weinraub in The New York Times, April 6, 1978, p. 38.

33. "Who's Who in the Carter Administration", The Washington Monthly, September 1977, p. 38.

34. Detailed reports on the results of Carter's appointments and staffing procedures include: Edward Walsh in The Washington Post, June 5, 1977, p. A-14; Robert G. Kaiser also in the Post, June 6, 1977, p. A-1; and Laura Foreman in The New York Times, July 16, 1977, p. 22. The front-page Kaiser story is recommended.

35. James T. Wooten reported these and other matters, such as Carter's failure actually to use his cabinet officers, in a front-page story in The New York Times, April 25, 1977. Although Wooten-- whose Carter biography Dasher was widely acclaimed --probably knows the President better than any other reporter, Press Secretary Jody Powell heatedly denied these Wooten descriptions, as was widely noted on April 26, 1977, for example, by Edward Walsh on p. A-3 of The Washington Post.

36. Hedrick Smith, "Problems of a Problem Solver," The New York Times Magazine, January 8, 1978, p. 30.

37. Berry, n. 21, supra. One is reminded of a definition of a fanatic sometimes attributed to Eric Hoffer: Someone who redoubles his efforts after losing sight of his goals.

38. The "Washington Whispers" column on p. 18 of the March 27, 1978, issue of U.S. News & World Report said that the President can be "so tough and intimidating that only three people have the stature to tell him to his face he is wrong--Ham Jordan, Jody Powell, and Vice President Mondale." But the column also said that, despite rumors of staff shake-ups, "...most top-level advisers feel safe, because, as one said: 'Carter just hates to

fire anybody.'" The same column in the same magazine, issue for July 17, 1978, p. 10, reported: "Latest word from White House aides is that there will be no changes in the cabinet this year. Why? As one explains: "It is typical of Carter's loyalty to advisers--and he doesn't want to admit a mistake."

39. Morton Kondracke, "Is There a Present Danger?" The New Republic, January 29, 1977.

40. "Carter's Foreign Policy: Jimmy in the Lion's Den," Time, August 8, 1977 (Cover Story).

41. "Foreign Policy by Committee--Can It Really Work?" U.S. News & World Report, February 21, 1977.

42. Ibid., p. 27.

43. Charles Mohr, The New York Times, October 23, 1977, p. 1.

44. Joseph Fromm, U.S. News & World Report, March 6, 1978, p. 23.

45. John Osborne, The New Republic, April 8, 1978.

46. Morton Kondracke, Ibid.

47. Morton Kondracke, The New Republic, April 15, 1978, p. 15.

48. "The Mishandled Bomb," The New York Times, April 6, 1978, p. 30.

49. Hedrick Smith, The New York Times, April 8, 1978, pp. 6-7.

50. Clyde Farnsworth, "Why U.S. Economic Policy Is At Loose Ends," The New York Times, April 2, 1978, p. 2 E, Section 4.

51. Hedrick Smith, The New York Times, April 8, 1978, p. 7.

52. U.S. News & World Report, April 17, 1978, p. 35.

53. U.S. News & World Report, July 24, 1978, (Cover Story). "Carter's 18 Months: What Went Wrong?" pp. 17-24.

54. *Public Opinion*, May/June, 1978, pp. 33, 35, and "Opinion Roundup" (Center Section).

55. "Washington Whispers," *U.S. News & World Report*, April 17, 1978, p. 16.

56. James Reston, *The New York Times*, April 26, 1978, p. 35.

57. Terence Smith, *The New York Times*, May 26, 1978, p. 1.

58. Richard Burt, *The New York Times*, May 31, 1978, p. 2.

59. James Reston, *The New York Times*, April 21, 1978, p. A27.

60. Terence Smith, *The New York Times*, April 23, 1978, p. 4, Section 4.

61. Martin Tolchin, *The New York Times*, May 19, 1978, p. A11.

62. Charles Peters, *The Washington Monthly*, July/August, 1978, p. 4.

63. Vernon A. Guidry, Jr., *Washington Star*, June 18, 1978, p. 1.

64. "Washington Whispers," *U.S. News and World Report*, July 31, 1978, p. 5. See also Richard Burt, *The New York Times*, April 21, 1978, p. 3.

65. *U.S. News & World Report*, July 31, 1978, p. 44.

66. *U.S. News & World Report*, July 24, 1978, p. 11.

67. "Postcript," *The Washington Post*, July 3, 1978, p. A3.

68. John Osborne, *The New Republic*, June 24, 1978, p. 9.

69. "Washington Whispers," *U.S. News & World Report*, June 26, 1978, p. 8.

70. Michael J. Robinson, "TV's Newest Program: The 'Presidential Nominations Game,'" *Public Opinion*, May/June, 1978, pp. 41-46.

71. Charles Peters, The Washington Monthly, July/August, 1978.

72. Sally Quinn, The Washington Post, June 25, 1978, pp. K1 and continuing.

73. U.S. News & World Report, July 24, 1978.

74. Time, July 31, 1978 (Cover Story).

75. Hugh Sidey, Washington Star, July 2, 1978, p. D3.

76. For more detailed comments on Kissinger, interested readers could inquire about the availability of remaining copies of an unpublished paper by Vincent Davis, "Henry Kissinger and Bureaucratic Politics: Some Disconnected Observations," written in October 1977 for a meeting of the Southern Regional Division of the International Studies Association; 64 pp.

77. In this writer's judgment, the most authoritative and detailed account in print on Brzezinski's NSC staff and its operations (obviously obtained in considerable degree from the man himself), is in a cover story by Dom Bonafede entitled "Brzezinski--Stepping Out of His Backstage Role," National Journal magazine, October 15, 1977, pp. 1596-1601. The best unpublished account is by Lawrence J. Korb, "The Structure and Process of the National Security Council System in the First Year of the Carter Administration," a paper presented at the February 1978 annual convention of the International Studies Association. All of this is put in a longer range historical perspective in an item of my own, Vincent Davis, "The Role of the President and His Advisors in Making U.S. Foreign Policy and Defense Policy," the text for a guest lecture at the Air War College, November 16, 1977.

78. On major continuing problems at the U.S. Department of State, see Robert Pringle, "Creeping Irrelevance at Foggy Bottom," Foreign Policy, Winter 1977-78.

79. In this writer's judgment, the best reporting on the Department of Defense in any daily newspaper is by Bernard Weinraub in The New York Times, particularly during the period of Secretary Brown's tenure thus far. See his article, "The Browning of

the Pentagon," in his newspaper's Sunday Magazine section for January 29, 1978. On the JCS, see Korb, n. 11 supra. A more recent and also quite useful analysis was the cover story entitled "Shaking Up the Pentagon," U.S. News & World Report, July 17, 1978, pp. 33-38.

80. One of the better recent articles on the roles of the key staff people on Capitol Hill on defense matters was entitled, "The New Power Elite in Defense," Business Week magazine, March 27, 1978, pp. 90-92. An earlier in-depth profile on one of these people, Richard Perle, who works for Senator Jackson, was written by Robert G. Kaiser in the "Outlook" section, The Washington Post, June 26, 1977, p. B1.

81. The New York Times, January 23, 1978, p. 1.

82. Vincent Davis, "Conference Proceedings," David M. Abshire and Gordon D. Gayle (eds.), Research Resources for the '70s (Washington, D.C.: Center for Strategic and International Studies, 1970), p. 41.

83. Thomas L. Hughes, Foreign Policy, Summer 1978, No. 3, pp. 34-35.

84. Joseph Fromm, U.S. News & World Report, March 6, 1978, p. 23.

85. Henry Bradsher, Washington Star, June 21, 1978, p. A-5, and June 22, 1978, p. 1.

86. The Washington Post, June 22, 1978, p. 1.

87. The Washington Post, June 25, 1978.

88. Charles Bartlett, Washington Star, June 22, 1978, p. A-13.

89. "When Huff Comes to Puff," Washington Star, June 22, 1978, p. A-12.

90. Joseph Kraft, The Washington Post, June 22, 1978, p. A27.

91. Kathleen Teltsch, The New York Times, June 26, 1978, p. A-3.

92. "Washington Whispers," <u>U.S. News & World Report</u>, June 19, 1978, p. 14.

93. Henry Bradsher, "Who Sets Foreign Policy, Vance or Brzezinski?" <u>Washington Star</u>, June 18, 1978, p. 1.

94. Don Oberdorfer, "Vance Presents a 'Positive' U.S. Foreign Policy," <u>The Washington Post</u>, June 20, 1978, p. 1.

95. "Tug of War over Foreign Policy," <u>U.S. News & World Report</u>, June 19, 1978, (Cover story).

96. "Washington Whispers," <u>U.S. News & World Report</u>, July 3, 1978, p. 5.

97. "'Not Going to Let Soviets Push Us Around'-- Carter Defends Brzezinski, Talks Tough on Foreign Policy," <u>Washington Star</u>, June 24, 1978, p. 1.

98. Marvin Stone, <u>U.S. News & World Report</u>, July 31, 1978, p. 72.

99. "Carter's next test: A hostile Kremlin-- repressive at home, expanding abroad--creates the biggest headache yet for the President," <u>U.S. News & World Report</u>, July 31, 1978, pp. 11-13.

100. James Gerstenzang, Associated Press report, July 21, 1978 (published in a number of newspapers).

101. Jeffrey Antevil, <u>New York News</u> Wire Service, July 29-30, 1978.

102. Perry, <u>Wall Street Journal</u>, n. 21 <u>supra</u>.

103. Copies of the Korb briefing could presumably be obtained from the American Enterprise Institute, where it was delivered.

104. Quoted by Dan F. Sullivan in a report on a McNamara speech to the National Association of Educational Broadcasters on November 7, 1967, in Sullivan's story in <u>The Denver Clarion</u>, November 14, 1967, p. 7.

105. See <u>The Fiscal Year 1979 Defense Budget: An Analysis</u>, a publication of the Association of the United States Army in Washington, D.C., 1978; p. 18.

106. For some further comments along these lines, see Vincent Davis, "The Changing International Environment and U.S. Military Policy in the 1980s: Some General Observations," presented at an IUSAFS meeting in Dallas, April 28, 1978.

107. John Osborne, The New Republic, April 8, 1978.

3
National Security Organization and Process in the Carter Administration

Lawrence J. Korb

INTRODUCTION

Since the creation of the National Security Council (NSC) in 1947, each President has designed an NSC system to suit his own decision-making style and to overcome the perceived inadequacies of the system used by his immediate predecessor. President Carter is no exception. During his first year in office, the current chief executive has shaped an NSC system whose structure and process bear his own trademark and which is alleged to overcome many of the shortcomings of the Nixon-Ford-Kissinger system.[1] This paper will compare the structure and process of the current NSC system to that used in the 1976-77 period and then analyze the strengths and weaknesses of the present arrangement.

THE NSC SYSTEM: 1969-1977

The NSC system which existed during the Nixon-Ford Administration was designed in 1969 by Henry Kissinger, then serving as the Presidential Assistant for National Security Affairs (NSA).[2] It remained essentially unchanged throughout the ensuing eight years.

The Nixon-Ford-Kissinger NSC structure consisted of the Council and an elaborate network of interagency bodies that supported the Council.

This is an updated and revised version of a paper prepared for delivery at the 19th Annual Meeting of the International Studies Association, Washington, D.C., February 22-25, 1978.

These groups were at two levels: Interdepartmental groups at the Assistant Secretary level and NSC subcommittees at the Undersecretary or Deputy Secretary level. The NSC structure as it existed in 1976 is depicted in Figure 3.1.

The Interdepartmental Groups (IGs) were organized on a geographical or functional basis and were chaired by an Assistant Secretary of State. They were responsible for preparing basic studies and developing policy options. If a specific issue did not fit neatly within a region or functional area, an ad hoc group was formed to deal with the subject.

Two of the NSC subcommittees, the Senior Review Group (SRG) and Undersecretaries Committee (USC), were the major supporting elements in the policy-making processes. The membership in these two groups was the same but the chairmanship was different. The USC, responsible for policy implementation, was chaired by the Deputy Secretary of State, number two man in the State Department, while the SRG, responsible for preparation of policy options was chaired by the Assistant to the President for National Security Affairs.

Two of the groups, the Committee on Foreign Intelligence and the Operations Advisory Group, were concerned with intelligence activities. The Committee on Foreign Intelligence, chaired by the Director of Central Intelligence, provided guidance on national intelligence needs and continually evaluated intelligence products. The Operations Advisory Board, under the chairmanship of the Assistant for NSA had the responsibility for advising the President on covert intelligence operations. This group was often referred to as the "40 Committee" after the identification number of a memorandum which set it up.

Three of the committees were established to deal with specific situations. The role of the Defense Review Panel was to evaluate the political, economic, and domestic consequences of changes in the size and distribution of the defense budget. This group was originally called the Defense Program Review Committee and chaired by the Assistant for NSA. Both the name and chairmanship were changed in 1975 when it was placed under the control of the Secretary of Defense. The Verification Panel under the chairmanship of the NSA Assistant, carried out the technical analyses necessary for developing U.S. positions at the SALT talks. The purpose of the International Energy Review Group,

THE NATIONAL SECURITY COUNCIL SYSTEM IN 1976
NATIONAL SECURITY COUNCIL
Pres;Vice-Pres;Sec of State;Sec of Defense;Sec of Treasury-OEP;Chairman,JCS;DCI;ACDA

| White House Situation Room | Asst to Pres for Natl Security Affairs | NSC Staff |

SENIOR REVIEW GROUP	COMMITTEE ON FOREIGN INTELLIGENCE	VERIFICATION PANEL
Asst to Pres for Natl Sec Aff(Chmn) Dep Sec of State Dep Sec of Defense Chairman, JCS DCI	DCI (Chmn) Dep Sec of State Dep Sec of Defense	Asst to Pres for Natl Sec Aff(Chmn) Dep Sec of State Dep Sec of Defense Chairman, JCS Director, ACDA DCI

WASHINGTON SPECIAL ACTIONS GROUP	OPERATIONS ADVISORY GROUP	INTERNATIONAL ENERGY REVIEW GROUP
Asst to Pres for Natl Sec Aff(Chmn) Dep Sec of State Dep Sec of Defense Chairman, JCS DCI	Asst to Pres for Natl Sec Aff(Chmn) Under Sec State for Pol Aff Dep Sec of Defense Chairman, JCS DCI	Asst to Pres for Natl Sec Aff(Chmn) State CIEP Treasury FEA Defense CEA OMB AEC CIA

UNDER SECRETARIES COMMITTEE

Dep Sec of State (Chmn)
Asst to Pres for Natl Sec Aff
Dep Sec of Defense
DCI

DEFENSE REVIEW PANEL

Sec of Defense(Chmn)
Dep Sec of State
Dep Sec of Defense
Chairman, JCS
Chairman, Council of Econ Advisors
Director, OMB
DCI

INTERDEPARTMENTAL GROUPS
(REGIONAL)

Figure 3.1

which had the widest membership of any NSC subcommittee, was to assess the effect of the energy shortage on national security issues.

The final committee, the Washington Special Action Group, handled crisis situations. It was created when North Korea shot down a U.S. EC-121 in 1969 and handled all of the major crises through the seizure of the Mayaguez in 1975.

The key to the NSC decision-making process in the Nixon-Ford era was the National Security Study Memorandum (NSSM). NSSMs identified a problem requiring study and assigned it to a specific subgroup of the NSC for action. A problem could be raised by any individual or group within the bureaucracy, but a NSSM would not be issued without specific presidential approval. During Nixon's first year in office, 85 NSSMs were issued and in the entire 1969-77 period 246 of these documents were promulgated.[3]

Each NSSM assigned responsibility for the problem to a specific standing interdepartmental group or an ad hoc group and set a time deadline for completion. Occasionally, the NSSM asked for a recommended solution to a problem, but usually it called for options and supporting arguments.

A study prepared in response to a NSSM was submitted to the SRG for review. The SRG ensured that the study met the stipulated requirements and that it presented the full range of meaningful options. When the SRG was satisfied that these criteria were met, a formal Council meeting was scheduled to debate the issue. Although the President attended the meetings, he did not make a decision on the issue until a week to 10 days later. During that period he would often call some of the Council members individually to discuss the subject with them. The presidential decision was published in the form of a National Security Decision Memorandum (NSDM). Subsequent to the promulgation of the NSDM, if any individual or group within the national security bureaucracy felt that there was a problem with implementation, a meeting of the Undersecretaries Committee was called to resolve it.

The Nixon-Ford-Kissinger NSC system was not without its flaws. Its main problem was the system's overdependence upon one man. At one time or another, Henry Kissinger, the Assistant to the President for National Security Affairs, was the chairman of every NSC subcommittee concerned with policymaking. The only group never chaired by him was the Undersecretaries Committee which focused on policy implementation.

Functioning of the entire NSC system was dependent on him. No NSSM could be issued nor could any item be approved for an NSC meeting without his passing on it. When he became involved in other areas, for example, the protracted negotiations with Le Duc Tho over the war in Vietnam, the SALT negotiations with the Soviet Union, or shuttle diplomacy in the Middle East, the NSC system simply ground to a halt.

Similarly, Kissinger's viewpoints dominated the entire process. The situation existed for two reasons. First, for most of the period, Kissinger held key positions all throughout the NSC system. Moreover, even when President Ford relieved him of his position as Assistant for National Security Affairs in late 1975, Kissinger continued to dominate the process. He was able to handpick Brent Scowcroft, the colorless Air Force Brigadier General who had served as his deputy from 1973 to 1975, to succeed him at the NSC. During the last year of the Ford administration, the NSC staff functioned as an adjunct to Kissinger's State Department staff, which itself was composed of many former members of Kissinger's NSC staff. Kissinger himself noted that in spite of losing his NSC hat he remained as influential as ever.[4]

Second, within the national security bureaucracy, there were few individuals as strong or opinionated as Kissinger. The only individual whose personality and intellect rivaled that of Kissinger was James Schlesinger and he was fired from his position as Secretary of Defense partly as a result of differences with Kissinger. Such advisors as Secretary of State Rogers and Secretary of Defense Rumsfeld were simply no match for Kissinger. Candidate Jimmy Carter characterized Kissinger's dominance of the NSC structure and process by referring to its results as "Lone Ranger" diplomacy.

NSC SYSTEM: 1977

The NSC structure used by the Carter administration is outlined in Figure 3.2 As indicated, the Interdepartmental Groups remain but are now called Interagency Task Forces. The eight NSC subcommittees have been reduced to two: a Policy Review Committee (PRC) and a Special Coordinating

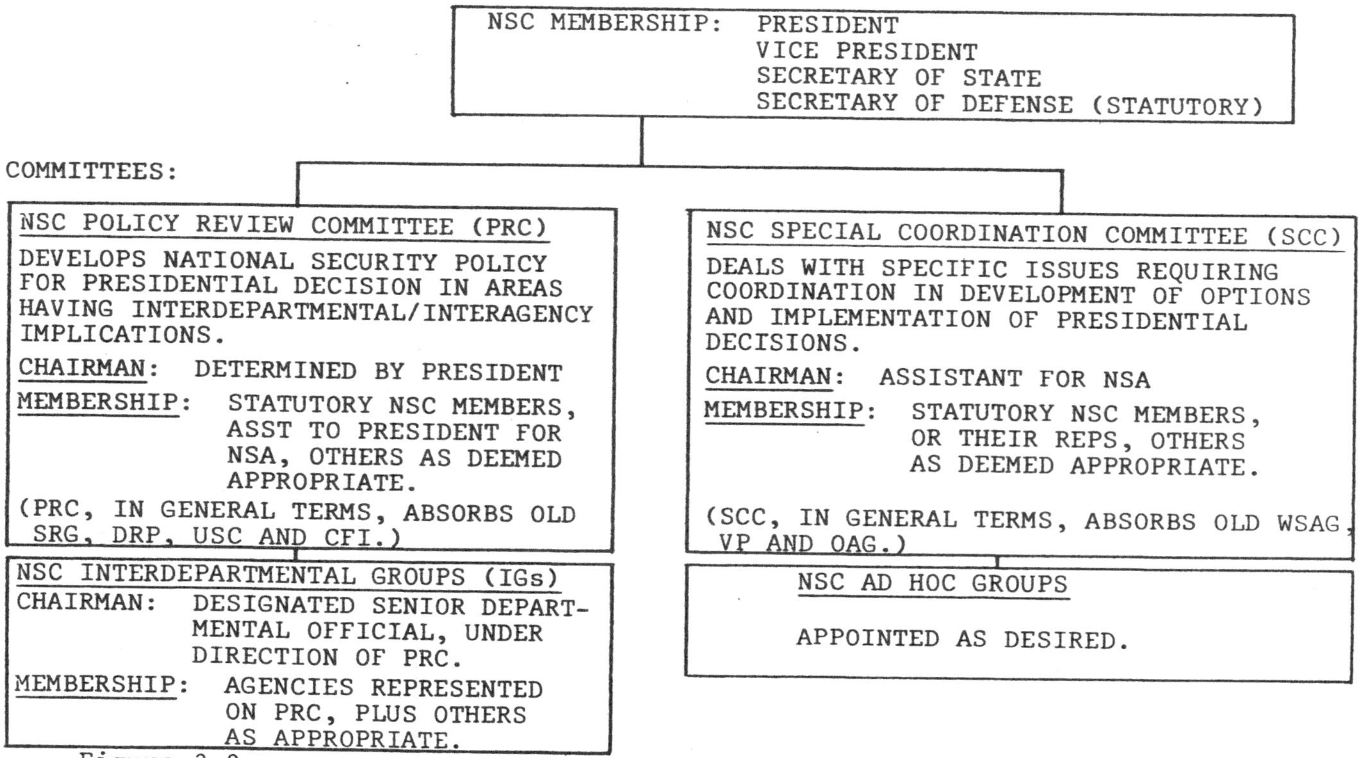

NSC MEMBERSHIP: PRESIDENT
                VICE PRESIDENT
                SECRETARY OF STATE
                SECRETARY OF DEFENSE (STATUTORY)

COMMITTEES:

NSC POLICY REVIEW COMMITTEE (PRC)

DEVELOPS NATIONAL SECURITY POLICY FOR PRESIDENTIAL DECISION IN AREAS HAVING INTERDEPARTMENTAL/INTERAGENCY IMPLICATIONS.

CHAIRMAN: DETERMINED BY PRESIDENT
MEMBERSHIP: STATUTORY NSC MEMBERS, ASST TO PRESIDENT FOR NSA, OTHERS AS DEEMED APPROPRIATE.

(PRC, IN GENERAL TERMS, ABSORBS OLD SRG, DRP, USC AND CFI.)

NSC INTERDEPARTMENTAL GROUPS (IGs)

CHAIRMAN: DESIGNATED SENIOR DEPARTMENTAL OFFICIAL, UNDER DIRECTION OF PRC.
MEMBERSHIP: AGENCIES REPRESENTED ON PRC, PLUS OTHERS AS APPROPRIATE.

NSC SPECIAL COORDINATION COMMITTEE (SCC)

DEALS WITH SPECIFIC ISSUES REQUIRING COORDINATION IN DEVELOPMENT OF OPTIONS AND IMPLEMENTATION OF PRESIDENTIAL DECISIONS.

CHAIRMAN: ASSISTANT FOR NSA
MEMBERSHIP: STATUTORY NSC MEMBERS, OR THEIR REPS, OTHERS AS DEEMED APPROPRIATE.

(SCC, IN GENERAL TERMS, ABSORBS OLD WSAG, VP AND OAG.)

NSC AD HOC GROUPS

APPOINTED AS DESIRED.

Figure 3.2
Source: PD/NSC-2, 20 January 1977

Committee (SCC). The PRC, whose chairman rotates according to the subject and whose membership is the same as the Council, works on long term projects, (i.e., areas having interdepartmental implications). The PRC is supposed to have absorbed the Senior Review Group, the Undersecretaries Committee, the Defense Review Panel and the Committee on Foreign Intelligence. The Special Coordinating Committee (SCC), whose chairman is always the Assistant to the President for National Security Affairs and whose membership also duplicates that of the Council, focuses on short term projects, (i.e., specific issues). The SCC is supposed to absorb the Washington Special Action Group, the Operations Advisory Group, the Verification Panel, and the Undersecretaries Committee.

At first glance, the Carter NSC structure appears to be more simplified than the Kissinger version. Indeed the President rejected a proposal made by Zbigniew Brzezinski, his Assistant for National Security Affairs, for an elaborate set of NSC committees, very similar to the Kissinger model. In reality the NSC structure has not been altered very much. Analysis of membership of the eight Kissinger subcommittees, which is depicted in Figure 3.1, reveals that the membership of each committee was essentially identical. The name of the committee varied according to the subject under discussion. For example, the group considering SALT were known as the Verification Panel, the same group focusing on Mayaguez were called the WASAG; if they were reviewing the Navy's shipbuilding program they were referred to as the Defense Review Panel.

Both the PRC and SCC have their own working groups. Depending upon the project, these working groups are composed of officials at either the undersecretary or assistant secretary level. For example, the Department of Defense representative on the PRC working group tasked with reviewing our military posture was the Assistant Secretary of Defense for International Security Affairs while the State Department was represented by the Director of the Bureau of Political-Military Affairs. In addition to its working group, the SCC also has a Net Assessment Group attached to it.

The name of the documents used in the NSC decision-making process also has been changed. As is indicated in Figure 3.3, the National Security Study Memoranda (NSSM) have been replaced by Presidential Review Memoranda (PRM) and the National

NSC SYSTEM DOCUMENTS*

REVIEWS AND ANALYSES

OLD	NEW
NATIONAL SECURITY STUDY MEMORANDUM	PRESIDENTIAL REVIEW MEMORANDUM
(NSSM)	(PRM/NSC-#)

PRESIDENTIAL DIRECTIVES

OLD	NEW
NATIONAL SECURITY DECISION MEMORANDUM	PRESIDENTIAL DIRECTIVE
(NSDM)	(PD/NSC-#)

Figure 3.3

Source: *PD/NSC-1, 20 January 1977

Security Decision Memoranda (NSDM) have been supplanted by Presidential Directives (PD).

As in the Kissinger era, a problem for review or study can be proposed by any member of the national security bureaucracy but presidential approval must be obtained before the NSC staff can issue a PRM. For long-term projects the PRM defines the problem, sets a deadline, and designates a member of the PRC to serve as a study chairman. This individual then assigns the project to the appropriate interagency task force for the preparation of alternatives. The designated PRC chairman also establishes a PRC working group, under the control of one of his subordinates, (either his deputy or one of his assistant secretaries).

Short term or more specific projects are assigned to the SCC, which, as noted above, is always chaired by the Assistant for National Security Affairs. The SCC chairman then appoints an ad hoc group to prepare alternatives.

About two-thirds of the PRMs have been assigned to the PRC and the Secretary of State has been designated as the chairman on most of them. The projects assigned to the SCC have been primarily in the area of arms control.

When the Interagency Task Force and ad hoc groups have completed a study, it is sent to the PRC or SCC working group for review. When this body is satisfied that the study has incorporated all of the meaningful options and supporting arguments, a meeting of the PRC and SCC is called to discuss the issue. The recommendations of either of these groups on an issue is then forwarded to the President who has acted in these different ways: on some occasions, he has accepted the recommendation as presented; on others he has consulted with individuals; and on still other occasions he has convened a meeting of the full NSC. Most of the decisions have been made by means of the first two methods. In his first nine months in office, the President held only seven formal NSC meetings.[5] When the President decides the question, a Presidential Decision or PD is promulgated.

During the initial days of the Carter administration, it appeared that the NSC would be used in much the same way as in the Kissinger period. In his few days in office, the President blitzed the National Security Bureaucracy with a total of 17 PRMs. Table 3.1 contains a list of these PRMs together with the committee responsible for the study. However, over the next twelve months, only

Table 3.1

PRESIDENTIAL REVIEW MEMORANDA (PRMs)

PRM 1. PANAMA CANAL ZONE (PRC-STATE)
2. SALT (SCC)
3. MIDDLE EAST (PRC-STATE)
4. SOUTH AFRICA/RHODESIA (PRC-STATE)
5. CYPRUS/AEGEAN (PRC-STATE)
6. MBFR (SCC)
7. WESTERN SUMMIT (ECONOMIC ISSUES) (PRC-STATE)
8. NORTH-SOUTH STRATEGY (PRC-STATE)
9. COMPREHENSIVE REVIEW/EUROPE (PRC-STATE)
10. COMPREHENSIVE REVIEW/MILITARY FORCE POSTURE (PRC-SECDEF)
11. INTELLIGENCE STRUCTURE/MISSIONS (VICE-PRESIDENT)
12. ARMS SALES REVIEW (PRC-STATE)
13. US POLICY/POSTURE KOREA (PRC-STATE)
14. PHILIPPINE BASE NEGOTIATIONS (PRC-SECDEF)
15. NUCLEAR PROLIFERATION (PRC-STATE)
16. NUCLEAR TESTING (SCC)
17. REVIEW OF U.S. POLICY-LATIN AMERICA (PRC-STATE)

15 additional PRMs were promulgated. The status of these 32 PRMs as of March 1978 is contained in Table 3.2. In contrast, Kissinger issued 85 during his first year in office. President Carter thus appears to be moving away from the formal NSC process to the informal arrangements which characterized the Kennedy-Johnson years. For example, the President now holds regularly scheduled Friday luncheons with presidential aide Hamilton Jordan and his top national security advisors and receives daily memoranda from the Secretary of State and Secretary of Defense.

STRENGTHS AND WEAKNESSES

The Structure

The present NSC system has overcome some of the structural weaknesses of the Kissinger years. The rotating chairmanship of the PRC keeps one viewpoint from dominating the process and makes smooth functioning of the process less dependent on one individual. In addition, by allowing the Secretary of State and the Secretary of Defense to coordinate many of the studies, it restores these officers to their rightful role in the NSC process.

However, like its predecessors, the Carter system also has some structural weaknesses. These fall into two categories. The first and main failing is that there is no interagency group, similar to the Operations Coordinating Board of the Eisenhower administration or Undersecretaries Committee of the Kissinger period, whose prime responsibility is to insure that decisions are implemented. Without such an interagency group acting as a control mechanism, the risk of NSC decisions being poorly implemented is increased greatly. The SCC does have responsibility in this area, but it has several other functions as well. Moreover, the size of the NSC staff which is in effect the SCC staff is composed of only 39 people; 25 fewer than in the Kissinger period.[6] One indication that the small NSC staff was unable to fulfill this role was the establishment of the Interagency Committee on U.S.-Soviet affairs to monitor U.S.-Soviet activities.[7]

Second, there are no clear distinctions between short and long term projects or specific and interagency problems. Theoretically, most of the projects or problems thus far identified could fall into either category. The jurisdictional problems

Table 3.2

STATUS OF PRM'S - MARCH 1978

PRM #	ISSUE DATE	SUBJECT	RESULTS
1	1-21-77	PANAMA	STUDY COMPLETED
2	1-24-77	SALT	PD-7 ISSUED
3	1-21-77	MIDDLE EAST	STUDY COMPLETED
4	1-21-77	SOUTH AFRICA AND RHODESIA	PD-5 ISSUED
5	1-21-77	CYPRUS/AEGEAN	STUDY COMPLETED
6	1-21-77	MBFR	STUDY COMPLETED
7	1-21-77	INTERNATIONAL SUMMIT	STUDY COMPLETED
8	1-21-77	NORTH/SOUTH STRATEGY	STILL MEETING
9	2-1-77	REVIEW EUROPEAN ISSUES	STUDY COMPLETED
10	2-18-77	NET ASSESSMENT FORCE POSTURE	PD-18 ISSUED, FOLLOW ON STUDIES
11	1-26-77	INTELLIGENCE STRUCTURE/MISSION	PD-19 ISSUED
12	1-26-77	ARMS TRANSFER POLICY REVIEW	PD-13 ISSUED
13	1-26-77	KOREA	PD-12 ISSUED
14	1-26-77	PHILIPPINE BASE NEGOTIATIONS	AWAITING DECISION
15	1-21-77	NUCLEAR PROLIFERATION	PD-8 ISSUED
16	1-25-77	NUCLEAR TESTING	AWAITING DECISION, ONGOING STUDIES
17	1-26-77	U.S. POLICY: LATIN AMERICA	PD-6 ISSUED, MAY BE REOPENED
18	2-1-77	LAW OF SEA	PD-4, PD-16 ISSUED, NEGOTIATIONS TO RESUME MAR 78
19	2-15-77	MICRONESIAN STATUS	PD-11 ISSUED
20	2-15-77	COOPERATION WITH FRANCE	CLOSE HOLD
21	3-17-77	HORN OF AFRICA	STUDY COMPLETED

Table 3.2 (continued)

22	3-24-77	NATN'L INTEGRATED TELECOM PROTECTION POLICY	STUDY COMPLETED
23	3-28-77	COHERENT U.S. SPACE POLICY	DRAFT PD DONE
24	4-5-77	PEOPLE'S REPUBLIC OF CHINA	STILL MEETING
25	4-7-77	ARMS CONTROL IN INDIAN OCEAN	STILL MEETING, LAST ROUND DEC 77
26	5-14-77	ABM TREATY REVIEW	STILL MEETING
27	5-19-77	CHEMICAL WARFARE	STUDY COMPLETED
28	5-24-77	HUMAN RIGHTS	STUDY COMPLETED
29	6-1-77	REVIEW OF CLASSIFICATION SYSTEM	DRAFT EXECUTIVE ORDER DONE
30	6-3-77	TERRORISM	STILL MEETING
31	8-18-77	EXPORT CONTROL OF US TECHNOLOGY	STILL MEETING: DOD GUIDANCE ISSUED
32	9-30-77	CIVIL DEFENSE	STILL MEETING

caused by the lack of clarity in the mandates of the PRC and SCC was illustrated by the dispute over PRM 10, the comprehensive review of our national strategy and military posture, which was supposed to lay the foundation for a new national security policy. Originally this project was assigned to the SCC. Zbigniew Brzezinski, the Assistant for National Security Affairs and Chairman of the SCC, asked his former Columbia colleague, Samuel Huntington, the Coordinator of Security Planning for the NSC staff, to direct the study for the SCC net assessment group.

Both the State and Defense Departments objected to this arrangement. State argued that it ought to have responsibility for developing foreign policy, while DOD contended that it ought to take the lead in developing force structure. As a result of their protests, the study was split. The SCC net assessment group analyzed the threat facing this nation and formulated general national strategies. A PRC working group, under the chairmanship of Lynn Davis, a Deputy Assistant Secretary of Defense for International Security Affairs, was given responsibility for preparing specific force structures to complement those strategies. This dichotomous structure for preparing PRM 10 is outlined in Figure 3.4.

Splitting the study into two parts created an organizational monstrosity. When Huntington's net assessment group completed its initial assessment of the military balance it was rejected by the State Department and NSC staff as too pessimistic. Huntington had argued that the Warsaw Pact forces had achieved dominance over NATO's forces in central Europe and could easily overrun NATO's defenses. The study was redone and changed to conform to the State Department view that there is a rough balance in central Europe.

The problem was compounded when Secretary of Defense Brown, under pressure from the Joint Chiefs of Staff, rejected the force packages developed by his own Deputy Assistant Secretary of Defense as conceptually unsound. As a result, the comprehensive review of national strategy and military posture which was supposed to do for the Carter administration what NSC-68 did for the Truman administration and NSSM-3 did for the Nixon administration, became an exercise in confusion and a missed opportunity partly because of structural differences.[8]

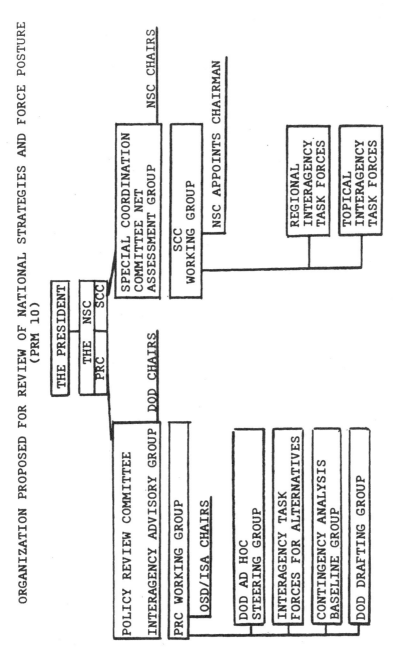

Figure 3.4

The Process

An effective NSC system should accomplish six goals. First, it should be compatible with the decision-making style of the President. He bears final responsibility for the quality of the decisions. Second, the system should enable the chief executive to obtain accurate information on all of the options available. Third, the system should be flexible enough to handle the various types of issues in a timely and efficient manner. Fourth, there must be some device to communicate presidential decisions throughout the national security bureaucracy. Fifth, the NSC decisions should provide guidance to the national security bureaucracy that is specific enough to serve as a guide for action. Finally, the system should have an effective control or feedback mechanism to ensure compliance with decisions of the Council.

The NSC system of the Carter administration accomplishes many of these goals. The system is certainly compatible with the President's decision-making style and has demonstrated that it is capable of handling a wide variety of issues in a timely manner. Within his first year in office the President was able to make some very significant decisions through NSC process. A comprehensive proposal on strategic arms was presented to the Soviets in March 1977, the process of withdrawing ground troops from Korea was begun in April, an arms transfer policy was formulated in May, production of the B-1 was terminated in June, and a review of our military posture and a reorganization of the intelligence community were completed in May. Table 3.3 contains a complete list of the major national security decisions made by President Carter in his first year in office.

All of the meaningful options on each of the issues have reached the President on each of his national security decisions. In his public statements on policy issues, the President has shown a clear grasp on all sides of the issues. This has occurred not only because of the openness of the NSC structure and process described above but also because of the wide range of viewpoints held by key members of the national security bureaucracy. Paul Warnke, Director of the Arms Control and Disarmament Agency, and Andrew Young represent one point of view on foreign policy, David Jones, Chairman of the JCS, another, while Zbigniew Brzezinski, the NSA Assistant, Secretary of State Vance, and Secretary

Table 3.3

PRESIDENTIAL DIRECTIVES AND OTHER UNNUMBERED PRESIDENTIAL DECISIONS

	SUBJECT	DOCUMENT DATE
PD/NSC-1	Establishment of Presidential Review and Directive Series/NSC	20 Jan 77
PD/NSC-2	The National Security Council System	20 Jan 77
PD/NSC-3	Disposition of National Security Decision Memoranda	11 Feb 77
PD/NSC-4	The Law of the Sea Policy Review	8 Mar 77
PD/NSC-5	Southern Africa	9 Mar 77
PD/NSC-6	Cuba	15 Mar 77
PD/NSC-7	No information available on subject, date, action, distribution	
PD/NSC-8	Nuclear Non-Proliferation	24 Mar 77
PD/NSC-9	Army Special Operations Field Office in Berlin	30 Mar 77
PD/NSC-10	Instructions for the Tenth Session of the Standing Consultative Commission	20 Apr 77
Presidential Decision on Proliferation		22 Apr 77

Table 3.3 (continued)

Presidential Determination on Arms Transfers		16 Apr 77
Foreign Intelligence Electronic Surveillance Legislation		25 Apr 77
PRM/NSC-23	Coherent National Space Policy Critical Issues--SPASAT-A Altimeter Data Collection Class	2 May 77
PD/NSC-11	Micronesian Status Negotiations	5 May 77
PD/NSC-12	U.S. Policy in Korea	5 May 77
	Sale of Hawk Missiles to the Republic of China	21 May 77
	AWACS for Iran	19 May 77
PD/NSC-13	Conventional Arms Transfer Policy	13 May 77
PD/NSC-14	Disposition of National Security Action Memoranda and National Security Decision Memoranda	10 Jun 77
PD/NSC-15	Chemical Warfare	16 Jun 77
PD/NSC-16	LOS	16 Jun 77
	Presidential Determination #77-77: Eligibility of Egypt for the Purchase of Defense Articles and Defense Services Under the Arms Export Control Act as Amended.	2 Aug 77
PD/NSC-17	Reorganization of the Intelligence Community	4 Aug 77

128

Table 3.3 (continued)

PD/NSC-18	PRM-10	24 Aug 77
PD/NSC-19	Intelligence Structure and Mission (Electronic Surveillance Abroad and Physical Searches for Foreign Intelligence Purposes)	25 Aug 77
PD/NSC-20	SALT	9 Sep 77
PD/NSC-21	Policy Toward Eastern Europe	6 Oct 77
PD/NSC-22	ABM Treaty Review	11 Oct 77
	Strategic and Critical Materials Stockpile	6 Oct 77
	FY-78 Underground Nuclear Test Program (CRESSET)	20 Oct 77
PD/NSC-23	Standing Consultative Commission	18 Nov 77
PD/NSC-24	Telecommunications Protection Policy	22 Nov 77
PD/NSC-25	Scientific or Technological Experiments with Possible Large Scale Adverse Environmental Effects and Launch of Nuclear Systems into Space	22 Dec 77
PD/NSC-26	Nuclear Weapons Stockpile	11 Jan 78
PD/NSC-27	Procedures for dealing with Non-Military Incidents	30 Jan 78

Table 3.3 (continued)

PD/NSC-28	U.S. Policy on Chemical Warfare Program and Bacteriological/Biological Research Program	3 Feb 78
PD/NSC-29	Nuclear Weapons Deployment Authorization FY 78-9	7 Feb 78

of Defense Brown stand somewhere in between.

The Presidential Decision Memorandum is an effective device to communicate presidential decisions. Not only do these documents provide written guidance but the President insists on clear concise language in his proclamations.

As discussed above, there does not yet exist an adequate interagency control mechanism to insure policy implementation. Thus far this has not been a major problem but it could be as more and more decisions are made.

However, there is one area where the NSC process has exhibited some serious shortcomings, i.e., providing specific guidance to the national security bureaucracy. This point can be illustrated by analyzing three of the most significant NSC studies: PRM 10 (the comprehensive review of military force posture), PRM 12 (the arms sales review) and PRM 11 (intelligence community reorganization).

PRM 10, the comprehensive review of our national strategy, and military posture, is the most ambitious project undertaken to date by the NSC system of the present administration. No less than 12 task forces, involving some 175 people from every agency in the national security bureaucracy, spent six months of full time work on the project. Yet, despite this massive effort, the output, PD 18, is only marginally useful. PD 18, which was issued on August 24, 1977 and is entitled "U.S. National Strategy" not only does not lay the groundwork for any new initiatives in national security policy, it obscures much of the present policy. Like the Basic National Security Policy documents of the Eisenhower administration, it can mean all things to all men and does not come to grips with many of the really difficult issues.[9]

The best example of the confusion generated by PD 18 concerns the level of defense spending for FY 1979.[10] The document postulates that beginning in FY 1979 there will be a 3 percent real increase in the level of defense spending, but it does not specify whether the increase applies to the entire defense budget, or to certain specific areas, e.g., NATO, the procurement account. Nor does the PD state what the base for the 3 percent increase will be. Is it the FY 1978 defense budget as submitted by the administration or as modified by the Congress? The ambiguity of PD 18 resulted in a series of confusing and chaotic battles between the Office of Management and Budget (OMB) and the Department of Defense (DOD) during the Fall of 1977 over the "correct" total for the FY 1979 budget. The military services argued that the 3 percent should be applied to the FY 1978 budget as submitted by the administration and thus sought $135 billion for FY 1979. The Office of the Secretary of Defense (OSD) countered that the base for the increase should be the figure approved by Congress and thus asked for a total of $130 billion. OMB interpreted PD 18 as applying only to the NATO posture of the defense budget and sought a $125 billion defense budget for FY 1979. The situation was complicated by the fact that in the midst of the PRM 10 process, the President had set a ceiling of $126 billion on defense for FY 1979.

Other parts of PD 18 were equally useless as guides to policy-making. For example, human rights will be emphasized but not at the expense of harming national security; Soviet strategic and conventional forces will be counterbalanced by the U.S., i.e., the U.S. will maintain an overall military balance at least as favorable as that which now exists! No mention is made of how that balance is to be measured; the U.S. does not intend to build a first strike nuclear offense; U.S. conventional forces must focus on meeting a massive thrust against NATO as well as maintaining the capability to fight lesser wars (no guidance on the priorities attached to each). The directive is equally unclear about such other controversial subjects as whether we will come to the aid of South Korea in the event of a North Korean attack.

PRM 12, is a comprehensive review of our conventional arms transfer policy. This review resulted in the proclamation of PD 13 on May 13, 1977. One week later, President Carter announced publicly the main points of PD 13.[11] According to the Chief Executive, henceforth, the U.S. would view arms transfers as an exceptional means of implementing foreign policy, and in the future the burden of persuasion would rest on those favoring a particular sale, not on those opposed. The President also stated that the U.S. will not be the first supplier to introduce into a region newly developed advanced weapon systems which would create a new or significantly higher combat capability. The dollar value of FY 1978 arms transfer will be reduced from its FY 1977 level, and a limited class of weapons will be considered for coproduction arrangements but with restrictions on third country imports.

However, nine months after the policy was

announced, the responsible agencies were still encountering difficulties in operationalizing the policy.[12] There does not yet exist a satisfactory way of determining what is an advanced weapon system or a higher combat capability. For example, it would seem that the Airborne Warning and Control System (AWACS) aircraft would fit the definition. It is the most advanced weapon system of its kind in the world, possessing a long range, look down radar with substantial jamming resistance, and at $200 million per aircraft the most expensive plane ever built. Not even the Soviets have a system as advanced as this, which General David Jones, Chairman of the JCS, stated "represents the single quantum jump in command and control since the development of radar."[13] Yet President Carter, despite vigorous opposition from many members of the Congress and from his own Director of Central Intelligence, approved the sale of seven of these planes to Iran for $1.2 billion.

Similarly in December 1977, the administration offered to sell a dozen F-5 aircraft to Sudan, while in February 1978, it announced its intention to sell 50 F-5E's to Egypt and 60 F-15's to Saudi Arabia. This is the first time that either Sudan or Egypt has ever been offered modern airplanes by the United States. While the Saudis have received U.S. aircraft in the past, they have never been offered anything as sophisticated as the supersonic, all weather, F-15, the most advanced tactical fighter in America's arsenal.

In the first three months of FY 1978, the President approved arms sales totaling about $10 billion. This is approximately the same as the total for the whole 12 months of FY 1977. Yet PD 13 states that the level for FY 1978 will be below that of FY 1977. It is no wonder that Senator Thomas Eagleton (D-MO) remarked "Since May 19, I've seen no guidance of any restraint in the arms race."[14]

The new arms transfer policy has also come into conflict with the President's goal of greater arms standardization in NATO.[15] Because the combined NATO market is insufficient to sustain the capacity of most European arms manufacturers, these companies must be able to export to third world countries in order to enter into coproduction arrangements which are economically feasible.

Since PD 13 limits their ability to do this, there is little motive for these companies to coproduce American weapons. For example, Augusta of

Italy is interested in leading a European combine to build the YAH-60, UTTAS, under lease from the U.S. But if PRM 12 precludes it from selling these helicopters abroad, the firm will probably team with other European firms to produce a European version of UTTAS for the NATO countries and for sale abroad.

PRM 11 analyzed the organization and functions of the intelligence community. The primary issue was the extent to which the Director of Central Intelligence (DCI) would assume control of the intelligence assets of the Department of Defense (DOD), particularly the National Security Agency, the National Reconnaissance Office, and the Defense Intelligence Agency. The results of this study were disseminated in PD 17 issued on August 4, 1977, and in an executive order signed on January 24, 1978.[16] According to these documents, the DCI will have responsibility for tasking, resources, and national analytical products of all intelligence agencies. If this is so, then the DCI would appear to have complete control over even the defense intelligence agencies. What else is left to control? Yet these documents also go on to state that DOD will maintain control over the day-to-day operations of its intelligence agencies just as they have in the past. Official Pentagon spokesmen state that the Presidential Decision does not weaken DOD's control over its intelligence agencies.[17]

CONCLUSION

Problems in the structure and process of the NSC system in the early days of an administration often are a result of the lack of experience on the part of the key players and usually disappear as these individuals mature. Secretary of Defense Brown has noted that one of the benefits of the PRM 10 exercise was that "all the participants learned a great deal - about bureaucracies as well as substance."[18] However, the organizational and procedural difficulties of the Carter NSC system appear to be getting worse instead of better as the administration moves well into its second full year in office.

The April 1978 decision to delay production of the neutron bomb provides an excellent example of the continuing chaos in the NSC decision-making process. Somehow, Secretary of State Vance, Secretary of Defense Brown, Presidential Assistant

Brzezinski, and their associates spent the nine months prior to the decision putting together a formula with our NATO Allies to allow deployment of the weapon on European soil without obtaining Mr. Carter's views on the matter. Similarly, the President allowed his national security bureaucracy to move to the brink of producing the weapon before he made his real feelings about the weapon known. Spring 1978, decisions about arms sales to the Middle East and navy shipbuilding were also made with the same lack of coherence.

Unless these problems are ironed out soon and the administration gets its act together, the President will continue to experience difficulties in the area of national security policy. While sound structure and process cannot guarantee good policy, a flawed decision-making apparatus will make it almost impossible to develop a coherent policy.

NOTES

1. Data for this paper comes primarily from interviews with members of the national security bureaucracy. Portions of the interviews included verifying press accounts of various aspects of the NSC decision-making process. None of the press accounts which are quoted in this paper were cited until they were checked with the interviewees. The best single source on the structure and process of the Carter NSC system is Dom Bonafede, "Brzezinski --Stepping Out of His Backstage Role," National Journal, October 15, 1977, p. 1596-1601.

2. The system is described in Richard Nixon, U.S. Foreign Policy for the 1970's, A New Strategy for Peace, February 25, 1971.

3. For a list of the first 138 NSSMs, see John Leacocos, "Kissinger's Apparat," Foreign Policy, Fall 1971-72, p. 25-27.

4. Quoted by Bernard Gwertzman in The New York Times, November 7, 1975, p. 19.

5. Bonafede, p. 1598.

6. According to one NSC staffer, "We have too big a plate and can't do justice to all the issues, particularly in view of the role they want us to

play." Quoted in Bonafede, p. 1599.

7. The committee is cochaired by Marshall Shulman, Special Advisor to the Secretary of State on Soviet Affairs, and George Vest, Assistant Secretary of State for European Affairs. Nine agencies are represented on the committee. For details on its role see the remarks of State Department spokesman, John Trattinger in "Administration Sets Up New Soviet Policy Group," <u>Washington Post</u>, July 20, 1977, p. A7.

8. It should be noted that PRM 10 may not have turned out any better even if these structural problems were not present. However, there is no doubt that the split study compounded the problem of developing a coherent national security policy.

9. Maxwell Taylor, <u>The Uncertain Trumpet</u>, New York: Harper, 1959, p. 82-83.

10. The best source on PD-18 is "Remarks by Harold Brown" at the thirty-fourth annual dinner of the National Security Association, September 15, 1977. See also George Wilson, "New Carter Directive Could Mean Rising, Not Falling Defense Budgets," <u>Washington Post</u>, August 27, 1977, p. A6.

11. Bureau of Public Affairs, U.S. Department of State, <u>U.S. Conventional Arms Transfer Policy</u>, November 1977.

12. See for example Harold Logan, "Bureaucracy Still Struggling to Restrain U.S. Arms Sales," <u>Washington Post</u>, November 12, 1977, p. A2 and <u>Herbert Schandler</u>, "Arms Sales Policy: The Problem of Implementation," <u>Washington Post</u>, January 2, 1978, p. A21.

13. Quoted in Center for Defense Information, "U.S. Weapons Exports: Can We Cut the Arms Connection?" <u>Defense Monitor</u>, February 1978, p. 5.

14. Quoted in Logan, p. A2. It is estimated that foreign military sales for FY 1978 will be $13.2 billion, about 20 percent above FY 1977. Unless some drastic changes are made sales for FY 1979 will rise to $13.5 billion.

15. Benjamin Schemmer, "Pentagon Reevaluates Carter's Arms Transfer Policy," <u>Armed Forces Journal</u>,

August 1977, p. 12.

16. Edward Walsh, "Turner's Powers, Duties, Expanded in Reorganization," Washington Post, August 5, 1977, p. A1; Office of the White House Press Secretary, August 4, 1977, and Edward Walsh,"Carter Centralizes U.S. Intelligence Authority, Draws Fire," Washington Post, January 25, 1978, p. A2.

17. See for example the statement of Thomas Ross, Assistant Secretary of Defense for Public Affairs, quoted in Walsh, August 5, 1977.

18. Remarks by Harold Brown, September 15, 1977.

4
The Policy Impacts of the Carter Defense Program

Lawrence J. Korb

INTRODUCTION

In defense "dollars are policy." Plans become irrelevant and operations virtually impossible until the forces and weapons to support them have been purchased through the defense budget. Conversely, the weapons and forces which are available often determine the policies which are undertaken. For example, the massive introduction of American ground troops into Southeast Asia in the mid-1960s was possible only because the budgetary decisions of the early 1960s had equipped our ground forces for such contingencies.

The FY 1979 defense budget is the first defense budget produced entirely by the Carter administration. Because of the time constraints imposed by the Congressional Budget and Impoundment Act of 1974, the incoming administration had only one month to modify the FY 1978 budget. Within that short period of time, President Carter was able to make only 31 marginal changes to the budget prepared by the outgoing Ford administration. These changes reduced the size of the FY 1978 defense budget by only 2.3 percent.

Preparation of the defense budget in any year is one of the most important undertakings of the executive branch. It is during the process of putting together this document that the administration must face up to questions which not only will determine the shape of our present and future national security policy but will also reflect its own sense of priorities in regard to social and military issues and fiscal policy. Drawing up the first defense budget of a new administration is especially critical. As President Carter noted in the message which accompanied the FY 1979 budget,

"The first complete budget of any new administration is its most important."[1] This is the budget which normally lays the foundation for the defense policy of the entire administration and signifies our national security intentions to our allies and adversaries. For example, the FY 1955 budget, the first defense budget of the Eisenhower administration, laid the foundation for the policy of massive retaliation and an era of level defense budgets. Eight years later, in the FY 1963 defense budget, John Kennedy moved away from the policy of massive retaliation toward a strategy of flexible response, and established the groundwork for a force designed to fight two major and one minor war simultaneously (2-1/2 wars) and for a period of rising defense expenditures. In the FY 1971 defense budget, the newly installed Nixon administration restructured our armed forces so that they would have to handle only "one and one half wars" simultaneously and laid a foundation for several years of declining defense expenditures. This decision led to a deterioration of our military position vis-a-vis the Soviets who had been increasing their defense expenditures by about 4 percent a year in real terms since 1962. However, during the presidency of Gerald Ford a remarkable consensus, that the real decline in defense spending must be halted, developed.[2] Ford's first defense budget, the FY 1976 version, arrested the decline in the level of defense expenditures and consequently laid the groundwork for reversing the deterioration in the military balance. In Ford's two and one half years in office, defense spending increased by $16.6 billion or 15.6 percent in real terms and our military capabilities began to improve markedly. The pattern of defense spending of the five administrations, which preceded this one, is depicted in Figure 4.1.

Thus, it is not surprising that both President Carter and Secretary of Defense Harold Brown devoted substantial amounts of their time to the preparation of the FY 1979 defense budget. Because he recognized that it would be his first full statement of priorities, policies, and proposals, the chief executive literally spent hundreds of hours focusing on the size and distribution of the defense budget which was unveiled on January 23, 1978.[3] The Secretary of Defense personally reviewed about 300 program packages and 2000 decision elements in formulating the budget.[4] Neither man intends to devote similar amounts of time to the

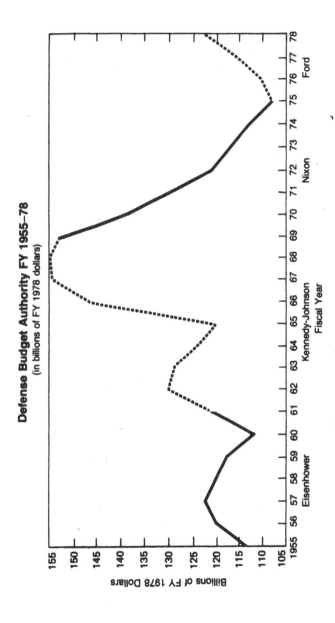

Figure 4.1 Defense Budget Authority FY 1955-78 (in billions of FY 1978 dollars)

Source: Office of the Assistant Secretary of Defense (Comptroller), National Defense Budget Estimates for FY 1978, p. 138.

subsequent defense budgets of this administration.

A useful way to analyze the defense program of any new administration is to compare the size and distribution of its proposed defense budgets to that of the previous administration. Just as the Eisenhower program served as an excellent benchmark for the Kennedy initiatives, so the Ford program can serve as a useful benchmark for determining whether this administration has established new priorities in defense. Indeed in his press conference unveiling the FY 1979 DOD budget Secretary Brown used the last Ford budget as a yardstick.

SIZE

The size of the defense budget is usually measured in three distinct ways: in obligational authority or outlays; in current or constant dollars; and in absolute or relative terms. All of these perspectives are useful and each of them presents different insights into the significance of the size of a specific defense budget. Moreover, confusion about the meaning of the size of a particular defense budget often is attributable to the mixing of those categories. Therefore, it is important to discuss briefly the meaning of each of these concepts before comparing the size of Ford and Carter programs.

Outlays

Outlays are a measure of the funds which will be spent in a given fiscal year, for example, FY 1979. The amount of outlays for a particular year results from authority granted in previous years plus authority requested for the present year. In the Department of Defense (DOD) budget, about 30 percent of the outlays are a result of authority approved in previous years, while the other 70 percent comes from the current request. Conversely, Total Obligational Authority (TOA) is a measure of the funds requested in a particular fiscal year, all of which will not be spent in that year. However, the authority once granted usually is not rescinded. Therefore, the TOA for a given year directly influences the size of the outlays for subsequent years. For example, TOA of $116.6 billion in FY 1978 resulted in projected outlays of $115.2 billion in FY 1979.

Current Dollars

Current dollars measure the amount of outlays of TOA in terms of the year in which the funds are actually spent, for example, TOA for FY 1979 in FY 1979 prices, outlays for FY 1980 in FY 1980 prices. Constant dollars adjust for the impact of inflation by presenting the cost of the defense program in terms of a base year, for example, the FY 1955, FY 1963, FY 1971, and FY 1978 budgets in FY 1978 prices. The contrast between using current and constant dollars as a basis for comparison can be exemplified by examining the size of the defense budget for FY 1955 (the first Eisenhower budget) and FY 1978 (the last Ford budget). In current dollars, the FY 1955 budget was $35.6 billion, while the FY 1978 budget was $116.6 billion, a difference of $81 billion or 228 percent. However, in constant FY 1978 dollars, the first Eisenhower budget was $120.5 billion or $3.9 billion higher than the last Ford budget.

Absolute and Relative Terms

The DOD budget can also be expressed in relative rather than absolute terms. Defense outlays for a given year are normally related in percentage terms to the GNP and to the total federal budget. These two standards aid in measuring the impact of defense spending on the economy and serve to highlight the priority given to defense programs within the government.

THE CARTER AND FORD BUDGETS: DOLLARS AND PRIORITIES

Table 4.1 contains the TOA and outlay projections for the Carter and Ford defense programs, expressed in both current and constant FY 1979 dollars, for the FY 1977-83 period. As indicated in that table, President Carter has proposed that the defense budget consume $861.6 billion in TOA and $790.2 billion in outlays during the FY 1978-83 period. This would mean an average annual increase of $10.4 billion or 9.4 percent in TOA, and $10.2 billion or 10.3 percent in outlays. In real terms or constant dollars, the growth will be about $2.9 billion or 2.4 percent in TOA and $3.1 billion or 2.7 percent in outlays.

Although the growth in the proposed Carter defense program is substantial, it is less than

Table 4.1

THE DEFENSE BUDGET FY 1977-78 IN CURRENT AND CONSTANT DOLLARS
(in billions of dollars)

BUDGET CATEGORY	FISCAL YEAR							TOTAL FY 77-83	AVERAGE ANNUAL INCREASE FY 77-82	
	1977	1978	1979	1980	1981	1982	1983		AMT.	%
TOA (CURRENT DOLLARS)										
FORD	110.2	122.2	134.4	144.8	155.7	166.8	180.1	904.0	11.7	10.5
CARTER	110.2	116.6	126.0	137.7	148.6	160.5	172.7	861.6	10.4	9.4
DIFFERENCE AMT.	---	6.6	8.4	7.6	7.1	6.3	7.4	42.4		
%	---	5.4	6.3	5.2	6.6	3.8	4.1	4.7		
TOA (CONSTANT FY 1979 DOLLARS)										
FORD	122.6	129.5	134.4	136.6	139.3	141.9	146.3	828.0	3.9	3.2
CARTER	122.6	123.7	126.0	129.4	133.0	136.6	140.3	789.0	2.9	2.4
DIFFERENCE AMT.								39.0		
%								4.7		

Table 4.1 (continued)

	1977	1978	1979	1980	1981	1982	1983	AMT.	%
OUTLAYS (CONSTANT FY 1979 DOLLARS)									
FORD	98.3	109.5	120.8	133.3	145.2	156.0	166.7	831.5	11.5
CARTER	98.3	105.3	115.2	125.8	136.5	147.9	159.5	790.2	10.3
DIFFERENCE AMT.	--	4.2	5.6	7.5	8.7	8.1	7.2	41.3	11.4
%	--	3.8	4.6	5.6	5.9	5.1	4.3	4.9	10.2
OUTLAYS (CONSTANT FY 1979 DOLLARS)									
FORD	111.3	116.0	120.8	125.7	129.9	132.7	135.1	760.2	3.9
CARTER	111.3	111.5	115.2	118.7	122.2	125.9	129.6	723.1	3.1
DIFFERENCE AMT.								37.1	3.5
%								4.8	2.7

Source: Donald Rumsfeld, *Annual Defense Department Report, FY 1977* January 17, 1977, p. 8 and Harold Brown, *Annual Defense Department Report, FY 1979*, p. 12.

that projected by the previous administration. As Table 4.1 demonstrates, the program proposed a year ago by the outgoing Ford administration was higher in both TOA and outlays, whether measured in current or constant dollars. The Carter projections are $42.4 billion or 4.7 percent below those of the previous administration in TOA and $41.3 billion or 4.9 percent less in outlays. Compared to FY 1977, the average annual increase in both TOA and outlays for the Carter administration is approximately 1 percentage point less than that of the Ford program.

Table 4.2 compares the relative priority given to the defense budget by the Carter and Ford administrations. As indicated in that table, defense outlays for FY 1979 are estimated to consume 5.1 percent of the GNP and 23.0 percent of the entire federal budget, approximately the same as FY 1978. According to the assumptions in the FY 1979 Carter budget, defense outlays will receive a slightly decreasing share of the GNP over the next five years and a slightly increasing portion of the federal budget. In the FY 1978-83 period, DOD is projected to receive about 5 percent of the GNP and 23.6 percent of the federal budget.

Compared to the previous administration, President Carter has altered the priority to be given to defense spending and eased the burden of defense spending upon the economy. By FY 1983, the Ford program would have raised the share of GNP allocated to defense to 5.4 percent and increased the DOD share of the federal budget to 28.5 percent. During the FY 1978-83 period, President Carter proposes to allocate about one-half a percentage point less of the GNP and about four and one-half percentage points less of the federal budget to the defense program than his predecessor. If the Carter projections hold up, FY 1981 will be the first year since FY 1950 that defense will receive less than 5 percent of the GNP, and his administration will be the first in the entire post-World War II period to spend less than 25 percent of the budget on defense. The changing emphasis on defense is illustrated by the fact that a decade ago defense consumed almost 10 percent of the GNP and 40 percent of the federal budget, and as recently as 5 years ago the Department of Defense (DOD) received almost 7 percent of the GNP and 30 percent of the entire federal budget.

Table 4.2

DEFENSE AND THE ECONOMY, FY 1978-83

	1978	1979	1980	1981	1982	1983	Average
Outlays as a % of GNP							
FORD	5.4	5.3	5.3	5.4	5.3	5.4	5.4
CARTER	5.2	5.1	5.0	4.9	4.9	4.8	5.0
Outlays as a % of Federal Budget							
FORD	25.0	26.0	26.9	27.6	28.0	28.5	27.0
CARTER	22.8	23.0	23.1	23.7	24.5	24.5	23.6

Source: The Budget for Fiscal Year 1978, pp. 24, 51, and 53 and The Budget for Fiscal Year 1979, pp. 33, 43 and 44.

DISTRIBUTION

The distribution of the defense budget is also expressed in three different ways: by budget title or appropriation account; program; and component. Like the situation which prevails with size of the defense budget, confusion about the actual distribution often results from mixing the different categories. Unfortunately, some mixing is almost inevitable because the executive branch formulates the budget in program categories while the Congress appropriates funds to the individual components or agencies by budget title.

Budget Title

The defense budget is presently composed of 6 primary budget titles or appropriation accounts. Table 4.3 displays the Ford and Carter programs by budget title for the FY 1978-83 period. Analysis of that table reveals that both administrations anticipated growing defense budgets for the period and that each projected an increase in every category.

Overall the Carter program envisions spending about 5 percent less than the Ford plan for the six year period. Except for two categories, Operations & Maintenance (O&M) and procurement, their proposals are not markedly different. Ford would have spent slightly more on personnel because his force levels were about 20,000 higher, but his retirement projections were somewhat lower because his administration had anticipated lower levels of inflation. Both Ford and Carter were committed to increasing spending on Research, Development, Test and Evaluation (R,D,T & E) by significant amounts, but, Ford would have spent about 2 percent more during the period. Spending for military construction is virtually identical for both presidents.

However, their O&M and procurement projections are significantly different. The Carter administration anticipates spending $19 billion or 8 percent more on O&M than the Ford administration. These additional funds are being spent primarily to increase the readiness of the conventional forces oriented toward NATO. Readiness of these forces will be increased in four different ways. First, the backlog of weapon systems awaiting overhaul and repair will be reduced through increased funding. Second, European units are being manned at full

Table 4.3

DEFENSE AUTHORITY BY BUDGET TITLE, FY 1978-83, THE FORD AND CARTER PROPOSALS
(in billions of current dollars)

Title	1978	1979	Fiscal Year 1980	1981	1982	1983	Total
Military Personnel							
Ford	27.7	29.1	30.5	31.9	33.5	34.9	187.6
Carter	27.3	28.7	30.1	31.4	33.0	34.3	184.8
							2.8 (1.5%)
Retired							
Ford	9.1	9.8	10.5	11.2	11.9	13.8	66.3
Carter	9.2	10.2	11.1	12.1	13.0	13.8	69.4
							-3.1(-4.6%)
O&M							
Ford	34.9	36.6	38.3	40.6	42.3	45.1	237.8
Carter	35.0	38.1	40.2	43.7	47.7	51.7	256.4
							-18.6(-7.8%)
Procurement							
Ford	35.1	39.8	46.1	51.3	55.3	61.5	289.1
Carter	30.3	32.0	35.7	39.8	43.9	48.5	230.2
							58.9(20.3%)

Table 4.3 (continued)

	1978	1979	1980	1981	1982	1983	
R, D, T & E							
Ford	12.0	13.0	14.5	15.1	16.8	18.4	89.8
Carter	11.4	12.5	14.0	15.5	16.5	17.9	87.8
							2.0 (2.2%)
Construction							
Ford	1.4	4.5	3.2	3.6	3.6	3.7	20.0
Carter	1.9	2.7	4.3	4.0	4.1	3.9	20.9
							-0.9 (-4.5%)
Other							
Ford	1.9	1.7	1.8	2.0	2.5	2.7	12.6
Carter	1.7	1.8	1.8	2.1	2.3	2.6	12.3
							0.3 (2.4%)
Total							
Ford	122.2	134.4	144.8	155.7	165.8	180.1	903.0
Carter	116.8	126.0	137.2	148.6	160.5	172.7	861.1
							41.9 (4.6%)

Source: The FY 1978 Budget, p. 53 and The FY 1979 Budget, p. 43.

strength and they are being given priority in receiving new equipment or systems completing overhaul. Third, more equipment is being prepositioned in the European theater by the Army and Air Force. By FY 1983 the Army will have prepositioned 5 sets of unit equipment in Europe. This will allow five divisions based in the U.S. to deploy rapidly by air to Europe and "marry up" with their equipment over there. Similarly, the Air Force will have additional runway repair kits, secondary items, and heavy construction equipment prepositioned in Europe. Fourth, the war reserve material stockpile, which was depleted during the October 1973 war in the Middle East, is being replenished.

This increase in current readiness will be more than offset by a huge sacrifice in future combat capability. Estimates for procurement are now a whopping $59 billion or 20 percent below those of last year. The size and scope of the Carter reductions in the procurement account are vividly illustrated in Table 4.4. This table compares the amounts projected for major procurement programs by former President Ford to those of President Carter for FY 1978 and FY 1979. As indicated in that table, the present administration plans to spend less money on the major programs for strategic forces, land forces, naval forces, and tactical air forces.

In the strategic area, both the M-X and B-1 programs have been virtually wiped out, while the Minuteman program received a slight reduction and the cruise missile and Trident programs received small increases. The 84 percent reduction in funding for the M-X mobile missile will slow the program down by at least three years. Because of the funding levels of this administration, the missile cannot achieve an initial operating capability (IOC) before the late 1980s. The 89 percent cutback in the B-1 program reflects President Carter's June 30, 1977 decision to halt B-1 production at four aircraft. The $106 million outlay for FY 1979 will complete the R,D,T & E phase and will keep open the option of moving into production through FY 1979. The 5.8 percent cut in the Minuteman improvement program reflects a decision not to modernize the Minuteman II missiles because of the increasing vulnerability of our ICBM force.

The $211 million increase in the cruise missile program is indicative of the increased reliance upon this option as a near term replacement for a new manned bomber. This level of funding

Table 4.4

MAJOR PROCUREMENT PROGRAMS, FY 1978-79
(In millions of current dollars)

	1978		1979		Total		Difference Ford-Carter	
Program	Ford	Carter	Ford	Carter	Ford	Carter	Amt.	%
Strategic Forces								
Minuteman Improvements	338	333	146	123	484	456	28	5.8
M-X	294	134	1533	158	1827	292	1536	84.0
Trident^{a/}	3626	3435	2339	2789	5965	6224	-259	-4.3
B-1	2162	443	2915	106	5077	549	4528	89.2
Cruise Missile^{a/}	358	382	229	416	587	798	-211	-35.9
Land Forces								
Tanks (M-60, XM-1)	1021	807	1187	909	2208	1716	492	22.3
AAH (YAM-64)	200	165	179	177	379	342	37	9.8
Patriot^{a/}	215	216	287	307	502	523	-21	-4.2
Roland^{a/}	131	131	216	225	347	356	-9	-2.6

151

Table 4.4 (continued)

Program	Ford	Carter	Ford	Carter	Ford	Carter	Amt.	%
Naval Forces								
CVV	14	--	1262	--	1276	--	1276	100.0
Major Escorts (CGN-42, DDG-47, CSGN)	1181	1149	1325	30	2506	1179	1327	53.0
FFG-7	1616	1218	1986	1548	3602	2766	836	23.2
SSN-688	531	311	548	474	1079	785	294	27.2
LSD-41	6	--	232	--	238	--	238	100.0
Support Ships	1182	389	973	626	2155	1015	1140	52.9
Tactical Air Forces								
F-16A/	1696	1685	1542	1595	3238	3280	-42	-1.3
F-15	1766	1667	1715	1416	3481	3083	398	11.4
A-10	841	832	969	925	1810	1757	53	2.9
F-14	941	891	1208	674	2149	1565	584	27.2
F-18A/	627	654	431	865	1058	1519	-461	-43.6
AV-8B	60	60	167	86	227	146	81	35.6

A/Carter increases

Source: Department of Defense, Program Acquisition Costs by Weapon System, FY 1978 and FY 1979.

will enable the first B-52 to be armed with cruise missiles in June 1981. The $259 million increase in the Trident program will not purchase any more submarines nor will it speed up the program. Rather it reflects the cost of paying for a 59 percent overrun on the first Trident or Ohio class submarine.

In the area of land force programs, the present administration has speeded up slightly the Roland and Patriot surface to air missile programs. However, these increases have been more than offset by larger cutbacks in the proposed rate of tank and attack helicopter procurement.

Compared to the projections of a year ago, the important programs in the category of naval forces have been devastated. Two major programs, the medium size carrier (CVV) and amphibious lift ship (LSD-41) have received no funding, in either FY 1978 or FY 1979. Funding for support ships, like oilers has been cut in half, while expenditures for the frigate (FFG-7) and attack submarine (SSN-688) programs have been reduced by approximately 25 percent.

Within the area of tactical air forces, the funding for only one aircraft has been increased significantly. The Navy's low cost fighter, the F-18A, has received about 44 percent more funds. The Air Force's two "low-mix" planes, the F-16 and A-10 are virtually unchanged, but the Navy's F-14A and the Marine's AV-8B programs have been slowed down markedly. Funding for the F-14A, the Navy's sophisticated fighter, has been cut in half for FY 1979. This will reduce the projected buy from 60 to 24. The AV-8B, Harrier, the Marine Corps' vertical takeoff and landing aircraft will remain in development for at least another year, thus saving about $81 million in the FY 1979 budget.

Program

The defense budget is presently divided into nine major program categories, which reflect the major mission and support objectives of DOD. Table 4.5 displays the Ford and Carter budgets in these program categories for the FY 1978-83 period.

Analysis of that table reveals that the present administration had reduced the projections made last year in every combat related category. Only the support categories, for example, central supply and maintenance and training, show any

Table 4.5

DEFENSE AUTHORITY BY PROGRAM, FY 1978-83 THE FORD AND CARTER BUDGETS
(In Billions of Dollars)

PROGRAM	FISCAL YEAR						TOTAL
	1978	1979	1980	1981	1982	1983	1978-83
Strategic							
FORD	11.0	12.5	15.1	16.0	17.0	19.1	90.7
CARTER	9.3	9.8	11.0	12.5	14.2	15.6	72.4
							18.3 (20.1)
General Purpose							
FORD	44.3	49.8	54.4	59.8	63.8	68.7	340.8
CARTER	42.6	46.9	51.0	54.4	59.9	63.9	318.5
							22.3 (6.5)
Intelligence and Communications							
FORD	8.2	9.2	9.4	9.8	10.7	11.8	59.1
CARTER	7.8	8.3	9.4	9.7	10.2	11.4	56.8
							2.3 (3.8)
Airlift and Sealift							
FORD	1.7	1.7	1.8	2.8	4.1	5.1	17.2
CARTER	1.6	1.8	2.0	2.9	3.4	4.4	16.1
							1.1 (6.3)

Table 4.5 (continued)

	1978	1979	1980	1981	1982	1983	1978-83
Guard and Reserves							
FORD	7.2	7.3	7.4	7.6	8.4	9.1	47.0
CARTER	6.7	6.7	7.0	7.1	7.5	8.0	43.0
							4.0 (8.5)
R&D							
FORD	11.1	12.6	14.0	14.6	15.6	17.0	84.9
CARTER	10.2	11.0	11.9	14.0	15.1	16.5	78.7
							6.2 (7.3)
Central Supply and Maintenance							
FORD	11.8	12.5	12.6	13.6	14.2	15.1	79.8
CARTER	12.0	12.8	13.6	14.3	15.0	15.9	83.6
							-3.8 (-4.7)
Training, Medical and Other							
FORD	24.3	26.2	27.5	28.8	30.2	31.5	168.5
CARTER	24.0	26.0	28.6	31.0	32.4	34.2	176.2
							-7.7 (-4.5)

Table 4.5 (continued)

	1978	1979	1980	1981	1982	1983	1978-83
Administration and Support							
FORD	2.6	2.6	2.6	2.7	2.8	2.7	16.0
CARTER	2.5	2.7	2.7	2.8	2.8	2.8	16.3
							−0.3 (−1.9)

Source: Estimated from The FY 1978 and FY 1979 Defense Reports and The FY 1978 and FY 1979 Budgets.

increases over the Ford program and these are quite small. The most significant cutbacks have come in the strategic, general purpose, guard and reserve, research and development (R&D), and airlift and sea-lift programs. The intelligence and communications category is essentially the same.

The 20 percent decrease in the strategic program results primarily from the decision not to move into production with the B-1, and to slow down the M-X program by three years. The 7 percent decrease in general purpose forces is a reflection of the cutback in building the forces of the Navy and Marine Corps.

The $1.1 billion cutback in the airlift and sea-lift program comes primarily in the sea-lift area. This administration proposes to spend less than 15 percent of the budget for mobility forces on sea-lift programs. The 8.5 percent cut in the guard and reserve is a reflection of a proposal to shift some 35,000 Naval reservists from the selected reserve (a pay status) to the individual ready reserve (non-pay). The difference in the R&D program comes primarily in the first half of this period and reflects the slowdown in M-X development.

Department or Component

DOD is composed of three large military departments: the Army, the Navy, and Air Force. In addition, there are a number of smaller components, like the Office of the Secretary of Defense and the Joint Chiefs of Staff, whose budgets are separate from the military departments. Table 4.6 displays the Carter and Ford budgets by department or component.

Analysis of that table leads to two salient conclusions. First, the present administration has reduced the budgets of all of the armed services below the levels projected a year ago. Second, the Army's budget has suffered only a slight reduction, but the budgets of the other two services have been reduced more sharply. The Air Force budget has been lowered by about $19 million or 7 percent while the Navy's has been cut by over $23 billion or almost 8 percent. As noted above, the lower Air Force budgets are a result of the B-1 cancellation and the slowdown of the M-X. The Navy's reduction stems from a cutback in construction funds for the new ships and planes.

The extent of the reduction in shipbuilding

Table 4.6

DEFENSE AUTHORITY BY DEPARTMENT, FY 1978-83
(in billions of current dollars)

DEPARTMENT		1978	1979	FISCAL YEAR 1980	1981	1982	1983	TOTAL 1978-83
Army								
FORD		30.2	33.0	35.2	38.2	40.4	42.7	219.7
CARTER		28.9	32.1	35.1	38.0	40.2	42.4	216.7
DIFFERENCE	AMT.	1.3	0.9	0.1	0.2	0.2	0.3	3.0
	%	4.3	2.7	0.2	0.5	0.5	0.7	1.4
Navy/								
FORD		41.1	45.8	48.7	52.3	56.4	61.0	305.3
CARTER		39.7	41.7	44.3	48.0	52.4	56.0	282.1
DIFFERENCE	AMT.	2.3	4.1	4.4	4.3	4.0	5.0	23.2
	%	5.6	9.0	9.0	8.2	7.6	8.2	7.6
Air Force								
FORD		36.0	39.7	43.9	47.1	49.7	54.0	270.4
CARTER		33.2	35.6	39.8	43.5	47.6	51.9	251.6
DIFFERENCE	AMT.	2.8	4.1	4.1	3.6	2.1	2.1	18.8
	%	7.7	10.3	9.3	7.6	4.2	3.8	6.9

Table 4.6 (continued)

		1978	1979	1980	1981	1982	1983	1978-83
Defense Agencies and Defense-wide[2]								
FORD		16.3	16.9	18.0	19.1	20.3	22.4	113.0
CARTER		14.8	16.5	18.0	19.1	20.3	22.4	111.1
DIFFERENCE	AMT.	1.5	0.4	---	---	---	---	1.9
	%	9.2	2.3	---	---	---	---	1.7
Total								
FORD		122.2	134.4	144.8	155.7	166.8	180.1	904.0
CARTER		116.6	126.0	137.2	148.6	160.5	172.7	861.6
DIFFERENCE	AMT.	6.6	8.4	7.6	7.1	6.3	7.4	42.4
	%	5.4	6.3	5.2	4.6	3.8	4.1	4.7

[1] Includes funding for the Marine Corps. About 19% of the Navy Budget supports the Marine Corps and its amphibious mission.

[2] Examples of this area include Office of the Secretary of Defense, Joint Chiefs of Staff, and military retirement.

Source: Estimated from The FY 1978 and FY 1979 Defense Reports and FY 1978 and FY 1979 Budgets.

funds is illustrated in Table 4.7. As indicated in that table, the shipbuilding budget has been reduced by almost $26 billion or nearly 41 percent in the FY 1978-83 time frame. For FY 1979, the Navy's shipbuilding account is 20 percent below the level of FY 1978 and about half of the level projected a year ago. The impact of the Carter reductions in shipbuilding can be found by examining Table 4.8.

The Ford administration proposed a program that envisioned building 25 ships in FY 1978 and a total of 157 ships at a cost of $44.6 billion over the FY 1978-1982 time frame. This proposal would have raised the number of ships in the Navy, which then was 476, to about 500 in the mid-1980s, to 550 by 1990 and to about 600 by the turn of the century. The essentials of this shipbuilding plan were based upon a May 1976 National Security Council study which concluded that our national security interests required a Navy composed of about 600 ships.[5]

In February 1977, the Carter administration reduced the Ford FY 1978 program from 25 to 22 ships and the overall program to 152 ships by cutting two frigates (FFG-7), one attack submarine (SSN-688), and two strike cruisers (CSG-N) from the Ford plan. The FY 1978 program was cut to 18 ships by the Congress despite complaints from some segments of the legislature. For example, the House Armed Services Committee stated that the shipbuilding program was grossly inadequate in numbers and types and failed to consider the threat adequately.[6]

In January 1978, the Carter administration did not present a new five year shipbuilding plan to the Congress. It promised that the five year plan would be made public as soon as a Navy force planning study was completed. However, the administration did reveal two things. First, for FY 1979 only $4.7 billion would be available for shipbuilding, sufficient funds to build 15 ships in the upcoming year. The amount is about 50 percent less than the sum that was projected a year ago.

Second, the total funds available for shipbuilding in the FY 1979-83 period would be $42 billion, $15 billion below the level projected by the Ford administration. This amount would buy 60 ships less than the Ford program.

In early March, the Navy completed its force planning study, named Sea Plan 2000. The study presented the President with three options. Option one or the high-risk option called for spending $6.3 billion (FY 1979 dollars) annually. The

Table 4.7

SHIPBUILDING AUTHORITY FOR THE NAVY, FY 1978-83
(in billions of current dollars)

	_____Fiscal Year_____						
	1978	1979	1980	1981	1982	1983	1978-83
Ford	6.5	8.5	9.9	10.7	13.1	15.0	63.7
Carter	5.8	4.7	5.9	6.6	7.3	7.5	37.8
Difference							
Amt.	0.7	3.8	4.0	4.1	5.8	7.5	25.9
%	10.8	44.7	40.4	38.3	44.2	50.0	40.7

Source: Estimated from The FY 1979 Budget, p. 328.

second or minimum acceptable risk option advocated spending $8.8 billion annually, while option three, the lower risk option, required the expenditure of $9.5 billion annually.

On March 23, 1978, the President submitted his plan to Congress. He recommended spending only $5.6 billion (FY 1979 dollars) annually over the next five years. This is 11 percent lower than an "high-risk option" in the Sea Plan 2000 Study and will enable the Navy to construct only 70 new ships in this time frame. This is 83 less ships than Ford had approved and will mean that the size of the Navy will continue to decline to about 450 in 1990 and to about 400 in the year 2000. As enumerated in Table 4.8, the present administration has accomplished its reduction in the number of new ships in the FY 1978-1982 period by delaying the medium size or 50,000 ton carrier (CVV) program by an additional year, eliminating the strike cruisers (CSGN) and new frigate (FFG-X) programs altogether, cutting the large destroyer escort (DDG-47) program in half, slowing down the ballistic missile (SSBN) and attack submarine (SSN) and frigate (FFG) programs by significant amounts and virtually wiping out the amphibious lift ships (LSD-41), mine countermeasures ships (MCM) and oilers (AO).

The Carter administration treated naval aviation in a similar fashion. As indicated in Table 4.9, the outgoing Ford administration had envisioned purchasing 630 fighter and attack aircraft in the FY 1979-83 period, an average of 126 per year. President Carter proposes to buy only 525 planes in that same period or about 105 per year. Since the Navy needs to procure at least 120 fighter and attack aircraft annually in order to prevent excessive aging and to replace aircraft lost through accidents, the Carter program will result in an annual shortfall of at least 15 planes per year. This will mean that by the end of the five year period the Navy will be forced to reduce the number of carrier air wings below the present level of 12.[8] Moreover, the Carter program will result in the procurement of a greater percentage of less sophisticated aircraft. About 25 percent of the planes which this administration plans to buy are A-4M and A-6E aircraft, which were developed over a decade ago. On the other hand, these older planes would have accounted for only 4 percent of the Ford program.

The contrast between the situations of the Army and Navy Departments in the Carter

Table 4.8

SHIPBUILDING PROGRAMS, FY 1978-82

Ship Type	Ford	Carter	Difference, Amt.	Ford-Carter %
SSBN	8	7	1	12.5
SSN	8	5	3	37.5
CVV	2	1	1	50.0
CSGN	2	---	2	200.00
DDG-47	10	6	4	40.0
FFG-7	56	32	24	42.9
FFG-X	2	0	2	100.0
LSD-41	6	1	5	83.3
MCM	19	3	16	84.2
AO	14	1	13	92.9
OTHER	30	18	12	40.0
TOTAL	157	74	83	47.1

Table 4.8 (continued)

COST	$48.7	$30.3	18.4	37.8
Active in October 1978	456	456		
Active Ships in 1990A/	550	440	110	20.0
Active Ships in 2000A/	600	400	200	33.3

A/ Assumes same shipbuilding rates continued through 1980s.

Source: FY 1978 Defense Report, p. 190, FY 1979 Budget, p. 328, The FY 1979 Defense Report, p. 167-185, George Wilson, "Pared Navy Shipbuilding Plan Unveiled," Washington Post, March 25, 1978, p. A2.

Table 4.9

NAVY FIGHTER AND ATTACK PROCUREMENT FY 1979-83

AIRCRAFT (TYPE)	NAME	FORD	CARTER
A-4M	SKYHAWK	--	72
A-6E	INTRUDER	27	48
A-7E	CORSAIR II	--	--
AV-8B	HARRIER	90	--
F-14A	TOMCAT	162	118
F-18	HORNET	351	287
TOTAL		630	587

Source: Program Acquisition Costs by Weapon System, FY 1978 and FY 1979; FY 1978 Defense Report, p. 221; and FY 1979 Defense Report, p. 215.

administration is illustrated in Table 4.10 which displays Army procurement trends for the FY 1975-83 period. As that table indicates, this administration is continuing the program begun by its predecessor of sharply increasing spending on every area of Army procurement. In his three budgets, President Ford more than doubled Army procurement, raising it from $2.4 billion in FY 1975 to $5.2 billion in FY 1978. In FY 1979 alone, Carter proposes to increase Army procurement by an additional $1.5 billion or 28 percent. By FY 1983 Army procurement will be more than double its FY 1978 level.

IMPLICATIONS

Every proposed defense program generates concern about its size and distribution. This is particularly true when the program is presented as part of the first full defense budget of a new administration, which had made the size and distribution of the defense budget a campaign issue, and when that program deviates significantly from the projections of the previous administration. Even before the FY 1979 budget was officially unveiled, there was a great deal of criticism about its size and distribution. For example, in December 1977, Ron Brown, Vice President of the National Urban League, stated that he was concerned that President Carter would not fulfill his commitment to slash the defense budget. In Brown's view, "No longer can we have both guns and butter. We believe we should choose butter."[9] During that same month, similar sentiments were echoed by Syracuse Mayor Lee Alexander, President of the United States Conference of Mayors. The upstate New York official stated that the reported increases in defense "indicated devastating consequences for urban America."[10] In late December, columnists Rowland Evans and Robert Novak accused Carter of being markedly closer to (Senator) George McGovern (D-S.D.) than to (Senator Henry) "Scoop" Jackson (D-Wa) and quoted an embittered naval officer as complaining that the FY 1979 DOD budget put the Navy in a Coast Guard status.[11]

The cacophony continued after the budget was unveiled officially. Speaker Thomas P. O'Neill, Jr. (D-Mass) suggested that the budget might have too much money for the Pentagon and not enough for jobs. He said further that the Democratic Party

Table 4.10

ARMY PROCUREMENT, FY 1975-83
(in millions of dollars)

CATEGORY	1975	1976	1977	1978	1979	1983	TOTAL CHANGE 75-83		AVERAGE CHANGE 75-83	
							AMT.	%	AMT.	%
Aircraft	247	331	534	657	1017	1400	1153	466.8	144	58.4
Missile	392	415	473	536	773	1600	1208	308.1	151	38.5
Weapons and Tracked Combat Vehicles	415	679	1089	1421	1636	1750	1335	321.6	167	40.2
Ammunition	647	682	897	1171	1420	3250	2603	402.3	325	50.3
Other	655	895	1383	1400	1789	3000	2345	358.0	293	44.8
TOTAL	2356	3002	4376	5185	6635	11000	8644	366.8	1082	45.9

Source: The Budget for Appropriate Years.

was not going to sacrifice the unemployed to a defense increase.[12] Representative Parren Mitchell (D-Md), Chairman of the House Budget Committee Human Resources Task Force, accused the President of reneging on his campaign promise to trim defense spending.[13] Senator George McGovern (D-S.C.) simply called the size of the defense budget almost unbelievable.[14] However, three other senators criticized the proposed FY 1979 budget as too low. Senator Gary Hart (D-Co) called the budget disappointing and purely negative.[15] John Tower (R-Tex) criticized Carter's first defense budget as being far too modest to respond to the seriousness of the Soviet military challenge, while Senator Dewey Bartlett (R-Okla) characterized the FY 1979 defense proposal as dangerously inadequate.[16] Finally, in his press conference, outlining the FY 1979 defense budget, Secretary of Defense Harold Brown was attacked not only for not reducing the budget enough, but also for reducing it too much in certain specific areas.[17]

The final part of our analysis will discuss the implications of the choices made by the President in deciding upon the size and distribution of his first defense budget. We will begin with the issue of the level of the defense budget and then move on to a discussion of the substantive implications of the new priorities in defense.

The Level of Defense Spending

Deciding upon the appropriate level of defense expenditure is always a difficult problem for a President. The size of the defense budget is often viewed by our adversaries and allies as a sign of our determination to carry out our commitments. This phenomenon has been referred to as the "defense budget's message to the world."[18] Former Secretary of State Henry Kissinger recognized the symbolic importance of the size of defense budgets, particularly in dealing with the Soviet Union. At National Security Council meetings, called to discuss defense budgets, the former Secretary of State would normally support the highest option. On the other hand, resources given to defense must be taken from non-defense areas or added to the budget deficit. Normally, neither of these options is appealing to a chief executive.

Deciding on the appropriate size of the FY 1979 budget was particularly difficult for President Carter because of his public pronouncements on the subject. The current chief executive was faced with the problem of reconciling his campaign commitments to reduce defense spending by $5 to $7 billion below the level of the Ford administration[19] and to balance the federal budget by FY 1981 with his post-election pledge to our NATO allies and to his own national security bureaucracy to increase the level of defense spending by 3 percent in real terms and to maintain an overall military balance with the Soviet Union as least as favorable as that which now exists.[20]

Before analyzing how the President tried to reconcile those apparently contradictory promises in his FY 1979 budget, it would be useful to discuss the background of these statements. Such a discussion should shed some light on why such disparate comments were made. President Carter's pre-election pledge to cut the defense budget apparently stems from a Brookings Institution seminar on the defense budget he attended in the Spring of 1975. At that time, the FY 1976 budget was being considered by the Congress. When candidate Carter asked Barry Blechman, then a member of the Institution's Defense Analysis Staff, how much the defense budget could be safely cut, the answer given was about $5 to $7 billion. In fact, Congress did reduce that particular budget by $7 billion that same summer. Moreover, in late 1975, President Ford reduced his own FY 1977 request by $5 billion below the figure he had projected for that year. Thus, in a real sense, the $5 to $7 billion cut had already been made before the presidential campaign began. Nonetheless, in remarks during the campaign, in the debates with President Ford, and in the Democratic platform, candidate Carter, apparently unaware of the reductions made by the Congress and the Ford administration, continued to insist that the defense budget could be safely cut by $5 to $7 billion below its present level.

The promise to increase defense spending by a figure of 3 percent in real terms is attributable to Soviet efforts in the defense area. Even people not sympathetic to our current National Security Policy agree that since 1962, the Soviets have been increasing their defense budget by about 3 to 4 percent a year in real terms. Therefore, President Carter's commitment to raise the United States level of defense spending was a signal to the Soviets of our willingness to match their resolve and a goad to our NATO allies to do likewise.

Both President Carter and Secretary of Defense Harold Brown claim that in his FY 1979 defense budget, the President has fulfilled both his apparently contradictory pre and post election promises. In one sense, he has. As noted in Table 4.11, the FY 1979 defense budget is $8.4 billion in TOA and $5.6 in outlays below the amounts projected by President Ford for the upcoming fiscal year. Moreover, TOA in this defense budget request is $9.2 billion or 7.9 percent above the level approved by Congress for FY 1978 and $9.9 billion or 9.4 percent higher in outlays. This translates into a real increase of $2.3 billion or 1.9 percent in TOA and $3.7 billion or 3.5 percent in outlays. Thus, compared to President Ford's projection for FY 1979 and to the Congressional level for FY 1978, the FY 1979 budget is both "lower and higher" by the necessary amounts in at least certain categories.

However, the administration is in reality practicing sophistry in trying to reconcile these contradictory positions, that is, the President and the Secretary of Defense are guilty of using a rubber yardstick and are comparing apples and oranges. If it wished to be consistent, this administration ought to compare its requests for FY 1979 to the amount it requested of Congress in FY 1978. When this is done, a different picture emerges. As indicated in Table 4.11, in current dollars, the administration's TOA request for FY 1979 is only $6.6 billion or 5.5 percent above the level of the request made a year ago, while its outlay request is $6.1 billion or 5.6 percent higher. In constant FY 1979 dollars, the President's FY 1979 TOA request is $0.5 billion or 0.4 percent below the level of FY 1978 and $0.3 billion or 0.3 percent smaller in outlays.

What Table 4.11 implies is that if Congress makes a 4 percent reduction in the President's FY 1979 request, TOA will be $121.0 billion and outlays $110.6 billion. In current dollars, this will mean an increase in TOA of $4.4 billion or 3.8 percent above last year and a jump of $5.3 billion or 5.0 percent in outlays. However, in real terms, a 4 percent congressional reduction will result in an actual decrease of $2.7 billion or 2.2 percent in TOA and $0.9 billion or 0.8 percent in outlays. In order for defense authority to remain at the FY 1978 level, the congressional reduction in this year's request cannot exceed $2.3 billion or 1.8 percent. A real increase of any kind of defense spending will mean virtually no reductions by the

Table 4.11

DEFENSE BUDGET TOTALS FOR FY 1978 AND 1979

BUDGET CATEGORY	1978	1979	CHANGE AMT.	%
TOA (CURRENT DOLLARS)				
Ford	122.2	134.4	12.2	9.9
Carter	119.4	126.0	6.6	5.5
Congress	116.6	121.0*	4.4	3.8
TOA (CONSTANT FY 1979 DOLLARS)				
Ford	129.5	134.4	4.9	3.8
Carter	126.5	126.0	-0.5	-0.4
Congress	123.7	121.0*	-2.7	-2.2
OUTLAYS (CURRENT DOLLARS)				
Ford	109.5	120.8	11.3	10.3
Carter	109.1	115.2	6.1	5.6
Congress	105.3	110.6*	5.3	5.0

Table 4.11 (continued)

	1978	1979	AMT.	%
OUTLAYS (CONSTANT FY 1979 DOLLARS)				
Ford	116.0	120.8	4.8	4.1
Carter	115.5	115.2	-0.3	-0.1
Congress	111.5	110.6*	-0.9	-0.8

*Assumes a 4% Congressional Reduction

Source: Donald Rumsfeld, Annual Defense Department Report FY 1978, January 17, 1977, p. 8 and Harold Brown, Annual Defense Department Report, FY 1979, p. 12.

Congress, a situation unheard of in the last decade.[21] A 3 percent real increase in defense TOA means that Congress will have to add $1.4 billion in authority to Mr. Carter's proposed budget.

The Carter defense program will most likely result in a real decline in the level of defense spending between now and FY 1983. This point is illustrated in Table 4.12. As is indicated in that table, if President Carter's requests for FY 1979 and future years are reduced by an average of 4 percent by the Congress and he raises the following year's budget by the same amount above the congressional level that he did in FY 1979, total defense spending is likely to grow by less than 6 percent per year above its FY 1978 level. This is less than the projected rate of inflation for the FY 1979-1983 period. The only way for the President to change this state of affairs is to request an amount that is 9 percent above his request of the previous year and not base his increase on the congressional level of the previous year as he did this year.

Even if the FY 1979 defense budget of the Carter administration will not result in a 3 percent real increase in defense spending, cannot the chief executive be given credit for fulfilling his pre-election pledge of reducing the budget by $5 to $7 billion? Not in the eyes of many of his supporters.[22] In their view, Carter's pledge referred to the present, that is 1976, level of defense spending, not some future projection.

The implications of the predicament which the President has created by his contradictory statements may be quite serious. On the one hand, both our NATO allies and the Soviet Union could perceive that we do not intend to match the size of the Soviet effort in the area of defense spending. This may undermine the willingness of the other NATO countries to increase their defense budgets and lead the Soviets to doubt our commitment to a strong national defense. On the other hand, members of the Democratic Party in Congress, like Speaker O'Neill, Senator McGovern, and Representative Mitchell, may feel that the President has not kept his campaign promise. This opinion could lead them to demand that Congress make reductions in the defense budget which are not warranted by the international situation.

Table 4.12

PROJECTED AND ANTICIPATED ACTUAL EXPENDITURES FOR DEFENSE, FY 1978-83
(in billions of current dollars)

	1978	1979	1980	1981	1982	1983	Total Increase 1978-83 Amt.	%	Average Increase 1978-83 Amt.	%
TOA										
Projected	116.6	126.0	137.2	148.6	160.5	172.7	56.1	48.1	11.2	9.6
Anticipated[1]/	116.6	121.0	126.6[2]/	132.4[2]/	138.5[2]/	144.9[2]/	28.3	24.3	5.7	4.9
Outlays										
Projected	105.3	115.2	125.8	136.5	149.9	159.5	54.2	51.5	10.8	10.3
Anticipated[3]/	105.3	110.2	116.8	121.0	126.6	132.4	27.1	25.7	5.4	5.1

[1]/ 4% Congressional Reduction
[2]/ Increase before congressional reduction
[3]/ Keyed to TOA Reductions

Source: The Budget for Fiscal Year 1979, pp. 43-44.

Distribution

As noted above, President Carter has reduced defense spending about 5 percent below the levels projected by the Ford administration. This cutback has been achieved primarily by reducing the strategic programs of the Air Force and the general purpose or conventional force programs of the Navy. The Carter administration has placed the same emphasis on Army procurement programs and slightly more emphasis on current readiness. The final part of this paper will analyze the impact of these actions on the strategic and conventional components of our defense policy.

STRATEGIC POLICY

Cancellation of the B-1 program and the three year slowdown of the M-X will have certain benefits. In the near term, these actions can reduce the defense burden or make funds available for other areas in the defense budget without undermining deterrence. However, these decisions could have potentially disastrous long term consequences. These consequences can be demonstrated by examining the strategic balance with the Soviets and the condition of all three components of our nuclear forces, that is, the triad.

The Strategic Balance

Table 4.13 summarizes the essential characteristics of the strategic nuclear forces of the United States and the Soviet Union as they are presently configured, and projects the shape of these forces over the next decade, on the basis of the Vladivostok accords. As indicated in that table, the two superpowers are presently in a condition of what the administration refers to as essential equivalence. The Soviet Union has more delivery vehicles than the United States and exceeds the United States by a large margin in missile throw-weight. On the other hand, this nation has significantly more warheads and bomber payload and a slight advantage in equivalent megatonnage (EMT).

However, as Table 4.13 makes clear, over the next decade that picture could change significantly. This projection is based upon the programs currently underway in both countries, and it

Table 4.13

Strategic Forces of the
U.S. and U.S.S.R. for Selected Years

(Vladivostok Accords)

Category	1977 U.S.	1977 U.S.S.R.	1982 U.S.	1982 U.S.S.R.	1987 U.S.	1987 U.S.S.R.
Delivery Vehicles						
Missiles						
MIRVed						
ICBM	550	277	550	800	550	900
SLBM	496		608	328	770	328
Non-MIRVed						
ICBM	504	1,000	504	534	504	500
SLBM	160	982	-	638	-	622
Long Range Bombers						
Penetrating	420	135	350	100	150	50
Cruise Missile	-	-	10	-	150	-
Total Delivery Vehicles	2,130	2,400	2,022	2,400	2,124	2,400
Lifting Capacity						
Missile Throw-weight	3.3	9.1	3.4	12.0	3.6	15.0
Bomber Payload[1]/	22.8	4.7	18.5	3.0	15.0	1.5
Warheads	11,300	3,826	12,200	7,000	15,000	13,000
EMT[2]/	6.7	4.6	6.8	6.5	7.0	11.0

Table 4.13 (continued)

1/ Excluded are the U.S.' FB-111 and Soviet Backfire.

2/ Equivalent megatonnage, a measure of destructive power based on both yield and accuracy.

SOURCE: The FY 1979 Defense Report p. 47; The International Institute for Strategic Studies, The Military Balance, 1977-1978, pp. 3, 4, 5, 8, 77, 78, 79, and 80; Herbert Scoville, "A Starting Point for a New SALT Agreement," Arms Control Today, April 1977, p. 5; Center for Defense Information "SALT: A Race Against the Arms Race," The Defense Monitor, July 1977, p. 6, and John Collins, "American and Soviet Armed Services, 1970-76," Library of Congress, March 17, 1977; Representative Les Aspin (O-W-IS), "Study on SALT II," January 8, 1978; Congressional Budget Office, Counterforce Issues for U.S. Strategic Nuclear Forces, January, 1978, pp. 16, 18, 19; and FY 1979 Defense Report, p. 104.

assumes that the essentials of the Vladivostok accord remain in effect, that is, each side can have no more than 2400 delivery vehicles and 1320 MIRVed missiles. If these assumptions are valid, by 1982 the Soviet Union will cut into our advantages in warheads and EMT, and by 1987, it will have forged ahead in EMT and virtually drawn even in warheads, while maintaining its lead in the number of delivery vehicles. A decade from now, the only clear United States advantage will be in bomber payload. If this situation should develop, it is difficult to see how this nation can claim that the strategic forces of the two superpowers are still in a state of essential equivalence or that the strategic balance is not less favorable. Moreover, if the Vladivostok limits are not observed, the situation will be even less favorable for the United States. Without Vladivostok, the Soviets will be able to MIRV almost their entire ICBM and SLBM force. This could increase the number of warheads by 45 percent to almost 19,000, EMT by 36 percent to 15.0, and throw-weight by 33 percent to 20.0. This would give them a clear lead over the United States in every category.

Some would argue that, given the vast number of strategic nuclear weapons possessed by both sides, such concerns are meaningless. However, what is often crucial in the international arena is not reality, but perceptions; perceptions of strength and perceptions of the strategic balance. Secretary of Defense Harold Brown has noted this phenomena by pointing out that if the balance turns, he would be concerned because there would start to be a psychological effect with respect to our allies and ourselves, or the Soviets might think that they had an advantage that they could use politically.[23]

There are three reasons why the strategic situation may change so markedly. First, the Carter administration cancelled the B-1 bomber and drastically slowed the pace of the M-X missile. Had these programs been funded in accordance with the schedule laid down by the Ford administration, our nuclear forces would have had approximately 125 B-1s and 100 M-X missiles in 1987. This would have given the United States force the same number of delivery vehicles and EMT as the forces of the Soviet Union, maintained the significant United States lead in total warheads, and closed the gap in missile throw-weight.

A second reason for the changing strategic

situation lies in the potential of the Soviet forces. The Soviets have more and bigger missiles than the United States, that is, their missiles have more yield and can lift larger payloads than their United States counterparts. The United States has only 54 heavy ICBMs, the Titan II, which has a 5 to 10 megaton warhead and a lifting capacity of 7500 pounds. On the other hand, the Soviets have 505 heavy ICBMs, half of which have 25 MT warheads and can lift 15,000 pounds. The United States is ahead in EMT now only because its missiles are more accurate. None of our missiles has a Circular Error Probable (CEP) in excess of 0.5 nautical miles, while over 100 Soviet missiles presently have CEPs of more than 1 mile. Similarly, the United States advantage in the number of warheads results from our lead in MIRV technology. Approximately 97 percent of our ICBM and SLBM force has been MIRVed. The Soviets lagged about seven years behind us in MIRV technology and are just beginning to MIRV a significant portion of their forces. At this time, only about 20 percent of the Soviet ICBM force is MIRVed. However, over the next decade, the Soviets will be able to close the technology gap to such an extent that they will be able to MIRV their entire missile force if they so desire. In addition, the accuracy of their missiles will begin to approach that of ours. By 1985, most of the Soviet ICBM force will have achieved a CEP of less than 0.15 nautical miles. This situation will enable them to exploit fully their advantages in size and numbers.

Third, the Soviets simply have more strategic programs underway than the United States. The Soviets are now deploying a fourth generation of ICBMs, a new manned bomber, and two ballistic missile submarines; modifying four other strategic missiles; and developing four new ICBMs, that is, a fifth generation. The United States is not standing still in this area, but the scope of its current effort does not come close to matching that of the Russians, especially with the 20 percent cutback in strategic programs made by the Carter administration.

The Condition of the Triad

In addition to the fact that the strategic balance is tilting against the United States, the Triad, the keystone of our nuclear deterrent, is in such precarious shape that the strategic situation could be even worse than currently projected a decade hence. The troubles with the Triad can be illuminated by taking a close look at the present and future condition of each of its components.

ICBM Vulnerability

At the present time, the Soviets can destroy about 50 percent of our ICBM force with a first strike. If the Soviets continue to improve their accuracy as rapidly as they have in the past three years, by 1985 they will have the capability to destroy 90 percent of our silos by launching two warheads per silo. Such a strike would require that they use less than one-third of the warheads in their ICBM force.[24]

The vulnerability of the ICBM can be offset partially by adopting some type of a "launch on warning" or "launch under attack" strategy, that is, a policy of firing our missiles before the Soviet missiles actually impact on our silos. Improving our early warning and command and control systems would facilitate the adoption of such a strategy. However, a launch on warning policy could be quite destabilizing and would be a departure from the current policy of configuring our force to absorb a full scale first strike.

Other than adopting a launch under attack posture, the only real defense that the United States would have against this development is to make its ICBM force mobile. Hardening of our Minuteman force will help somewhat but will not alter the essential fact that by the mid or late 1980s, the only leg of the Triad which currently possesses a prompt, high confidence, counterattack capability against a broad spectrum of both hard and soft targets, will be in jeopardy.

Some six years ago, DOD began work on an advanced ICBM to be deployed in a mobile mode. The original plan called for moving this system, designated the MX-1, into production in 1978 and actual deployment in 1984. In late 1976, the outgoing Ford administration, alarmed by Soviet advances in strategic weaponry, accelerated the MX program by a year. However, within the past year, the Carter administration has twice cut back on funding for the program. In its FY 1978 budget changes, the present administration reduced $160 million from the MX program, and its FY 1979 budget cut funding back by another $1,375 million, an 84 percent reduction over a two-year period. Because of these reductions, the earliest date at which the MX can become operational is 1986. By that time, less than 10 percent of our Minuteman force will be able to survive a Soviet first strike.

President Carter's initial decision to slow down the MX in February 1977 appeared to be a wise choice because he intended to try to conclude quickly a comprehensive arms limitation agreement with the Soviets. MX is such an extremely powerful and accurate missile that it could be construed by the Soviets as a counterforce weapon. Moreover, placing it in a mobile mode would make verification nearly impossible. However, the President's decision to slow the MX even further in spite of the fact that no SALT agreement was concluded with the Soviets in 1977, that an agreement in 1978 now seems unlikely, and that the Soviets have not slowed down any of their missile programs is open to question. Such a delay may give us the worst of all possible worlds. If no agreement is reached, we risk having a period where the bulk of our ICBM force is vulnerable. Moreover, our bargaining position during the negotiations may be weakened because we have unilaterally slowed down our most sophisticated program.

Manned Bombers and Cruise Missiles

The Carter administration plans to rely primarily upon the air launched cruise missiles (ALCM) to maintain the viability of the bomber leg of the Triad. Approximately 150 B-52Gs will be equipped with some 3000 ALCMs. Each of these extremely accurate missiles will have a range of 1500 nautical miles and carry a 200 kt warhead. From a fiscal standpoint, this is an attractive option. The cost of equipping the bombers with cruise missiles will amount to some $4 billion (FY 1978 dollars).

However, there are two problems with the emphasis on cruise missiles. First, if the missiles are going to be capable of destroying a significant portion of Soviet industrial targets and ICBM fields, their carriers must be able to approach within 400 nautical miles of the Soviet border. As indicated in Figure 4.2, at that distance, they can reach about 55 percent of the Soviet missile fields and 80 percent of the industrial targets. If Soviet defensive forces, such as the MIG-25 or MIG-27 interceptors, can keep the B-52 forces away, the effectiveness of the cruise missile declines rapidly. At a standoff distance

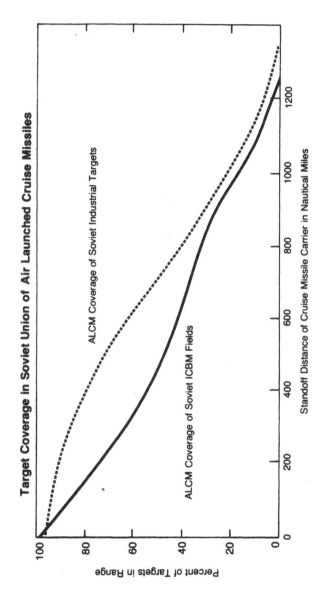

Figure 4.2 Target Coverage in Soviet Union of Air Launched Cruise Missiles With a Range of 2500 KM

Source: Clarence Robinson, "Carter Warned on Soviet Nuclear Advantage," Aviation Week and Space Technology, November 7, 1977, p. 19.

of 800 miles, the ALCMs can cover only 35 percent of the ICBM fields and 45 percent of the industrial targets. Beyond 800 miles, the target coverage of the cruise missile declines rapidly.

Moreover, even if the Soviets cannot force the cruise missile carrier out of its effective range, they may still be able to blunt the impact of this subsonic cruise missile by developing the capability of shooting it down. This can be done with sophisticated surface to air missiles or interceptor aircraft equipped with look down shoot down radar. Indeed, there are some indications that the new Soviet surface to air missile, the SA-10, which is nearing deployment, has that capability. Given the traditional Soviet emphasis on strategic defense and given the fact that their defenses no longer have to work on coping with a new penetrating bomber like the B-1, it is not unlikely that they will develop the ability to deal with the cruise missile simply by increasing the depth and density of their current system.[25] At the present time, the Soviets already have the most sophisticated strategic defensive system in the world. It consists of over 10,000 surface to air missile launchers, 6500 air defense surveillance radars, and 2600 interceptor aircraft. (By way of comparison, the United States has no launchers, 57 radars, and 330 interceptors.)

Second, a new standoff bomber or cruise missile carrier will have to be developed comparatively soon. The B-52Gs were first deployed about 20 years ago. Even with modifications, it will be difficult to extend their useful life much past the middle of the next decade. Research and development on a new carrier must be begun now if a replacement is to be ready on time. Exploratory studies on the B-1 began 15 years before the first aircraft rolled off the production line and industry proposals on B-1 were submitted eight years before production first began.

The administration apparently recognizes this situation. Both this year and last year it requested long lead funding for a cruise missile carrier. Present estimates are that a fleet of 50 carriers would cost about $5.8 billion, while a force of 100 would come to about $10.4 billion or $104 million per aircraft.

The Carter administration also plans to maintain a penetrating capability in its bomber force. Present plans call for using B-52D and H models in that capacity. However, for two reasons, the penetration capabilities of the B-52Hs are rapidly declining. First, there is the age problem common to all B-52s. Second, Soviet air defenses are becoming so much more sophisticated that the B-52s are losing their capabilities. Even now, the B-52, with a low altitude penetration height of 400 feet at a speed of mach .53, does not pose an overwhelming problem for the Soviet strategic defensive system.

If the United States wishes to maintain a penetration capability, it has three options: the B-1, the FB-111H or an entirely new bomber, the BX or B-2. To date, the Pentagon has spent $4.3 billion to produce 4 RDT&E B-1 aircraft. The administration proposes to spend some $200 million in FY 1979 and FY 1980 to continue the 4 aircraft B-1 RDT&E program to completion. This would allow DOD the option to begin procurement of the B-1 anytime between now and 1979 without excessive start-up costs. Beginning production in 1979 would mean an initial operating capability by the mid-1980s. Completing the B-1 program, that is, purchasing 240 production aircraft would cost an additional $18 billion.

Some five years ago, General Dynamics proposed the FB-111H as a replacement for the B-52. The FB-111H is a derivative of the FB-111A medium bomber, with which it shares a 43 percent common structure. The H model is 12 feet longer than the A model, has a more restricted wing arc, uses B-1 engines and electronics, and carries a modified tail section. Proponents of the FB-111H envision modifying 65 FB-111s and manufacturing 100 new FB-111Hs. Total production costs for this program would be about $7 billion. The administration did not seek any funds for this aircraft in its FY 1979 budget, but, if the FB-111H is to become operational by the middle of the next decade, RDT&E funding must begin no later than FY 1980 and a production decision must be made the following year.

The BX would be a new manned penetrating bomber altogether. Last year the Senate added $5 million to the defense appropriation bill to study this program. Congress deleted funds for this program and the administration did not request funds for it this year. Even if Congress should add funds for a BX this year, this notional plane could not achieve an IOC before the 1980s.

Two interrelated questions arise concerning the penetration bomber. Do we need one, and if so, which one? In light of the vulnerability of the

ICBM and the potential target coverage programs of the cruise missile, the prudent answer to the first question would seem to be yes. The question then becomes which one. The choice really boils down to the B-1 or the FB-111H. The BX is only a notional aircraft and will not be fully operational until too late to adequately replace the aging B-52s. If this option is selected, there would be a gap in our penetrating bomber capability.

The FB-111H would not appear to be a good choice. It is less capable and less cost effective than the B-1. A force of 165 FB-111Hs would have the same penetrating capabilities as a force of only 61 B-1s. The 20 year life cycle cost of 165 FB-111Hs would be $17 billion compared to an equal alert force of 61 B-1s at $11.5 billion. In many ways, the FB-111H is even less capable than the B-52. For example, it has about half the cruise missile capability and less range regardless of the assigned mission.

Despite the fact that President Carter has chosen not to move ahead with production of the B-1, it continues to compare favorably with its competition. This point is illuminated in Table 4.14. Building 240 production models of the B-1 would cost about $18.0 billion or about $75 million per plane. This force could be capable of carrying 5760 cruise missiles and would have an 0.7 probability of penetrating Soviet air space to deliver an additional 5760 nuclear bombs on target. For the same cost, DOD could purchase a mixed force of 100 cruise missile carriers and 165 FB-111H aircraft. This mixed force would be capable of carrying 7980 cruise missiles, but would have only an 0.6 probability of penetrating Soviet defenses to deliver 660 nuclear gravity bombs.

Thus, President Carter's decision not to build the B-1 appears to have been a mistake. While it may save money in the short run, it could present him or some future chief executive with some painful options, for example: accept vulnerability of two legs of the Triad, build an equally expensive but less capable force of cruise missile carriers and FB-111Hs, or build the expensive ($40 billion) and potentially destabilizing M-X system.

The SLBM Force

The United States' fleet ballistic missile force is presently composed of 41 submarines. Ten of these submarines carry Polaris A3 missiles while

TABLE 4.14

CHARACTERISTICS OF MANNED BOMBERS

Type	Number	Cost[a]	Unit Cost[b]	Cruise Missile Capability	Internal Nuclear Payload	Penetrating Capability (Probability)
Cruise Missile Carrier	100	10.4	104	60	0	0.0
B-1	240	18.0	75	24	24	0.7
FB-111 H	165	7.0	42	12	4	0.6

[a] In billions of current dollars. Does not include cost of arming the aircraft.

[b] In millions of current dollars.

Sources: Ronald Tammen, "The Bomber Debate; Is There a B-2 in Our Future?" Arms Control Today, November 1977, pp. 1-4; "U.S. Detente Policy and the B-1 Bomber Controversy," Congressional Digest, December 1976.

the other 31 are equipped with Poseidon missiles. These boats were build on a crash basis between December 1959 and January 1967. The normal useful lifetime for a ballistic missile submarine is considered to be about 20 years. After that time, reliability considerations and maintenance costs make the continued operation a risky proposition. Therefore, between 1979 and 1987 the entire force ought to be replaced.

As indicated in Table 4.15, these boats were originally scheduled to be replaced with Ohio Class submarines equipped with Trident I missiles beginning in 1979, at the rate of three every two years. Simultaneously, the 12 youngest Poseidon submarines were to be backfitted with Trident I missiles. Thus, in the mid-1980s, the United States SLBM force would have had 44 FBMs; 13 Ohio Class, 12 Lafayette Class equipped with Trident I missiles, and 19 Poseidon submarines. This force would possess 152 or 23 percent more missiles and some 2192 or 43 percent more warheads than at the present time. In addition, the range accuracy, and yield of the force would have been increased significantly. These improvements in the quantity and quality of our submarine force were considered to be a hedge against the anticipated weaknesses of the other legs of the Triad.

However, like the other parts of the Triad, the SLBM program is also experiencing difficulties. Its problems arise from a combination of production delays and escalating costs. The first Ohio Class submarine will be delivered almost two years late. In addition, the next four boats are also behind schedule. Thus, the Navy will not be able to replace its ten Polaris submarines with Ohio Class submarines at the 20 year point. Both the Undersecretary of Defense for Research and Engineering and the primary contractor, Electric Boat, claim that the program will be back on schedule with the sixth submarine, that is, the one which is scheduled to be completed in June 1982.[26] But, past experience causes some skepticism regarding that claim.

Even if Electric Boat can get the program back on its original schedule, the Navy and DOD may not be able to afford to pay for three of these boats every two years. The first Ohio Class submarine came in at $1.2 billion, some $400 million or 50 percent higher than anticipated. Equipping the boat with missiles will add another $300 million to the cost of the weapon system, thus making the cost

Table 4.15

The Original U.S. Fleet Ballistic Missile Program, FY 1978-95

Ship Number	Ship Name	Missle	1978	1979	1980	1981	1982	1986	1990	1995
SSBN 598	Washington	Polaris A3	5	4	3	3				
SSBN 608	Allen	Polaris A3	5	5	4	1				
SSBN 616	Lafayette	Poseidon	9	9	9	9	9	9		
SSBN 627	Lafayette	Poseidon	10	10	10	9	7	7		
SSBN 640	Lafayette	Poseidon	12	12	9	8	6	3	3	
SSBN 627	Lafayette	Trident I				1	3	3		
SSBN 640	Lafayette	Trident I			3	4	6	9	9	
SSBN 726	Ohio	Trident I		1	3	4	6	12	12	12
SSBN 726	Ohio	Trident II						1	7(A)	13(A)

188

Table 4.15 (continued)

Total Ships.........			41	41	39	37	44	31	25
Total Missiles......		656	664	680	656	608	808	648	600
Total Warheads......	5120	5264	5264	5760	5824	7312	6288	6672

(A) Trident only approved for 14 at the present time. This number assumes continued rate of 3 every two years beyond the approved level.

SOURCE: Estimated from Jane's Fighting Ships and FY 1973 through FY 1979 Defense Reports.

of the first FBM about $1.5 billion. Unless the price of the following ships drops significantly, the Navy will be forced to spend about $4.5 billion every two years on the Trident program. Since the total Navy shipbuilding budget for FY 1978 and FY 1979 will be $10.6 billion, the Trident program could consume 42 percent of the entire shipbuilding program. Up to now, it has consumed some 20 percent. Neither the administration nor the Congress is liable to permit this to happen.[27]

Therefore, unless the delays and costs in the Trident program drop or the Carter administration expands the Navy shipbuilding budget, this leg of the Triad could also be in jeopardy.

Taken separately, the problems being experienced by each leg of the Triad are not significant. However, taken together, they are indeed serious because this nation could experience a situation where simultaneously its ICBM force becomes vulnerable, its cruise missile carriers incapable, its penetrating bombers too slow, and its FBM fleet too old.

Therefore, unless a SALT II agreement is forthcoming soon or the troubles with the Triad alleviated, this administration could be faced with the painful choice of allowing the strategic balance to deteriorate or increasing the amount of money it had planned to spend on mobile missiles, penetrating bombers, or Ohio Class submarines.[28] The pressures on President Carter to adopt the latter course could be great indeed, especially since his choices in the FY 1979 budget contributed to the situation.

CONVENTIONAL POLICY

There is no doubt that this administration is placing its primary emphasis on preparing our general purpose forces to wage a short intensive war in Central Europe, that is, along the border dividing West Germany from Eastern Europe.[29] This is not a new phenomenon. Ever since the United States began to withdraw its forces from Southeast Asia, DOD has begun to focus its attention on the military situation in Europe which was allowed to deteriorate during our deep involvement in Asia. Approximately four years ago, during the first year of the presidency of Gerald Ford, the Pentagon began to accelerate sharply the rate of spending on its NATO oriented forces. It was in that year that the Army's force planning goal was increased from 13 to 16 divisions and the Air Force's goal from 22 to 26 tactical air wings. During the Ford presidency, real procurement costs of major weapons and items of equipment for NATO forces rose at an average annual rate of 22.8 percent.[30]

What is new with the Carter administration, is its emphasis on preparations for a short intensive war on the central front at the expense of certain other areas. The previous administration was attempting to strengthen our forces all across the board by providing a five percent per year real increase in the level of defense spending. As has been discussed above, the Pentagon has been placed in the position of having to build up its NATO forces, within a level budget. The Carter administration wishes to do this by taking funds from such other areas as shipbuilding, and strategic nuclear forces.

Before assessing the advantages and disadvantages of the NATO emphasis, one point should be emphasized strongly. In absolute terms the administration is not spending more on NATO than its predecessor. This point is illustrated in Table 4.16, which compares the funds to be allocated to the major NATO related programs by the Carter and Ford administrations for FY 1979, and by the fact that the Carter administration has deferred production of the neutron warhead.

Analysis of Table 4.16 reveals that in none of the six categories of NATO related procurement does the present administration propose to allocate more funds than its predecessor had planned. Although President Carter does provide more funding for certain programs, these are more than offset by reductions in other programs. Overall, this administration allocates about $9 billion to these 31 NATO programs. This is $1.4 billion or 13 percent less than former President Ford had projected. The two administrations project similar amounts for helicopters, air defense and tactical air, but in the areas of fire support, close combat, and airlift there are significant differences. The Carter program would provide some 10 percent less funding to airlift, 15 percent less to close combat, and about 50 percent less to fire support.

Strengthening the capabilities of our forces on the central front in Europe, even at the expense of our non-NATO forces, has some obvious advantages. First, it focuses our general purpose forces toward meeting the primary threat to the security of the

TABLE 4.16

Proposed Allocation of Funds for FY 1979 to
Major Procurement Programs Related to NATO
(In Millions of Dollars)

CATEGORY	FORD	CARTER	DIFFERENCE	
			AMT	%
Close Combat				
M-60	731	502		
XM-1	456	497		
APC	58	75		
Tow/Dragon	72	51		
Total	1317	1125	192	14.6
Helicopters				
Cobra	138	141		
AAH	179	177		
Hellfire	68	65		
Blackhawk	377	377		
Total	762	760	2	0.3
Air Defense				
Hawk	90	72		
Patriot	287	296		
Chaparral/Vulcan	1	39		
Roland	216	225		
Stinger	167	123		
Total	761	755	6	0.8
Fire Support				
Pershing	140	88		
Lance	9	78		
Rocket System	24	71		
Howitzers	180	51		
Artillery/Ammunition	1311	546		
Command & Control	310	195		
Total	1974	1029	945	47.9
Tactical Air				
F-16	1542	1700		
F-15	1715	1333		
F-4/F-111	144	215		
A-10	969	886		
AWACS	510	361		
F-4G	40	2		
EF-111A	105	264		
AAM	205	286		
Total	5230	5047	183	3.5

TABLE 4.16 (continued)

CATEGORY	FORD	CARTER	DIFFERENCE AMT	%
Airlift				
C-5	37	37		
C-141	88	66		
CRAF	15	69		
ATCA	227	159		
Total	367	329	38	10.4
Total NATO	10411	9045	1366	13.1

SOURCE: FY 1978 Defense Report, pp. 159, 160, 161, 162 and 213; FY 1979 Defense Report, pp. 160, 161, 162 and 223.

Western World, without increasing the defense burden. Second, strengthening the ability of our conventional forces to fight a war in Europe makes it less likely that the U.S. and NATO allies will have to resort to nuclear weapons to repel a Warsaw Pact Blitzkrieg. Third, the emphasis on NATO will help to redress the conventional balance in central Europe where the Warsaw Pact currently outnumbers the NATO forces by approximately 2 to 1 in ground troops, 3 to 1 in tanks, and 1-1/2 to 1 in tactical aircraft.[31] By FY 1983, the Carter program will give DOD the ability to double the numbers of ground troops and tactical aircraft in Central Europe within 7 days. Such a situation on the Central European front should make an attack by the Warsaw Pact less likely.

However, this NATO first strategy could also have some serious effects. First, the policy weakens U.S. capabilities on the northern (Norwegian Sea) and southern (Mediterranean) flanks of NATO and in the Pacific, where the power protection forces of the Navy play the major role. These weaknesses may tempt the Soviets to believe they can fight a one-front war. Such a mind set could make it easier for the Soviets to start a war. Moreover, our allies on the flanks and in the Pacific may come to doubt our intentions. This could lead to such undesirable actions as: a weakening of the NATO alliance; a desire on the part of the Japanese to rearm, or even a Sino-Soviet rapprochement.

Second, the NATO emphasis decreases the flexibility of U.S. forces to be used outside of Central Europe. Since the end of World War II, the American people have been unwilling to pay for the forces needed to carry out our national security objectives and to keep our military commitments. Traditionally, DOD has dealt with the situation by relying upon flexible forces, that is, forces usable in more than one place and for more than one purpose. Without this flexibility our ability to protect our interests outside of NATO is diminished.

Third, the NATO central front strategy is too defensive, that is, it directs our efforts into those areas where the Soviets are most capable and fails to exploit those areas where we have more capability than the USSR. For example, our power projection forces are much greater than those of the Soviets. The Navy has 12 carrier air wings consisting of approximately 1000 aircraft and it has the capability to lift 1-1/3 Marine amphibious forces (102,000 troops). The Soviets have only 65 carrier aircraft and no capability to move their 14,500 man Naval Infantry. Instead of exploiting this area, the Carter defense program will result in cutting back the number of carrier air wings and our lift capacity in order to try to match the Soviet strength, that is, ground and tactical air forces in Central Europe.

CONCLUSION

The Carter administration appears to be recognizing the impact of its budgetary choices on American defense policy. On February 20, 1978, Secretary of Defense Harold Brown, in a speech to the Los Angeles World Affairs Council, tried to assure Asian nations that we are not weakening our military posture in the Pacific. According to the Secretary of Defense, "We cannot be strong in Europe and weak in Asia. Indeed our strength in Asia supports our strength in Europe and vice versa. They are two sides of a coin."[32]

Approximately one month later, President Carter himself, in a speech at Wake Forest University, on March 17, 1978, warned the Soviet Union that the United States will match Soviet expenditures and military force levels. The President stated that we will not allow any nation to gain military superiority over us and that this nation can readily afford to increase the level of defense spending.[33]

However, words are not enough. It is dollars that determine policy. The administration cannot have it both ways. It cannot cut the strategic budget by 20 percent, and slash procurement for naval power projection forces and maintain essential equivalence with the Soviet Union and retain the capability to project power in the Pacific, nor can it defer production of the neutron bomb while maintaining that it wishes to counter the Soviet advantage in Central Europe.

In a certain sense, the administration has fallen into the same trap as the Eisenhower administration. Twenty-four years ago, the former Army general proposed to keep defense spending level by relying on a strategy of massive retaliation at the sacrifice of conventional forces. This strategy was loudly criticized by many experts, some of whom now walk the halls of the Pentagon, for its lack of flexibility. None of the critics argued that

Eisenhower was spending too much on our strategic nuclear forces, but rather that he should be spending more in other areas. Similarly, no one disputes the emphasis which the former naval officer is now placing on programs designed to strengthen the central front in Europe. Rather, the concern is with cutbacks in other areas necessary to support the NATO emphasis within a level budget. It remains to be seen whether critical analysis will change the defense policies of this administration in future years.

NOTES

1. <u>The Budget of the United States Government, Fiscal Year 1979</u>, p. 3. Unless otherwise specified, all figures used in this text are drawn from the Fiscal 1979 Budget.

2. Rudolph Penner, <u>The FY 1978 Budget in Transition: From Ford to Carter to Congress</u> (Washington, D.C.: American Enterprise Institute, 1977), p. 101; and Henry Owen and Charles Schultze (eds.) <u>Setting National Priorities: The Next Ten Years</u> (Washington, D.C.: Brookings Institution, 1976), p. 127.

3. According to the one source, Carter spent more hours studying the budget than any of his predecessors. Rowland Evans and Robert Novak, "The Defense Budget's Message to the World," <u>Washington Post</u>, December 24, 1977, p. A19.

4. Department of Defense, <u>FY 1979 Budget Briefing with Secretary of Defense Harold Brown</u>, January 23, 1978, p. 1.

5. The study was made public by Representative Les Aspin (D-Wis.) on March 6, 1977.

6. <u>Congressional Quarterly</u>, April 16, 1977, p. 721.

7. Between now and the year 2000, 360 ships will drop from the active inventory. About 270 will be major combatants. The Carter program would not be able to replace these ships on 1 for 1 basis. Because of the number of ships authorized, but not delivered, there will be slight increase in fleet size in the mid-1980s. This will only be a

temporary phenomenon.

8. The Navy has already cut the number of carrier wings from 15 to 12.

9. Quoted in Susanna McBee, "Coalition Armed with Study Pursues Defense Cuts," *Washington Post*, December 22, 1977, p. A2.

10. *Ibid.*

11. Rowland Evans and Robert Novak, "The Defense Budget's Message to the World," *Washington Post*, December 29, 1977, p. A19.

12. Quoted in Adam Clymer, "Congress Praises Budget in General, But Some Reservations are Voiced," *New York Times*, January 24, 1978, p. 14M.

13. Quoted in James Rowe and Hobart Rowen, "Liberals and Conservatives Decry Carter Economic Policies," *Washington Post*, February 1, 1978, p. A8.

14. Quoted in Hobart Rowen, "Plan to Penalize High Wage Boosts Hit," *Washington Post*, February 9, 1978, p. D9.

15. Quoted in James Hessman, "The New Strategy: A Redistribution of Weakness," *Sea Power*, March, 1978, p. 23.

16. The statements of the two Republicans are quoted in Art Pine, "Lean and Tight: Carter Budget Seeks $500.2 Billion," *Washington Post*, January 24, 1978, p. A19.

17. Department of Defense, *FY 1979 Budget Briefing with Secretary of Defense Harold Brown*, January 23, 1978, pp. 6, 7, 10.

18. See, for example, Rowland Evans and Robert Novak, "The Defense Budget's Message to the World," *Washington Post*, December 29, 1977, p. A19.

19. On June 10, 1976, President Carter told the Democratic Platform Committee "Without endangering the defense of our nation or our commitments to our allies, we can reduce defense expenditures by about $5 to $7 billion annually."

20. Carter's post-election pledges on defense are summarized in a speech by Secretary of Defense Harold Brown to the Thirty-Fourth Annual Dinner of The National Security Industrial Association, Washington, D.C., September 15, 1977.

21. In the last five years, Congress has reduced TOA for Defense by an average of $5.5 billion per year. However, there are indications that Congress will treat the defense budget more kindly in the future.

22. See for example the remarks of Representative Mitchell quoted above.

23. Quoted in Bernard Weinraub, "The Browning of the Pentagon," New York Times Magazine, January 29, 1978, p. 59.

24. FY 1978 Defense Report; Clarence Robinson, "Carter Warned on Soviet Nuclear Advantage," Aviation Week & Space Technology, November 7, 1977, pp. 18-21, and "House Debate Intensifies on Strategic Vulnerability," Armed Forces Journal, February 1978, p. 8. It should be noted that in the past DOD has underestimated Soviet missile accuracy advances by about four years, and on March 11, 1978, the Pentagon announced that the ICBM Force could become vulnerable as early as 1983.

25. John McLucas, "The Case for a Modern Strategic Bomber," AEI Defense Review, Volume 2, Number 1, p. 19. Estimates on the cost of such modifications range from a low of $10 billion to a high of $50 billion.

26. George Wilson, "The Trident: History's Most Expensive Weapon," Washington Post, March 3, 1978, p. A3 and Stephen Baron, "Navy's Trident Program is Good News for EB," Providence Sunday Journal, January 15, 1978, p. C8.

27. In its report on the FY 1979 shipbuilding program, the House Armed Services Committee recommended not funding a Trident in FY 1979 and putting the funds into building a Nimitz carrier and a nuclear cruiser. The Carter 5 year shipbuilding program deletes a Trident submarine in FY 1980.

28. Representative Les Aspin (D-Wis) estimates that without SALT II, the U.S. would have to

increase defense spending by a total of $20 billion just to stay even with the U.S.S.R. George Wilson, "Aspin See $20 Billion Saving in SALT II," <u>Washington Post</u>, January 9, 1978, p. A2. The White House puts the increase at about $3.3 billion annually.

29. In addition to the Central Front, NATO must also be concerned about defending its northern and southern flanks. The northern flank consists primarily of the Scandinavian Peninsula, while the southern sector is in the eastern Mediterranean. Loss of either sector could have grave consequences for the Central Front. For example, control of the Scandinavian Peninsula would enable the U.S.S.R. to use its fighters and bombers to extend its sea denial capabilities far out over the North Atlantic. Defense of the flanks is primarily a mission for forces from the Navy and Marine Corps.

30. Congressional Budget Office, <u>U.S. Air and Ground Conventional Forces for NATO: Overview</u>, January 1978, p. xi.

31. The International Institute for Strategic Studies, <u>The Military Balance 1977-78</u>, pp. 102-107.

32. Bernard Weinraub, "Brown Says U.S. Will Strengthen Its Forces in Asia," <u>New York Times</u>, February 21, 1978, p. 7.

33. Edward Walsh, "Carter Warns U.S. Will Match Soviet Military," <u>Washington Post</u>, March 18, 1978, p. A1.

5
Intervention Policies of the Carter Administration: Political and Military Dimensions

Doris A. Graber

INTRODUCTION

No man is an island. Certainly, no politician and no policy can be understood without examining the context of surrounding and preceding events. The political and military intervention policies of the Carter administration thus can be neither appraised nor understood appropriately without indicating their historical context. Our examination of the intervention policies of the Carter administration will therefore begin with a brief excursion into the past. This will be followed by a more detailed analysis of the types of constraints imposed on intervention policy by the current domestic and international setting. Next we will look at the intervention policies of the first year of the Carter administration to assess whether they reflect the policy constraints which we have identified. Finally, we will attempt to project present trends into the future years of the Carter administration.

What is "Intervention"?

At the outset, we must define "intervention" as we shall use the term in this essay. We need to discuss its legal status under international law. We also must explain why definitions of intervention have been controversial and why it is difficult to fully delineate the boundaries of actions that fall within the definition and to determine their legality in specific cases.
Stated in simplest form, intervention is unsolicited interference by a state in those affairs of another state which are customarily deemed to be within the latter's exclusive purview. Under the principle of sovereignty, a state's domestic

affairs and its foreign relations which do not affect the intervening state are customarily considered inviolable. Intervention may take the form of military action by the intervening state, or overt or covert economic or political pressures. Examples are offers or refusals of economic aid when the purposes are interventionary, or grants or denials of diplomatic recognition in order to influence the target state's internal affairs, or support for dissident forces to help them overthrow an established government. These activities of the intervening state impose its will on the target state or force it to choose policies contrary to its own inclinations. States act in conformance with interventionary pressures because they fear the coercive powers of the intervening states or because they are unable to stop its agents and their activities.

Since members of the international community are interdependent, the policies of many states automatically impinge on the foreign and domestic policies of other states. The occurrence of intervention is therefore difficult to pinpoint because of disagreement about the circumstances under which these effects can be labelled as going beyond the bounds of normal international intercourse.[1]

The Legality of Interventions

Interventions may be legal or illegal under international law. Under most modern interpretations of the doctrine of state sovereignty, the presumption is that unsolicited interference by one state in the affairs of another is illegal, unless it has been sanctioned by treaties or general international law. Bilateral and multilateral treaties presently sanction a wide range of collective and individual interventions in situations which have been identified as dangers to peace, or serious, imminent threats to the most vital national interests of intervening states. Interventions by an individual state to protect its national security from imminent disaster and counterinterventions against illegal interventions usually are legal under general international law.

Despite numerous debates and ratification of treaties which attempt to spell out the circumstances under which intervention is either legal or illegal, the boundaries remain unclear and controversial. The definition of "vital interests" and "dangers to peace" is problematical when one devises a general, <u>a priori</u> definition and then tries to apply it to a particular situation. Likewise, it is difficult to specify in general, and in actual interventionary situations, the degree of severity of threats and the degree of imminence of danger which justify intervention politically and legally.[2]

The fact that many interventions undertaken by small and large powers have been illegal, has led to semantic obfuscation. The term "intervention," which is frequently used as a term of opprobrium, has become a synonym for illegal intervention. To avoid this taint, politicians and scholars often use masking language for legal interventions, calling them by other names, such as interposition or police action. In this essay, we shall eschew such subterfuges and shall use the term "intervention" for legal as well as illegal acts which meet the criteria of our definition. Since we are concerned with the full range of American interventions, irrespective of their legality, we shall not attempt to pass judgment in disputed cases about the legality of particular American interventions, past or present. Likewise, we shall not attempt to determine in specific borderline cases where the boundary lies between unsolicited interference in a state's affairs which is "normal" in international intercourse and unsolicited interference which goes beyond normality. Instead, we shall use pragmatic criteria. Actions which have been widely designated as interventions by members of the international community, will be within the realm of this essay. We shall also ignore the legal and definitional problems raised when the validity of prior consent to interventions is challenged because the legitimacy of the consenting power is in doubt or when its authority is challenged by internal groups who claim the status of belligerents in a civil war.[3]

THE HISTORICAL ANTECEDENTS OF CARTER'S INTERVENTION POLICIES

When one traces U.S. intervention policies throughout American history, one is struck by the fact that there are two major strands which seemingly mesh at times and diverge at other times. These strands are the doctrine of nonintervention, on the one hand, which has been espoused by the United States throughout its history, and the actual policy of intervention and nonintervention carried out for the past two hundred years.

The Patterns of Intervention

Although nearly every American President and Secretary of State has pledged support for the rule of nonintervention, the United States has always included intervention among its foreign policy options. The frequency and extent of exercise of the option have hinged on its presumed usefulness in particular circumstances, and on the ability or willingness of the United States to bear the costs entailed by the policy. Since intervention costs have generally been high, intervention has been used sparingly and usually only when stakes are high.

A variety of means have been used for interventions, ranging from direct military action, through various types of material assistance, to verbal admonitions and refusals to recognize a country diplomatically. The desire to keep intervention costs low has meant that political and economic pressures have been preferred over military pressures, especially since military costs have skyrocketed in recent years. When military pressures have been considered unavoidable, comparatively cheap forms, such as weapons aid to other countries, or American naval or air strikes have been selected in preference to massive American ground force involvement.

In the early days of the nation, intervention was comparatively rare because the weakness and vulnerability of the country precluded it. Opportunities for intervention which might have been seized at a later date were therefore avoided. As the country grew stronger and expanded its sphere of interests, interventions became more plentiful and farflung. By the turn of the twentieth century, they had become a nearly standard response to situations of turmoil in areas in which the United States was greatly interested. Then the policy became less fashionable among great powers and its use declined considerably.

The major vital interest which the United States has sought to protect through intervention has been its hegemony in the Western hemisphere. When this appeared to be threatened by European colonial powers in the early days of the nation and by imperialist European and Asiatic powers during the nation's second century, intervention has frequently been considered, and intermittently adopted as a suitable policy to safeguard the national interest.

Protection of American hegemony has involved preventing other countries from establishing footholds in the Western hemisphere which might become bases for attack on the United States. It has also involved forestalling dangerous power combinations in Europe and Asia which might ultimately lead to an attack on the Western hemisphere. Additionally, interventionary pressures have occasionally been used to establish American strategic and economic bases abroad to protect access routes to the Western hemisphere and safeguard its overseas supplies of strategic resources.

The most massive and lasting threat in the twentieth century to the security of the Western hemisphere has been the danger of communist imperialism. Its opponents have feared that it might extend itself by direct conquest or infiltration in the Americas, or through establishing jump-off points in Europe, Asia and Africa, after acquiring control over strategic areas in these continents. Accordingly, the bulk of recent U.S. interventions has been spawned by the desire to fend off communist intrusion into the power sphere of the United States.

During the cold war years, any communist takeover any place in the world was labelled as a major threat to U.S. survival. Under the 1947 Truman Doctrine, the United States claimed a right to intervene anywhere in the world to protect countries against communist rule, alleging that America's and the world's peace were at stake. The Eisenhower Doctrine, ten years later, narrowed the proclaimed sphere of interest of the United States and pinpointed the areas which the United States would be willing to protect from communist control. The Middle East, battleground for American and Soviet client states, was singled out as a prime area for potential interventions, if states there requested aid against overt armed aggression by communist forces. The Nixon doctrine, enunciated in 1970, further narrowed the contingencies under which the United States pledged itself to a policy of intervention. According to the doctrine, the United States will not automatically assume that its security interests require it to protect other countries against communist intervention. Rather, interventions will hinge on a specific determination in each case that American security interests are involved. When communist activities threaten the United States or any other country, intervention was deemed to be the collective duty of all countries opposed to communist expansion.

One can argue about the reality of the communist threat now, and in the cold war years, and about the seriousness of its potential consequences for the United States in particular cases. One can also argue about the wisdom of anti-communist interventions and their appropriateness for achieving the desired goals. But one cannot dispute that U.S. intervention in the postwar years were inspired by a genuine belief among American foreign policy makers that the country was seriously threatened by communist imperialism. These policy makers responded to the reality, as they saw it, with a policy they considered to be appropriate and potentially effective.[4]

Before World War II, most American political leaders deemed interventions a useful tool to protect the national interest. After the second world war and the anti-colonial revolutions which followed it, a series of interventions to stop insurgent movements and stabilize tottering regimes in the Third World were unsuccessful. They failed to stop guerrilla wars, failed to stop communism, and failed to produce democratic regimes. They often stimulated counterinterventions which made the intervention costlier and less successful than had been anticipated. They also raised fears that interventions might escalate into a major international war where the dreaded thermonuclear weapons might be used. These failures of intervention policies and the fears about disastrous consequences led the United States and other powers to question the value of interventions as a foreign policy tool. They therefore became increasingly reluctant to engage in interventions.

In the mid-twentieth century, in addition to the direct costs of interventionary operations, and the dangers of counterintervention, interventions carry heavy indirect political costs as well. These include loss of international prestige, severe hostility from target states and their populations, and domestic opposition which may cause internal civil disturbances and political upheavals in intervening states. The damage done to American prestige abroad and at home by the Vietnam intervention is an example of such political costs. In the heydays of interventionism, at the turn of the twentieth century, comparable political costs were minimal. The right of strong states to interfere in the affairs of weaker members of the world community was axiomatic. In fact, interventions then were considered the mark of a great power which exercised its leadership for important objectives.

The Nonintervention Doctrine

While intervention has always been considered as a policy option open to policy makers and advisable under certain conditions, the United States has steadfastly proclaimed a preference for nonintervention. In fact, the principle of nonintervention has often been labelled as one of the major pillars of American foreign policy.

The seeming contradiction between a policy which has permitted a substantial number of interventions and the nonintervention doctrine is easily explained. In the first place, it is not at all unusual for policy makers to proclaim ideal ends and means, fully knowing that these ideals will not be attainable. Most modern policy makers genuinely prefer to achieve their goals through non-coercive measures, without intervention, particularly military intervention. Yet few are able to forego intervention entirely. The proclamations of ideal policies are nonetheless valuable because they provide a standard which policy makers attempt to approach.

Secondly, doctrines and policy pronouncements serve distinct purposes quite aside from the reality which they ostensibly describe. America's leaders in the early days of the Republic proclaimed a preference for nonintervention because they hoped that this pronouncement would protect America's security. If the country pledged to leave others alone, the reasoning went, then it could reasonably expect that they would leave the United States alone. America's leaders could also better resist internal pressures to intervene in European affairs at the risk of being drawn into costly conflicts abroad.

In the nineteenth century, adherence to the nonintervention principle became a hallmark of young nations who were proclaiming their independence from monarchs and colonial powers. The United States, as the presumed champion of such nations because it had only recently won its own freedom from a colonial power, saw support for nonintervention as a badge of honor and a symbol of democratic behavior. Even when the country became deeply involved in interventions at the turn of the century, its leaders tried to explain them as permissible exceptions to a general policy of nonintervention. They also tried to paper over the contradictions between policy and doctrine by labelling interventions with innocuous names, like 'protective mission' or 'police action.'

In the post World War II era, which saw the break-up of colonial empires and the sanctification of the concept of self-determination, support for the nonintervention principle has continued to be an appropriate policy stance for democratic countries. The United States has therefore continued to pay homage to it. It has been particularly important to do so to enhance the U.S. image among Western hemisphere countries. Latin American nations, as frequent targets of intervention, have been among the strongest champions of the principle. They have fought for its incorporation into most of the recent inter-American organizational compacts and their implementing treaties, primarily as a way to curb intra-hemispheric intervention by the United States.

THE SETTING FOR THE INTERVENTION POLICIES OF THE CARTER ADMINISTRATION

Presidential Commitments

Like all administrations since the days of the Good Neighbor Policy of Franklin Roosevelt, the Carter administration is officially committed to the nonintervention doctrine, but has reserved and exercised the right to define what that commitment entails. The President has repeatedly stressed that the United States respects the independence and right of self-determination of other nations and that it will not interfere with their rights.[5] For instance, when he was asked about American policy in the Middle East, Cyprus, and Panama, during his second month in office, he declared flatly that "we can't impose our will on other people." He promised good offices, if asked for help, but said that the nations in these areas would have to carry the main burden of their problems.[6] Similarly, he would not comment on the separatist movement in Quebec, stating that he "would certainly make no private or public move to try to determine the outcome of that great debate."[7] When reporters suggested that the United States was meddling in South Africa's internal affairs, he denied it contending that deploring blatant violations of human rights did not constitute intervention by American standards.[8]

He also excluded a variety of economic pressures from the scope of intervention. Intervention, he argued, was not involved whenever the United States decided

> ...to either enhance or reduce our trade with a country, depending upon its own policies that are important to us and the world. I think it's important for us to decide when we should and should not invest in another country, when we should and should not encourage Government programs, loans and grants to apply to another nation. I don't look upon that as an interference in the internal affairs of another country.[9]

Like other administrations, the Carter administration has also stressed that the United States will not forego the right of self-defense or the right of counterintervention to protect its major national interests. Nonintervention is the preferred policy, but interventions are not totally precluded.[10] For instance, the United States feels justified to intervene in Middle Eastern politics through the supply of military and economic assistance. When asked about an increase in arms supplies planned for a variety of Middle Eastern nations, the President pointed to the defense needs of the country, in light of Soviet Middle Eastern policies. In his view, it was preferable that arms for these nations were supplied by the United States rather than the Soviet Union. He said:

> Saudi Arabia is our ally and friend. Egypt is our ally and friend. Israel is our ally and friend. And to maintain security in that region is important.... The Soviets are shipping massive quantities of weapons into the Middle Eastern area now, into the Red Sea area or Ethiopia, into Syria and Iraq, Libya. And we cannot abandon our own friends. So I don't think that it's wrong at all to insure stability or the right to defend themselves in a region with arms sales.[11]

Beyond impromptu verbal commitments to a policy of nonintervention, the Carter administration is bound to such a policy by the nation's contractual agreements. The United Nations Covenant imposes prohibitions on interventions, particularly military interventions, in Article 2 (4), and the prohibition has been further clarified by General Assembly Resolution 2131 (1965). A similar prohibition has been part of various inter-American treaties and conventions to which the United States is a party, beginning with the Montevideo Convention on the Rights and Duties of States of 1933. Articles 18 to 22 of the Charter of the Organization of American States also proscribe interventions. Article 18 states:

> No State or group of States have the right to intervene, directly or indirectly, for any reason whatsoever, in the internal or external affairs of any other State. The foregoing principle prohibits not only armed force but also any other form of interference or attempted threat against the personality of the State or against its political, economic, and cultural elements.[12]

Despite the explicitness of this provision, the United States has always claimed that the right of self-defense supersedes any nonintervention pledge. There is little doubt that President Kennedy's 1961 interpretation of this provision still holds. Kennedy declared:

> Should it ever appear that the inter-American doctrine of noninterference merely conceals or excuses a policy of nonaction --if the nations of the hemisphere should fail to meet their commitments against outside Communist penetration--then I want it clearly understood that this Government will not hesitate in meeting its primary obligations, which are the security of our Nation.[13]

Public Opinion Factors

More formidable in many respects than treaty commitments are the constraints imposed on policy makers by national and international moods, attitudes, and opinions. In the wake of the Vietnam war and the spectre of atomic holocaust, the

Western world's mood has been isolationist and noninterventionist. Military interventions in particular have been disfavored because they run counter to the strong public opinion trends in favor of self-determination, and because they invite counterintervention which may then escalate into a major war.

Until very recently, social scientists have predicted that the worldwide mood against intervention represented a long-range trend which would certainly last into the 1980s. For instance, Bruce Russett noted in 1975 that:

> It is not a short-term phenomenon in reaction against the Vietnam disaster; rather it appears likely to be prevalent for a long period, probably more than a decade, and to be manifest in the very same influential circles of the American populace which formally supported the "internationalist" . . . American foreign policy of the cold war years.[14]

However, public opinion experts have detected in the late 1970s a swing away from the isolationist, noninterventionist mood. They perceive it as a reaction to Soviet-Cuban activities in Africa and the declining belief in the viability of detente and coexistence policies.[15] It is too early to tell whether this presents a definite change in the public mood or merely a transient fluctuation.

The noninterventionist, isolationist mood which has characterized recent years has manifested itself in several ways which have weakened the capacity of the United States to intervene. For instance, there has been marked opposition to military spending. This opposition rose sharply in the seventies when over 50% of the respondents in nationwide polls wanted a cutback in spending. This compares with an average of less than 35% in the previous thirty years. Recent polls (1977) indicate that opposition to defense spending is lessening, but it still remains at a level substantially above the pre-Vietnam era.[16]

After 1968, those who wanted defense budget cuts were no longer the low income groups of yesteryear. Rather they were people of high income and education who were most likely to make themselves heard in decision-making circles. The substantial reduction in ordinary military spending in the post-Vietnam years may well reflect the opinions of these attentive publics. The public has also shown less willingness to support military foreign aid. In a recent poll (1976), 52% of the respondents considered it "extremely important" to reduce arms sales abroad.[17] The reluctance to give military foreign aid has even overtaken the traditional opposition to give economic foreign aid. This represents a reversal of longstanding trends.

The bulk of Americans also appear to be unwilling to assist countries attacked by foreign communist forces, even if they request American help. The hypothetical victims of attack in the poll which disclosed these findings were Brazil, India, Japan, Mexico, Thailand, West Germany, and Yugoslavia. The respondents showed greatest willingness to rescue Mexico and West Germany.[18] While willingness to protect countries from outside communist aggression was low, it was even lower when assistance was required against a serious insurgency led by an indigenous communist movement. Two-thirds of the respondents indicated that they believed the United States should abstain from intervention under these circumstances.[19] The slogan of "No more Vietnams," apparently has taken firm hold, at least when hypothetical questions are asked. Faced with real situations, the response might be different.[20]

Public opinion evidence also shows that "Americans in general, and elites in particular, see international affairs as less threatening than they once did."[21] Traditional cold war concerns no longer rank very high among the problems mentioned as "most serious" by the public.[22] In Russett's view, "The great backlog of popular anticommunism and determination to fight just no longer exists."[23] Whether or not there is good reason to abandon cold war fears does not matter. What matters is how the public and its representatives assess the situation because this affects the calculus within which policy makers work. In making these calculations, it is important to remember that fear and its reactions are volatile sentiments. Whatever the attitudes may be at any particular time, they may change rapidly and significantly. The events of the Carter years could produce such a change.[24] If they do not, anti-intervention sentiments will make it progressively more difficult to maintain American troops in Europe and elsewhere. It will also be tough to sustain the level of current military intelligence and foreign operations spending and to obtain other resources necessary for successful interventions.

Another potentially major obstacle to an active intervention policy is the fact that the United States is in a period of legislative assertiveness and Congress appears to be in no mood to authorize interventions. The passage of the War Powers Act of 1973, which reduced the president's power to deploy troops abroad is proof, as is the denial of presidential requests for funds for military purposes in Vietnam and Angola, and the perennial hassle over funds for foreign economic and political operations.

Congressmen, as well as the public, believe that domestic goals have priority over assistance to foreign countries. This feeling is translated into resentment of most foreign ventures, particularly those in far off lands where the relationship between the intervention and American interests may not be readily apparent. Psychologically and politically, the nation is thus geared in the Carter era to forego interventions which would have been undertaken in other times.[25]

Threats to U.S. Security

While nonintervention is obviously the preferred policy of the American public and many political leaders, the major dangers which have led to interventions in the past still persist. For example, interventionary activities of the Soviet Union and other communist powers in Africa and the Middle East threaten to upset the world balance of power to America's detriment. America's access to vital oil resources could be seriously impaired by communist moves, particularly in the Persian Gulf region. In the Far East, further communist expansion in Southeast Asia and South Korea could endanger the survival of governments in that area which are still friendly to the United States. Should all of Asia fall into the communist sphere of power, it might become difficult to protect Alaska, Hawaii, and even the American West coast against invasion. It could also become impossible to keep strategic supply lanes to the Orient open.

In Europe, Soviet support for European communist movements endangers the NATO alliance which is deemed America's defensive shield to protect its Eastern flank. In the Western hemisphere, the presence of communist Cuba close to American shores continues to concern American policy makers. Communist influence is also strong in a number of other Latin American countries. Likewise, policy makers are apprehensive about the safety of the Panama canal, particularly once it reverts to full control by the Panamanian government.

THE CALCULUS OF INTERVENTION

What are the chances that the United States will intervene in the politics of these vulnerable areas? What is the calculus that will determine when, where, and how the United States will intervene? As was true in earlier years, the answers to three basic questions will determine whether or not intervention will be undertaken under a particular set of circumstances. These questions relate to (1) the presumed usefulness of the intervention in achieving the policy goals to be attained; (2) the costs of the projected intervention in relation to anticipated benefits; and (3) the ability and willingness of the American public to bear the political and economic costs of the intervention and its aftermath.

The Usefulness of Interventions

We have already indicated that faith has declined in the usefulness of interventions to counter communist intrusion into the politics of nations throughout the world. Specifically, the effectiveness of interventions to shore up governments which seem to be succumbing to domestic communist forces is being viewed with growing skepticism by contemporary political leaders. The failure rate of interventions has been high in the postwar period, especially in the Far East. Events in the People's Republic of China, in Vietnam, and in Laos and Cambodia epitomize these failures. In Latin America the success rate has been somewhat higher, despite conspicuous failures like Cuba and, for a time, Chile.[26] In Europe, success was good in the past, as shown by the defeat of communist interventionary efforts to take over Greece, Turkey, and Italy. But the success rate has been declining.

The will to counterintervene has seen parallel declines because the American political psyche has a low tolerance for failures. When they occur, the lessons from a particular failure often are generalized beyond the settings which produced them. Vietnam thus becomes the prototype for the consequences expected from interventions by military force which have been undertaken to halt communist insurgency.

Disastrous experiences in the recent past also have taught American policy makers that interventions are no longer useful to support friendly, yet unpopular and corrupt governments. Vietnam was the most graphic lesson. Despite massive military and economic support over long periods of time, Vietnamese governments continued to lose support and power. In the end, they were overthrown. Americans have also learned that interventions on behalf of a foreign government will not earn lasting gratitude and loyalty for the United States which will be translated into support of its policies and opposition to its enemies. Influx of massive aid may actually make a country less dependent and tractable. Hence interventions are not a useful tool to buy or control allies.

The soundness of engaging in interventions has become especially questionable in those regions of the world where regional formal and informal allies are willing and able to resist communist expansion. For instance, at the present time Brazil can be counted on to oppose communist intervention in South America. Zaire can serve as a watchman in southern Africa; Iran and Saudi Arabia guard the Persian Gulf region, and Indonesia has become a bastion in Southeast Asia. However, the instability of most third world governments always leaves policy makers with a troubling uncertainty about the steadfastness of regional allies in working for a common cause.

The failures of recent U.S. interventions, particularly the Vietnam war and similar failures by Britain, France, Belgium, and the Netherlands in defeating communist-supported insurgencies, have left the Carter administration heir to the knowledge that interventions may not only fail in their objectives, but that they may be counterproductive as well.[27] For instance, the forces which interventions may seek to suppress may actually receive psychological and material boosts when they can prove foreign opposition to them. The forces which are receiving the support may, in turn, be scarred by the fact that they are allied with a foreign power. This may weaken them substantially. Examples of this phenomenon abound in U.S. relations with Latin America. The charge of CIA support has been used to discredit political parties and movements in countries like Chile, Bolivia,

Guatemala, and the Dominican Republic.

Interventions may also be counterproductive because they may disrupt indigenous life patterns in a way which is contrary to American purposes. For example, Vietnam mountain people, as a result of their collaboration with Americans during the Vietnam war, have become objects of persecution. They have been forced to abandon their traditional homes and customs. Many have been killed or have joined the ranks of displaced persons living in refugee camps.

Another drawback of interventions is their propensity to create permanent dependency on the part of their beneficiaries. That appears to be the case in South Korea. Intervention may encourage a client state to overextend its resources, forcing the intervening state to spend beyond its intended range. Israel, for instance, is currently pursuing a costly policy of instant retaliation against its enemies. The United States, because of its ties with Israel, is forced to underwrite these Israeli ventures, even though it may object to them.

When interventions succeed in shoring up regimes, it may be a Pyrrhic victory. If the regimes are not genuinely viable, the intervention may perpetuate a status quo which should have been allowed to change. Where new radical regimes come to power in the face of unsuccessful interventions, initial U.S. opposition against them may make them hostile. This happened in China, in Sukarno's Indonesia, and in Castro's Cuba. Finally, most interventions have involved third world people of non-white race. The actions taken to control their fate have tended to increase international racial tensions.[28]

While the prevailing view at the start of the Carter years has been that interventions are useless for many of the purposes for which they were employed in recent decades, and while there is evidence that they have often been counterproductive, there is also some evidence to the contrary. For instance, limited interventionary efforts have been useful in Africa, the Middle East and Asia to maintain governments which look to the West, rather than the Communist world for support. Somalia, Sudan, Zaire, Taiwan and the Philippines are examples. It has also seemed useful to give verbal support to non-communist parties in Italy and France where large communist gains were feared in elections in the mid-seventies. With the erosion of detente and the weakening of the hope for peaceful coexistence, the Carter administration may raise its faith in the usefulness of interventions to protect American interests, even when the chances for success appear severely limited and even when counterproductive developments must be risked.

Interventions have also remained useful in cases where granting or withholding of aid of various types could secure compliant behavior. The direct costs of such interventions have been low. In most cases, aid had already been allotted. Intervention consisted in making its delivery dependent on specific actions or promises by the recipient. The approach has worked with a number of Latin American and African nations. But it may also backfire. For instance, military aid to Turkey was cancelled when Turkey failed to comply with American requests regarding Turkey's relations with Greece and Cyprus. Turkey did not yield. Instead, it withdrew permission for America's use of various Turkish bases. After a three year interval, the Carter administration, concerned with the loss of the Turkish bases, finally recommended resumption of aid in the face of noncompliance.

The Costs of Intervention

Even when interventions are deemed highly useful, their direct and indirect costs must be appraised to determine whether the country can afford them and whether the anticipated benefits are worth the expected costs. The direct costs of intervention tend to be very high, particularly when military action is involved.[29] This fact was driven home forcefully by staggering personnel and matériel costs of the Vietnam war. The price of military intervention is especially high if ground forces have to be transported and maintained over long distances. It has therefore become American policy to avoid ground force commitment and depend on air and naval power instead. This is the gist of the Guam Doctrine of the Nixon administration under which the United States pledged sea and air power in support of indigenous ground forces. Given the fact that costs for transporting and sustaining military ground forces have risen steadily since the Nixon days, the Carter administration must be even more wary of ground force involvements.[30] However, it is as yet unclear whether military intervention can be successful without ground troops. Many observers doubt it. This may leave President Carter with the choice of paying the high costs of ground troop involvement or avoiding direct military intervention entirely.

Military interventions can also take the form of furnishing weapons and other military supplies to countries or political factions which the United States seeks to support, and training foreign forces in their use.[31] While less costly than direct participation in military activities, this form of intervention has the disadvantages of diminished American control over the forces. The same objection holds true when intervention takes the form of economic aid.[32] Recipient countries have frequently used such aid in ways which did not accord with American priorities. For instance, they have misdirected most aid intended to relieve the lot of population groups who were highly susceptible to recruitment by leftist forces. Even though the benefits of intervention through military and economic aid are often slow and uncertain, the cost-benefit ratio many times has seemed advantageous enough to encourage these forms of intervention. There is no reason to expect that this will change in the future. Hence future interventions are likely to take the form of military and economic assistance.

In the past, interventions by covert means have been common. Their costs have varied widely, depending on the number of spies and saboteurs which had to be financed, the amount and number of bribes which had to be paid, and the nature of the dummy businesses and other covering ventures which had to be set up. Judging from disclosures about CIA operations which came to light during congressional investigations in the mid-seventies, the success rate of these operations has been low. A large share of the expenditures has gone for naught. If the cost-benefit ratio is as low as these disclosures have indicated, interventions by covert means are not likely to receive wide use in the future.

Interventions in the form of veiled and not-so-veiled threats have carried the lowest price tag in the past. Words are cheap, except when the opponent calls a suspected bluff. Then the words must be matched by performance or reveal the speaker as weak and irresolute. The possibility of escalation from words to material contributions must always enter calculations of costs. If these costs are high, they may deter verbal interventions.

The indirect costs of intervention likewise tend to be discouragingly high. Interventions are apt to produce a great deal of international disapproval, particularly among Western democracies. For instance, the United States lost much prestige among its Western allies by its intervention in Vietnam. Interventions in the Dominican Republic and Chile cost it the good will of many Latin American countries. Support of the Bay of Pigs invasion of Cuba had worldwide adverse repercussions. Such losses would not be risked lightly by the image-conscious Carter administration.

Within the United States, the disaffection produced by the Vietnam war was a major factor in costly domestic upheavals. The unpopularity of the war cost many elected politicians, including those at the highest levels, their chance to remain in office. These are high prices which politicians will try to avoid.

High prices have been paid at bureaucratic levels as well. After the mass media gave plentiful adverse coverage to covert activities of military and civilian agencies, a number of congressional investigations ensued. They ultimately led to cutbacks in the powers of these agencies. Even the presidential level was not immune to congressional curbs. As mentioned earlier, the War Powers Act of 1973 and the repeal of the Gulf of Tonkin resolution are examples of the power curbs which have resulted from recent interventions.

The Capability to Intervene

Despite major economic problems and questions about declining ability to match Soviet military efforts, the United States, in the Carter era, retains the economic and military strength to muster the physical resources for intervention. However, the country's capacity for military intervention has, in the view of many observers, been sharply reduced by the creation of the All Volunteer Forces.[33] In this view, volunteers are less willing and less able to fight in foreign locations in situations short of purely defensive war. They cannot be counted on to meet the challenge of major operations, should an initially limited military effort escalate. As the high defection rate in the Vietnam war showed, many Americans are unwilling to serve in military operations of which they do not approve. Interventions in foreign countries are likely to fall into that category, making the risks substantial that troops will refuse to fight. Volunteer forces also are more dependent on the mobilization of reserves than are mixed forces (volunteer and selective service), and therefore less well suited for quick military intervention strikes. These weaknesses in the military forces enhance the reluctance to undertake interventions which have the potential for escalating to full-scale war.

The reductions in forward military bases have further weakened America's capability to attempt military interventions in far-off locations. Airlifts cannot carry big enough pay loads over long distances. It therefore becomes difficult to deploy military forces, sustain them, and resupply them, particularly if the enemy does have nearby bases which cannot be denied him. In 1973, for instance, when the United States wanted to airlift supplies to Israel, the NATO allies refused landing rights for planes involved in the operation. The airlift succeeded only because Portugal finally granted use of its bases in the Azores. Similar difficulties in locating staging areas are likely to arise in the future. To avert them, the President has instructed the Defense Department to prepare quickly deployable land, air and sea forces to defend American interests throughout the world.[34]

It has also become more difficult to muster physical resources for intervention. The President is committed to substantial cuts in the defense budget and substantial increases in funds for the alleviation of domestic hardships. This orientation appears to be shared by solid majorities in both houses of Congress and by a majority of the public. However, the tide of opinion could change rapidly on this score, if relations with the Soviet Union deteriorate further and attempts to conclude a new Strategic Arms Limitation Treaty fail. The President's speech on defense policy and Soviet ties, delivered at Wake Forest University in March, 1978 points to possible major changes at the executive level. "We will match," he said, "any threatening power through a combination of military forces, political efforts and economic programs." And he called it a myth that "this country somehow is pulling back from protecting its interests and its friends around the world" and that the public believes "that our defense budget is too burdensome and consumes an undue portion of our Federal revenues."[35]

We have already mentioned the restraints which

Congress has put on the President's military intervention power through the War Powers Act of 1973 and the International Security Assistance and Arms Export Control Act of 1976. These two acts severely curb the President's authority to assure military aid to foreign countries and to send troops abroad, without congressional approval. Congressional efforts have also severely diminished the prestige and power of intelligence agencies through the Rockefeller investigation and report in 1975, and through the disclosures of the Senate Committee on Intelligence, chaired by Senator Frank Church. Consequently, the chances are sharply reduced that these agencies will be available for extensive covert interventions in the future. As the quality of clandestine intelligence declines, the capacity to intervene is reduced.[36]

American dependence on Arab oil has made the country more vulnerable and less capable to intervene freely to protect America's national interests in the Middle East. Robert Tucker, who has watched this situation closely, contends that the United States will not use intervention to break the power of Arab states because it is afraid of oil flow stoppages and afraid that intervention may topple existing regimes and bring in more radical ones. By use of the oil weapon, small powers can thus force the United States to abstain from interventions which it might otherwise undertake.[37]

To a substantial degree, the ability to conduct major interventions effectively is also dependent on the quality of leadership at the presidential level. Thus far the Carter administration has not given evidence of great leadership ability in crises. It has been unable to swing the Congress behind major plans of the Carter program, and unable to arouse the country in support of presidential policies. It is therefore unlikely that the President could rally the country behind him for a major high-cost intervention.

Moreover, such an intervention would not accord with the Carter style of operation. He is not given to taking strong actions in the face of opposition. When other countries have resisted interventionary pressures and activities, the administration has not attempted to escalate the pressure. Examples are Rhodesia's refusal to accept Anglo-American plans for producing black rule, Germany's and Brazil's defiance of a request to stop the sale of nuclear plants, and the Soviet Union's failure to ameliorate the fate of dissidents.

As indicated earlier, the popularity of intervention among the general public is equally doubtful. Bruce Russett and Miroslav Nincic, who analyzed public opinion trends over a forty year span, found a sharp decline in willingness to use military forces in the defense of other countries, when the 1938-1941 period was compared with the span from 1969-1975. A similar drop was noted in support for military spending.[38] There also is increasing public opposition to a variety of covert activities, such as political assassinations, bribe payments, and spy activities.[39] Without public support and with possibly a great deal of opposition, which is likely to be mirrored by political leaders in Congress and the executive branch, the capabilities for successful interventions are sharply reduced.

THE CARTER INTERVENTION POLICIES--YEAR ONE

The major areas and goals which have tested Carter's willingness to pursue or forego intervention, and to continue with whatever policy he has chosen, have been the Middle East, Rhodesia and South Africa, Ethiopia and Somalia, Zaire, South Korea, Panama, Italy, and the desire to halt nuclear proliferation and to promote human rights. While interventions to promote respect for human rights do not involve national defense policies directly, they warrant appraisal here since they provide clues to the President's steadfastness.

Humanitarian Interventions

The bulk of humanitarian interventions have consisted of purely verbal admonitions. However, in a few cases, involving small countries which were of limited strategic interest to the United States, the interventions have taken the form of punitive reductions in military and other aid. A large number of the complaints about a country's treatment of its own people have been directed against the Soviet Union. For instance, in the winter of 1977, the State Department warned the Soviet Union that efforts to silence Andrey D. Sakharov, winner of the 1975 Nobel peace prize, would "conflict with accepted standards of human rights." Several weeks later, in a letter to Mr. Sakharov, the President proclaimed that "the American people and our government will continue our firm commitment to promote respect for human rights not only in our country but also abroad."[40] The President claimed that the United States, as a signer of the Helsinki agreements of 1975, had a right to complain.[41] Soviet authorities disagreed and accused the United States of illegal intervention in Soviet internal affairs.

The Carter administration also denounced President Idi Amin of Uganda for "horrible murders" of his political opponents, charged the Czech government with violations of the human rights of dissidents, criticized Brazil's policies towards political opponents, and complained about South Africa's suppression of blacks and the handling of civil rights activist Steve Biko who died in a South African prison.[42] The United States also reduced military aid to Ethiopia as a protest against human rights violations.

While there obviously has been willingness to speak out on human rights--though the pace slackened somewhat after the initial months of the Carter term--the Carter administration has been far more timid in taking the second step, withdrawal or reduction of aid or other restraints on intercourse with the offenders. Nothing was done when American protestations were met with outright rebuffs by the Soviet Union. Nothing ensued when Brazil failed to change its ways but cancelled a military aid treaty with the United States to protest the interference in its domestic affairs. Likewise, when Ethiopia registered its objections to American human rights complaints by closing U.S. offices in the country, no further steps were taken. It seems fair to infer from these cases that the administration considers the costs of interventions very carefully. When they cannot be achieved at the price of the initial bidding, it drops the case.[43]

Africa and the Middle East

Talk also has been the main, though by no means exclusive, contribution of the Carter administration to solving problems in Africa involving shifts of political power from whites to blacks. For ideological and political reasons, the United States has sought to pursuade both Rhodesia and South Africa to take faster, more radical steps to transfer power to blacks. It has conferred with other African countries to make plans for power transfers in Rhodesia and South Africa and it has discussed pressures which might be brought to achieve compliance. It has tried to force Prime Minister Vorster of South Africa to pressure the government of Ian Smith in Rhodesia to accept British-U.S. plans for governance. It also has participated in economic sanctions imposed by the United Nations. Though concrete evidence is as yet lacking, there are signs that the United States may also be involved in clandestine operations in the area to counteract Soviet and Cuban interventionary activities.

To prevent shifts in the African power balance which might benefit the communist world, the Carter administration has made limited amounts of military supplies available to Zaire to help it ward off attacks from rebel exiles from Angola.[44] American transport planes were used to ferry troops to the country's embattled South and to evacuate troops already in the area. The United States has also given assistance to Somalia in its battle with Soviet-supported Ethiopia. It has continued heavy U.S. commitment of both military and economic support to the Middle East, particularly to Israel, but also to Egypt and selected other Arab powers. It has done so in hopes of stabilizing the area, preserving the peace, and preventing the Soviet Union from exploiting the Arab-Israeli confrontation to its own advantage.

The various transactions in the Middle East and Africa have been a mixture of normal diplomatic activities, responses to aid requests by legitimate governments, and overt and covert interventionary activities. The complexities of international politics in the area make it difficult to dissect out those actions which are definitely interventionary. One thing is certain, however: the United States is continuing its substantial involvement in that area and there is no evidence that it is shunning the interventionary tools used by previous administrations. These include logistics support, political and economic pressures, and meddling in elections in which some parties receive support from foreign communist sources. There is no evidence on the other hand that the Carter administration is engaging more vigorously in interventions than has been customary in Africa and the Middle East in recent years.

Carter has stated his administration's positions in several news conferences. He reaffirmed the general desire for nonintervention on January 12, 1978, when he said: "We've taken a position concerning Africa that we would use our influence to bring about peace without shipping arms to the disputing parties and without injecting ourselves into disputes that could best be resolved by Africans."[45] With respect to Israel, he pledged continued supportive intervention, promising in his news conference on March 9, 1978, to honor all previous agreements guaranteeing "the adequate defense capabilities of Israel."[46] He also promised military aid for Saudi Arabia in accordance with prior agreements. Military aid for Egypt was recommended "because Egyptians, in effect, have severed their supply of weapons that used to come from the Soviet Union and have cast their lot with us--which is a very favorable development in the Middle East."[47]

The Far East, Europe, and the Western Hemisphere

In the Far East, the administration appears to be keeping hands-off in areas like Vietnam and Thailand, where previous administrations had already reduced American commitments. It is maintaining previous positions in the Philippines, Taiwan, and elsewhere. The plan for gradual withdrawal of ground forces from Korea, with total withdrawal accomplished over a period of four to five years, is apparently envisioned as a holding action, rather than a reduction of interventionary capabilities. Presumably, air power is being substituted for ground forces. This is in line with the Guam Doctrine proclaimed during the Nixon administration. Whether or not air power can substitute for ground forces is, of course, questionable. It has been the subject of heated debates which have resulted in a number of shifts in military personnel to assure that command in Korea rests with people who share the President's views.[48]

In the European theater, the Carter administration has also kept American commitments essentially stable. It has pledged continued and even stepped-up support for the North Atlantic Treaty Organization. But NATO support has rarely raised questions of intervention because NATO members are deemed capable of freely consenting to NATO policies. Moreover, NATO policies have been largely defensive, designed to rebuff military attacks on members of the NATO alliance. The alliance has not been used to interfere in the domestic policies of European countries.

Despite pledges that the United States would not interfere in the internal policies of Western

Europe and that the choice of their governments was up to them, the Carter administration has verbally opposed Eurocommunism. For instance, the State Department issued a statement in January 1978 urging Italy and other Western European countries to curb communist influence. This statement averred that the United States does not favor "Communist participation in West European governments... and would like to see Communist influence in any Western European country reduced."[49] European communist parties condemned the statement as interventionary, but the Carter administration disagreed. It claimed the right to publicly express its views on major political developments which concern the United States. The Carter administration apparently has not moved beyond the verbal level, however. It has not repeated the substantial efforts which the United States made in the immediate post-World War II period to keep the Italian government out of the hands of Italian Communists. At that time, large sums of money and other resources were covertly transferred to the Christian Democrats. It was also hinted that foreign aid to Italy would cease, should the people elect a communist government.[50]

The general impression which one gains from viewing Carter's initial record of interventions is that there have been no major changes from the policy of previous administrations. In fact, one is struck by the frequent assertions made by the President that his policies are a continuation of commitments and trends set in force by his immediate predecessors. Policy continuity is well illustrated by the one foreign policy issue which has involved explicit discussion of intervention as a policy option in the Western hemisphere. The issue is the right to protect the Panama Canal by intervention during the remaining years of U.S. control and even thereafter.

The Carter administration, like its Republican predecessors, was willing to negotiate withdrawal of American forces from the canal and to pledge nonintervention in Panama's internal affairs. But it was not willing to forego the right to intervene in this strategically important area if the need to protect passage rights through the canal should demand that. The lengthy debates in the Senate and in the country in general showed that this view was shared by the public. For instance, in January, 1978, 65% of the respondents in a national poll (NBC-AP) favored relinquishment of control over the

Panama canal if the United States retained the right to intervene whenever the canal was threatened by attack. 25% opposed and 10% were not certain. In the absence of the right to intervene, only 28% favored turning control of the canal over to Panama, 62% opposed it, and 10% were uncertain.[51]

Like other American administrations in this century, the Carter administration has strenuously objected to interventions by other powers. It has called these intrusions violations of international law, a judgment which provides a legal basis for counterintervention. For instance, it has condemned the Soviet Union for its support of the Ethiopians in their fight against Somalia and has blamed it for the presence of Cuban troops in Africa. But it has refused to use the threat of suspending SALT negotiations as a means to deter Soviet interventions.[52] This differs from behavior towards Cuba where objections against Cuba's military involvement in Africa were linked to a refusal to resume U.S.-Cuban relations until Cuban troops were withdrawn. The United States has also objected to arms sales by other powers when these have gone to underdeveloped countries or areas of high international tension. Objections have been particularly strong when arms sales have involved the transfer of nuclear capabilities, as happened between West Germany and Brazil during the first year of the Carter administration. But objections have not gone beyond words.

PROSPECTS FOR THE FUTURE

What do the policies and constraints of the present portend for the future? The intervention policies of the Carter administration, like those of the Nixon and Ford administrations, will continue to sail under the stars of the ill-fated Vietnam intervention. From the Vietnam experience, American policy makers generalize that most military interventions are unsuited to attain their major objectives, too costly in men and matériel and prestige at home and abroad, and that the United States is neither willing nor able to undertake them without sacrificing goals that currently have higher priorities. We can therefore expect that no military interventions are in the offing. Only the most compelling strategic and political reasons could overcome this reluctance to commit military forces.

There appears to be less reluctance to intervene through sales of military supplies or through political and economic pressures as long as operations are overt rather than covert.[53] Such interventions are likely to continue, particularly since many of them are based on long-standing commitments or on well-established traditions to intervene in areas of national security interest.

There is least reluctance to intervene with words, especially since the Carter administration claims the right--not claimed by its immediate predecessors--to comment publicly on other nations' political behavior, especially in the field of human rights. However, the guiding motto for interventionary pronouncements appears to be to "Speak loudly and carry a small stick," a reversal of Teddy Roosevelt's admonition to keep the stick large and the voice small. When the Carter administration faces opposition to its verbal skirmishes, it retreats. It is too early to tell whether such retreats are only temporary, permitting a revision of strategy and timing, or whether they are permanent. Given the propensity of the Carter administration to put a good deal of effort into image-making, the chances appear good that brave talk about human rights at home and abroad will continue, even if the effects are minimal in terms of improving the treatment of the world's oppressed people. Recent polls have shown that the American public approves human rights interventions by a two to one margin (55%-26%).[54] It is not clear whether this support extends beyond rhetorical battles.

What are possible intervention sites in the years to come? President Carter listed them in a speech which outlined the areas of great national interest to the United States which it would protect against communist aggression. He identified East Asia, particularly Japan and South Korea, the Middle East and the adjacent Persian Gulf and Indian Ocean areas, and the Western hemisphere. For these areas, he promised that the United States would "work with our friends and allies to strengthen their ability to prevent threats to their interests and ours. In addition, however, we will maintain forces of our own which could be called upon if necessary to support mutual defense efforts." Even though efforts required to halt communist expansion might be large, he pledged that "We will match, together with our allies and friends, any threatening power through a combination of military forces, political efforts, and economic programs."[55]

While it is not likely that military forces would be dispatched to these areas, there is a chance that forces which are already in place or nearby might be used, if needed. There are some who believe that this would most likely occur in Western Europe and Japan. Also included in this view is that Cuba, Mexico, and Canada might constitute a second echelon, because of their physical proximity to the United States. Troop dispatches to Central and South America and the Middle East would be far less likely because of the logistics problems.[56]

Patterns of intervention through supplying military hardware or economic and political aid can be gauged by recent assistance patterns. In 1976, for instance, Israel received half of the security assistance granted by the United States. Other priority recipients were Korea, Jordan, Greece, Turkey, the Philippines, Thailand, Indonesia, and Ethiopia.[57]

As in the past, the circumstances which may lead to the adoption of interventionary policies are most likely to involve fear of growing Soviet power and influence which might threaten the security of the United States. A decline in perceived aggressiveness by the Soviet Union would thus reduce the pressure for interventionary policies. So would a decline in Soviet interventions in third world countries which have tempted the United States to engage in counterinterventions. Since U.S. intervention policy has become primarily a defensive tool, a large number of the decisions made by American policy makers in favor of intervention begin with actions by the Kremlin. The United States currently lacks the power to prevent these actions and therefore lacks the power to resist being drawn into counterinterventions.

The chances for U.S. interventions which are not linked to security considerations are small, except for continued attempts to influence the internal politics of a haphazard array of states who are accused of violating human rights of their citizens. Given domestic and international political pressures and the danger of war and communist intervention in southern Africa, the United States is also likely to continue to pressure white-ruled states with nonwhite majorities to get them to increase the political power of nonwhites.

A variety of rationales will continue to be used to justify these types of interventions and reconcile them with the pledges of nonintervention to which the Carter administration is committed. Interventions to checkmate Soviet expansionism are going to be justified by either the principle of self-defense, the right of counterintervention, or previous treaty commitments or requests for aid by new client states. Similarly, the proclaimed rationale for intervention to change the power structure in Rhodesia and South Africa and their former dependencies will be self-defense on the grounds that these situations threaten a major war. Collective intervention rights, based on United Nations actions could also provide a rationale.

For interventions to protect human rights the justification will be either contractual rights under the Helsinki agreements, or under the guarantees of human rights embodied in the United Nations Charter. A natural law rationale may also be used to argue that any country has the right to protest against morally reprehensible behavior by other countries.[58] While most of the Carter intervention policies are a continuation of recent trends, set by post-Vietnam administrations, humanitarian interventions present a return to earlier traditions. A policy of humanitarian interventions flourished in the immediate post-Civil War period. Secretaries of State William Seward and Hamilton Fish and Presidents Theodore Roosevelt, William McKinley and William Howard Taft were its chief proponents. Since then, humanitarian interventions have been less common because the results have been poor and the costs in international tension high.

The image-conscious Carter administration appears to calculate the costs and benefits of humanitarian intervention in a somewhat different way. The fact that such interventions portray the American President as the spokesman for the world's oppressed people is prized highly, even if the effects on inhumane behaviors are small, and even if international tensions are increased. Like Woodrow Wilson before him, Jimmy Carter is willing to make substantial political sacrifices for the mantle of moral leadership. But, as in Wilson's case, this does not mean that traditional policies in defense of the national interest will be ignored. The moral leadership mantle will be cast around them, whenever possible. But where this fails, the mantle will be thrown to the winds in favor of the protection of the national interest. This is as it has always been: Plus ca change, plus c'est la meme chose.

NOTES

1. The following works define intervention more fully: D.A. Graber, Crisis Diplomacy: A History of U.S. Intervention Policies and Practices (Washington, D.C. Public Affairs Press, 1959), pp. 1-18; Ann Van Wynen Thomas and A.J. Thomas, Jr., Non-Intervention: The Law and Its Import in the Americas (Dallas: Southern Methodist University Press, 1956), pp. 167-212; R.J. Vincent, Nonintervention and International Order (Princeton: Princeton University Press, 1974), pp. 3-16.

2. For existing norms, see Derek W. Bowett, "The Interrelation of Theories of Intervention and Self-Defense," pp. 38-50 in John Norton Moore, ed., Law and Civil War in the Modern World (Baltimore: The Johns Hopkins University Press, 1974). Suggestions for new norms are discussed by John Norton Moore in the introduction to the volume, pp. xiii-xv.

3. We are also skirting the tricky question of boundaries between "intentional" and "unintentional" interferences and the question whether intent is an essential component of intervention. For a fuller discussion of these and related legal issues, see Vincent, pp. 281-325.

4. In 1976, 59% of the respondents in a nationwide poll considered "containment of communism" to be a "very important" goal of U.S. foreign policy. See Daniel Yankelovich, "Cautious Internationalism: A Changing Mood Towards U.S. Foreign Policy," Public Opinion, Vol. 1 (1), March/April 1978, pp. 13-14. The danger of Soviet intervention is carefully assessed in Grayson Kirk and Nils H. Wessell, eds., The Soviet Threat: Myths and Realities (New York: Academy of Political Science, 1978). Interventions to protect the lives and property of American citizens have been omitted from this essay because they are not a part of U.S. defense policy.

5. See, e.g., news conference reports in The New York Times, February 23, 1977 and October 28, 1977.

6. New York Times, February 24, 1977.

7. Ibid.

8. New York Times, October 28, 1977.

9. Ibid.

10. See his Wake Forest University speech, New York Times, March 18, 1978.

11. New York Times, February 18, 1978. For a recent statement on the moral obligation of counter-intervention, see Nathan Glazer, "American Values and American Foreign Policy," Commentary, vol. 62 (1), July 1976, pp. 32-37.

12. The status of intervention and nonintervention under the United Nations Charter is explained by Vincent, pp. 233-277.

13. John F. Kennedy, "The Lessons of Cuba," Department of State Bulletin, vol. 94 (No. 1141), May 18, 1961, pp. 659-661.

14. Bruce Russett, "The Americans' Retreat from World Power," Political Science Quarterly, Vol. 90 (1), Spring 1975, p. 2.

15. Yankelovich, pp. 12-16.

16. Ibid., p. 14.

17. Ibid., p. 13.

18. Russett, pp. 5-7.

19. Yankelovich, pp. 14-15.

20. A sample of military personnel reported that they would defend Germany, Mexico, Brazil, Japan, and Thailand from communist invasion, but only Mexico from communist insurgents. For the view that opposition to intervention has remained stable over the years, see John E. Mueller, "Changes in American Public Attitudes Toward International Involvement," pp. 331-337 in Ellen P. Stern, ed., The Limits of Military Intervention (Beverly Hills, Cal.,: Sage, 1977).

21. Russett, p. 8.

22. Ibid. For conflicting data, see Mueller,

p. 336.

23. Russett, p. 10.

24. The volatility of public support is discussed, by Stanley Hoffmann, "The Hell of Good Intentions," Foreign Policy, No. 29, Winter, 1977-1978, pp. 3-26.

25. For a fuller discussion of the retreat from interventionism, see Russett, pp. 1-21. The President's plea in his news conference on May 25, 1978, for fewer congressional curbs on foreign aid is likely to go unheeded.

26. A historical account of recent interventions in Third World countries is presented in Melvin Gurtov, The United States Against the Third World: Antinationalism and Intervention (New York: Praeger, 1974).

27. For a long list of disadvantages of intervention see Gurtov, pp. 210-215.

28. The impact of these problems on military decision making is discussed in Lawrence E. Grinter, "Nation Building, Counterinsurgency and Military Intervention" in Stern, pp. 237-256.

29. Klaus Knorr, On the Uses of Military Power in the Nuclear Age (Princeton: Princeton University Press, 1966). The conditions which may produce military intervention are set forth in Herbert K. Tillema, Appeal to Force: American Military Intervention in the Era of Containment (New York: Crowell, 1973), pp. 20-39, 179-200. Also see Frederic S. Pearson and Robert Bauman, "Foreign Military Intervention and Changes in United States Business Activity," Journal of Political and Military Sociology, Vol. 5 (1), Spring, 1977, pp. 79-97.

30. Use of unmanned "smart" bombs may be another cheap way for intervention. For development of this idea, see George H. Quester, "The Impact of Strategic Air Warfare," Armed Forces and Society, Vol. 4 (2) Winter, 1978, p. 202.

31. The interventionary impact of such military aid is discussed in Brian Jenkins and Caesar D.

Sereseres, "U.S. Military Assistance and the Guatemalan Armed Forces," *Armed Forces and Society*, Vol. 3 (4) Summer 1977, pp. 588-592.

32. For a discussion of the interventionary effects of economic aid, see Klaus Knorr, *The Power of Nations: The Political Economy of International Relations* (New York: Basic Books, 1975), pp. 134-206.

33. Thomas A. Fabyanic, "Manpower, Military Intervention, and the All-Volunteer Force," p. 291, in *The Limits of Military Intervention*, Ellen P. Stern, ed.,(Beverly Hills, Cal.: Sage, 1977).

34. Wake Forest University Speech, *New York Times*, March 18, 1978.

35. *Ibid*.

36. Grinter, p. 252. Also Paul W. Blackstock, "The United States Intelligence Community and Military Intervention," in Stern, p. 272.

37. Robert W. Tucker, "Oil and American Power--Three Years Later," *Commentary*, Vol. 65 (1) Jan. 1977, pp. 29-36.

38. Bruce Russett and Miroslav Nincic, "American Opinion on the Use of Military Force Abroad," *Political Science Quarterly*, Vol. 91 (3), Fall 1976, p. 414.

39. Blackstock, p. 262.

40. *New York Times*, January 28, 1977; *New York Times*, February 18, 1977.

41. The legality of humanitarian interventions is discussed by Ian Brownlie, "Humanitarian Intervention," and Richard B. Lillich, "Humanitarian Intervention: A Reply to Ian Brownlie and a Plea for Constructive Alternatives," pp. 217-251 in *Law and Civil War in the Modern World*, John Norton Moore, ed.,(Baltimore: The Johns Hopkins University Press, 1974).

42. *New York Times*, February 24, 1977.

43. For a similar appraisal, see Walter Laqueur, "The World and President Carter," Commentary, Vol. 65 (2), February 1978, pp. 56-63.

44. The background of this move is described in C.K. Ebinger, "External Intervention in Internal War: The Politics and Diplomacy of the Angolan Civil War," Orbis, Vol. 20 (3), Fall 1976, pp. 669-699. Direct military aid to Zaire hinges on a presidential declaration that such aid is required by U.S. security interests and on Zaire's repayment of overdue military credits.

45. New York Times, January 13, 1978.

46. New York Times, March 10, 1978.

47. Ibid.

48. Major General John Singlaub, third ranking U.S. officer in South Korea, was removed from his command because he publicly disagreed with the President's contention that removal of ground troops would not weaken South Korea's capabilities to defend itself.

49. New York Times, January 13, 1978.

50. These and other strategic psychological operations of the cold war are discussed in Robert T. Holt and Robert W. van de Velde, Strategic Psychological Operations and American Foreign Policy (Chicago: University of Chicago Press, 1960).

51. Everett C. Ladd, Jr. "The Great Canal Debate," Public Opinion, Vol. 1 (1) March/April 1978, p. 34.

52. New York Times, March 26, 1978.

53. Testimony by former CIA director Richard Colby indicates that the sharp decline in covert operations had already set in during the Nixon administration and continued under Ford. Blackstock, cited in note 36, p. 268.

54. Yankelovich, p. 14.

55. Wake Forest University Speech, New York Times, March 18, 1978.

56. Fabyanic, p. 300. Factors which appear to affect willingness to intervene are set forth in Russett and Nincic, pp. 411-431. Also see Richard G. Head, "Technology and the Military Balance," Foreign Affairs, Vol. 56 (3), April 1978, pp. 544-563.

57. Caesar D. Sereseres, "U.S. Military Assistance to Nonindustrial Nations" in Stern, pp. 217-219.

58. Past humanitarian interventions by the United States and their rationales are discussed in Graber, pp. 338-360.

6
Europe and the Superpowers
James A. Linger

INTRODUCTION

Any attempt to assess the major features of the Carter administration's defense policy vis-a-vis NATO and the Soviet Union during the course of Carter's first year and a half in office represents a complex and multifaceted task. Traditionally, a new administration's first year or more is a period of transition. It is in this period that a new administration must staff the defense and foreign policy bureaucracies with personnel reflecting its own Weltanschauung while simultaneously fulfilling defense and foreign policy commitments of previous administrations, articulating new national commitments in response to emerging problems and issues, and/or redefining previous national commitments to problems and issues of a more enduring character. Any conclusions drawn in the subsequent pages, therefore, must be considered to be of a tentative nature, for the changes in American defense and foreign policy initiated by the Carter administration with respect to NATO and the Soviet Union appear to be broad in scope and undergoing further evolutionary adaptation at this time. In this context, it is best to begin with a brief overview of a number of changes in American defense and foreign policy, initiated under previous administrations. These can then be used to identify the continuities and discontinuities of the policies of the Carter administration.

THE 1970s: THE NIXON-FORD/KISSINGER LEGACY

The Carter administration's legacy from immediately preceding administrations, particularly in light of the changes that have taken place since the beginning of this decade and the problems associated with these changes, pose a number of discrete but related complications for the formation and promulgation of American defense policy with respect to NATO and the Soviet Union.

American defense policy, beginning with the conclusion of the American involvement in Vietnam, has undergone a series of major reorientations. These reorientations have manifested themselves in at least three ways: 1) the restructuring of the American force posture for both conventional and nuclear combat in Europe; 2) the transition from a mixed conscription/volunteer armed force to an all-volunteer armed force; and 3) a new emphasis on the modernization and build-up of the American armed forces committed to NATO in response to the equipment and personnel "draw-down" during the Vietnam War.[1]

American defense policy with respect to NATO, under the Carter administration, will also have to adjust to the changes that have emerged since the beginning of the 1970s. These include, but are not limited to: 1) continuing Western European difficulties or failures to fulfill their force level commitments to NATO; 2) Greece having joined France in a withdrawal from NATO's integrated military command structure, with Turkey threatening to follow suit if the American arms embargo is not lifted; 3) the emerging phenomenon of "Eurocommunism" with particular relevance to the internal political situation in France, Italy, Portugal, and even Spain, in so far as communist participation in or control of the governments of these nations raises questions not only about the cohesiveness of NATO, but also regarding its very raison d'etre; 4) unresolved questions and issues touching on "cost-sharing" and "burden-sharing" among the NATO member states; 5) unresolved questions and issues touching on the degree of standardization and interoperability that should or could be established; 6) unresolved questions and issues relating to the role of NATO in the Mutual Force Reduction (MFR)/Mutual Balanced Force Reduction (MBFR) negotiations; and 7) Western European disagreement on the value and role of advanced weapons technologies and their application within a NATO context (i.e., the value and role of precision guided munitions (PGMs) and the so-called "neutron bomb," an enhanced radiation weapon).

In dealing with the Soviet Union, American defense policy will have to take into consideration and will have to adjust to: 1) the emergence of rough strategic parity between the United States and the Soviet Union; 2) the continuing build-up and modernization of Soviet and Warsaw Pact armed forces; 3) the increased capacity and willingness of the Soviet Union to globally project, either directly or indirectly, its military power and influence; 4) Soviet intransigence regarding the negotiations of a new Strategic Arms Limitation (SALT) agreement; and 5) the need to discover a way to regain the lost momentum of the deadlocked MFR/MBFR negotiations in a manner which is consistent and compatible with both American and Western European defense interests, without generating NATO and, especially, West German fears of a "decoupling" of the American commitment.

This brief overview of the American defense policy environment in the early and mid-1970s has, of necessity, been sketched in broad terms in order to highlight some of its most salient features with respect to NATO and the Soviet Union. Viewed from this perspective, the evolution of American defense policy, particularly as it has undergone change either in nature or in emphasis, had already established parameters within which the two previous administrations operated.

The Carter administration is, of course, not immune to similar considerations and constraints. Indeed, as it will be pointed out below, the Carter administration's defense policy orientation with respect to NATO and the Soviet Union appears to be in the process of being modified in response to both domestic and international criticisms.

THE CARTER ADMINISTRATION'S APPROACH TO DEFENSE POLICY FORMATION AND PROMULGATION

Presidential candidate Jimmy Carter, in the course of his campaign for the presidency, sought to disassociate himself, to the greatest extent possible, from the Nixon-Kissinger, Ford-Kissinger perspectives, styles, and policies. Carter's criticism of the two previous administrations in these three dimensions was both specific as well as comprehensive. He made it clear that, if he became President, there would be sweeping and dramatic changes in all three aspects of national security, policy making and implementation.

In the articulation of his own perspective, Carter rejected, out of hand, the commitment of the two previous administrations to the search for and the creation of "what Henry Kissinger called 'stable structures of peace,' built around great power relations and relying on traditional (largely personal) diplomacy."[2] Carter viewed Kissinger's dual role as presidential national security advisor and Secretary of State under both the Nixon and Ford administrations as a dangerous concentration of bureaucratic and executive power in the hands of a single individual who was not directly responsible to the American people, but who nevertheless possessed enormous influence in the formation and promulgation of both the national security policy and the foreign policy of the United States. Additionally, from Carter's perspective, Kissinger over-emphasized the role of the United States and the Soviet Union in terms of their mutual capacity to erect "stable structures of peace." Because of this over-emphasis on establishing and maintaining the Soviet-American relationship, Carter also felt that the two previous administrations had failed to be sufficiently "tough" with the Soviet Union in the negotiations on strategic arms limitation. In Carter's opinion, Kissinger's view, moreover, neglected to give adequate consideration to changes in the international milieu, particularly in the context of the changing role of new nations as international actors, whose views and activities must be re-evaluated and effectively integrated into newly emerging patterns of international politics. Finally, Carter felt that Kissinger's predisposition to focus on great power relations tended to reinforce his propensity to engage in secret as opposed to open diplomacy, a tendency which Carter felt could undermine the domestic base of political support necessary to effectively conduct foreign and national security policy.

Since assuming office, Carter and his national security advisor, Zbigniew Brzezinski, have attempted to delineate and describe a different perspective for the conduct of American foreign and defense policy, one whose foundations are rooted in a __Weltanschauung__ that is virtually diametrically opposed to that previously espoused by Kissinger. In broadly defined terms, this new Carter/Brzezinski perspective has been described as an attempt "to move from 'acrobatics' to 'architecture'; the wish to enhance consultation with other nations; the willingness to recognize new actors in international politics; and also the determination to grow fresh roots for American foreign policy in the domestic turf."[3] The

Carter/Brzezinski conceptualization also argues that the foreign and defense policy agendas need to be broadened with respect to both the range of issues considered and the number of nations involved in the deliberative or consultative process. "It sought more diversified objectives and a more complex agenda, and it wanted to rely on multilateral diplomacy."[4] Carter and Brzezinski, again in contradistinction to the pattern of diplomacy established by Kissinger under the Nixon and Ford administrations, indicated that great power relations would be de-emphasized by the new administration, and that multilateral diplomacy and interaction, rather than detente between the "Superpowers," would receive the highest priority. In a somewhat obtuse manner, this shift in emphasis was articulated as a manifestation of "administration wishes to develop a set of international relations not based exclusively on an entente of superpowers... "[5] (i.e., a set of international relations that would be more comprehensive as well as more globally integrative in scope).

Five Cardinal Principles

Although there has never been a precise description of what Carter and Brzezinski conceive as their alternative to the approach of previous administrations in the areas of defense and foreign policy, some insights can be tentatively obtained by a partial review of the public statements of Carter over the period of the last year and a half. In late May of 1977, Carter, in what has since become known as the "Notre Dame Address," presented a macroscopic overview of the defense and foreign policy rationales and objectives of his administration. In this speech, Carter argued that American "policy must be open; it must be candid; it must be one of constructive global involvement, resting on five cardinal principles."[6] In paraphrased form, these five cardinal principles were listed as: 1) a reaffirmation of America's commitment to human rights as an essential cornerstone of foreign policy; 2) the reinforcement of American ties with other democracies, especially including, but not limited to, NATO member states; 3) a desire to halt the strategic arms race with the Soviet Union, which was viewed as both dangerous and morally undesirable; 4) the initiation of new American proposals designed to facilitate the realization of a lasting peace settlement in the Middle East; and 5) a restatement of a strong American commitment to reduce the spread of nuclear proliferation as well as the spread of conventional weapons.[7] Carter also argued that the basis of the American relationship with the Soviet Union, which largely shaped the parameters of American defense and foreign policy in the period after World War II, had been fundamentally altered by a transformation of historical trends.

> Our policy during this period was guided by two principles: a belief that Soviet expansion was almost inevitable but that it must be contained, and the corresponding belief in the importance of an almost exclusive alliance among non-Communist nations on both sides of the Atlantic. That system could not last forever unchanged. Historical trends have weakened its foundation. The unifying threat of conflict with the Soviet Union has become less intensive even though the competition has become more extensive.[8]

Carter further argued that other changes in the international milieu since 1945, such as the breakdown of old colonial relationships with a corresponding increase in the number of newly independent nation-states, the emergence of new normative objectives for nation-states (e.g., such as redistribution of international wealth and power), and the creation of new centers of power and influence in the international environment, have abetted the decline of the centrality of the American-Soviet relationship. These changes, in turn, have led to a demand on the part of more nation-states for a more active role in the management of the international system, a new emphasis on their part with respect to questions of justice, equity, and human rights in both an absolute sense and in their relations with the United States and the Soviet Union.[9]

While Carter's early statements were consistent with his administration's alternative approach to the problems of defense and foreign policy formation, it must be observed that the five cardinal principles cited in the Notre Dame Address above are not so much principles as they are objectives. The changes in the international milieu that are cited, to be sure, have long been neglected; new issues and new actors have emerged and must be effectively integrated into the international system. Carter's statement of principles cited above notwithstanding, the question remains as to how these tasks can be accomplished.

Criticisms

This administration has consistently made itself vulnerable to both the domestic and foreign criticism that its defense and foreign policy agenda has been: 1) too ambitious; and 2) indifferent or insensitive to implicit contradictions and/or problems that have made themselves manifest since this administration has come into power. This has led to and reinforced the view, recently succinctly described by Thomas L. Hughes, that the Carter administration may not be aware of the implications of its defense and foreign policy initiatives.

> As always, language, truth, and logic are connected. Carter's semantics have tended to reinforce the historic American myth that there are no incompatibilities or contradictions in public life, and to perpetuate the old American view that all good things are simultaneously possible. His sense of conscious ambiguity is hard to discern, and contradictions continue to be reconciled by avoidance or denial, or else unconsciously displayed. This fortifies the ill-starred politics of pushing ahead indiscriminately on all fronts.[10]

In another sense, the position of the Carter administration on the centrality of the American-Soviet relationship appears to have undergone some change over the last 18 months. The failure of the United States and the Soviet Union to reach a new strategic arms agreement, the utilization of Soviet proxy forces in Africa, and the continuing build-up and modernization of Soviet and Warsaw Pact armed forces, have all tended to emphasize the importance of reaching a set of military and political agreements with the Soviet Union before the other goals and objectives of the Carter administration can be considered and some form of resolution attempted. Thus, as these problems have emerged, the Carter administration has been forced to reconsider its overall position on, and approach to, the Soviet Union. In practice, the response of this administration has been to reaffirm its objectives while it has simultaneously adopted, almost incrementally, a "tougher" line in its relations with the Soviet Union. Gradually, through speeches at Charleston, South Carolina in July 1977, at Wake Forest University in March 1978, and most recently in a speech at the United States Naval Academy at Annapolis, Maryland in early June 1978, Carter has been compelled to address himself to the problems posed by Soviet intransigence in the SALT negotiations and to Soviet actions and initiatives in various parts of the world which are potentially destabilizing and which threaten the continuation of the policy of detente on any meaningful basis. Indeed, in ·his Annapolis speech Carter adopted what a number of commentators referred to as his strongest stand to date vis-a-vis the Soviet Union, calling upon "the Soviet Union to choose between confrontation and cooperation and [he] said the United States is 'adequately prepared to meet either choice.'"[11] Carter further pointed out, moreover, that Soviet actions and initiatives were inconsistent with the American view of detente, implicitly warning that if the Soviet Union persisted the entire detente process would be at stake, for the Soviet interpretation of this process seemed "'to mean a continuing aggressive struggle for political advantage and increased influence.'"[12] The response of the Soviet Union to Carter's Annapolis speech was to reaffirm its commitment to the detente process and to question the sincerity of the American commitment in light of what it perceived as the vacillation of the Carter administration between a "cold war" posture and one conducive to detente, perceptions which were interpreted as reflecting inconsistencies in American foreign policy and/or internal divisions within the Carter administration.[13]

Changing Relations With the Soviet Union

While the Carter administration remains committed to its conceptualization of the dimensions of defense and foreign policy, the period since Carter took office has witnessed a gradual shift in its position with respect to the Soviet Union. The problems that this administration has encountered with the Soviet Union, particularly in the areas of the SALT negotiations and the indirect Soviet intervention in Africa, have demonstrated quite clearly that other items on the administration's defense and foreign policy agenda must assume a secondary or subordinate position until outstanding differences with the Soviet Union have been satisfactorily resolved. Insofar as these and other issues remain unresolved with the Soviet Union, the Carter administration will be severely limited in its ability to focus its attention on other issues and/or problems. This is patently true because of the capacity of the Soviet Union to unilaterally create problems for the promulgation of American defense and foreign policy when it perceives its interests as being affected by American actions and initiatives. This raises, for the Carter administration, the recurrent criticism that it must establish some rank order of priorities in the articulation and implementation of its defense and foreign policy initiatives in order to avoid contradictions and confusion, a problem which will be addressed again in a different context below.

THE NATIONAL SECURITY STRUCTURE

Carter and Brzezinski also felt that it was necessary to reorganize the entire national security policy formation and promulgation apparatus created during the Kissinger era. Whereas national security policy formation and promulgation had been highly centralized under Kissinger, Carter and Brzezinski sought to decentralize the process. Where Kissinger had created a number of committees to deal with national security affairs and policy making, Carter and Brzezinski created only two. Moreover, the committee structures that now exist are more corporately organized rather than being organized under the central direction and control of one man as they had been under Kissinger. In terms of style, then, the Carter/Brzezinski national security policy apparatus is much simpler. It attempts to emphasize decentralization, in terms of both powers and functions, and is less formally organized than it was under the Nixon-Kissinger and Ford-Kissinger administrations.

> Business in the West Wing, where Brzezinski operates, is conducted in a breezy style. Whereas Kissinger's NSC apparatus had a half-dozen committees, most of them chaired by him, now there are only two. One is the Policy Review Committee, presided over by the Cabinet member designated by Carter (the choice is made according to which department has the largest responsibility on a given issue) and the other is

Brzezinski's Special Coordination Committee. The latter appears to be the more important one, cutting, as it does, across departmental responsibilities.[14]

These two new committees, following the organizational predispositions of Carter and Brzezinski, have been functionally specialized in a broadly conceived manner. The Policy Review Committee is not to be concerned with the day-to-day consideration of the administration of defense and foreign policy. Instead, it is primarily charged with the responsibility for the consideration of the long-term requirements of American defense and foreign policy. The Special Coordination Committee, conversely, is primarily concerned with the day-to-day problems of defense and foreign policy implementation as well as short-term planning; it is crisis oriented, and manages the overall American intelligence effort as well as being charged with responsibility for the coordination of American arms control and disarmament negotiating positions.[15]

In contrast to the national security policy making institutions and procedures established by Kissinger, Carter and Brzezinski have elected to "open up" the decision making process through the creation of committee structures which they feel will facilitate the conduct of non-secretive diplomacy as well as the achievement of their national security policy objectives. As Richard Burt recently, in the New York Times, described the changes instituted by Brzezinski, they have been strongly supported by the White House as being consistent with the changes that Carter wanted to make with respect to the Kissinger apparatus and organizational style.

> To White House officers and aides, Mr. Brzezinski's operational style reflects the Administration's preference for an open, corporate approach to decision-making and a vindication of his own belief that a decentralized process is most likely to achieve the long list of objectives that the White House has set.[16]

To reiterate, the one man dominance of the entire national security policy making processes and institutions associated with Kissinger, is, under the Carter administration, evolving into a more corporate or collegial approach. Nixon and Ford relied, basically, upon Kissinger to shape policy; "Carter now relies on a four-man 'collegium'--Brzezinski, Secretary of State Vance, Defense Secretary Harold Brown and Vice President Walter Mondale--to help him shape policy."[17] Within this "collegium," however, Carter and Brzezinski have been described by some as being "aggressive activists,"[18] who tend to vigorously advocate and press for the acceptance of their own views and objectives; thus, they tend to play dominant roles or at least appear to be "more equal" than the other members of the "collegium."

It cannot be argued with any great certainty, however, that Carter and Brzezinski dominate the national security policy making processes and institutions that have been created. At various times over these last 18 months, analysts have concluded that other members of the "collegium" have played the most significant role on selected issues, e.g., Mondale superseding Andrew Young as the chief administration spokesman on American policy in Africa, Brzezinski recently taking a key role in the articulation of American policy with respect to the People's Republic of China, Vance playing a more prominent role in American-initiated attempts to bring the continuing Middle East situation to some acceptable conclusion, and Brown has emerged as the administration's chief spokesman on issues related to NATO and general requirements of American defense policy. These roles, however, do not appear to be fixed. Rather, what seems to have developed is a shifting set of defense and foreign policy responsibilities which the Carter administration can manipulate at its own discretion for the purpose of emphasizing the importance that it associates with various issues and/or nation-states or regions. Similarly, the flexibility of the administration, in terms of the personalities associated with important roles in certain issue areas is also consistent with Carter's long held predisposition to "open up" the national security decision making processes, for as these processes are presently organized more individuals have an opportunity to play a significant role in a number of issue areas than was possible under the last two administrations when these processes tended to be dominated by Kissinger. Whether the Carter administration will retain the national security decision making apparatus that it has erected for the remainder of its current term in office remains uncertain, however, just as the contemporary division of labor among the key personalities in the administration with respect to various other issue areas is also subject to further change.

A BALANCED PERSPECTIVE

Over and beyond the organizational/bureaucratic transformations described and analyzed above, the conceptual perspective of the Carter administration on the formation and promulgation of American defense policy has also emerged. The Carter administration's deemphasis of the primacy of the American-Soviet relations, predicated upon the emergence of strategic parity and a mutuality of American-Soviet interests, suggests that the interests of Western Europe and the so-called "Third World" nations will receive greater attention than under the two previous administrations. This view does not mean to imply, however, that relations between the Soviet Union and the United States will not continue to be viewed as important, particularly in the strategic political/military context, but rather that the new administration views questions related to military, economic and social issues in remaining areas of the world to be of great importance as well. This suggests that the Carter administration will continue to take a "tougher" line with the Soviet Union on the substantive issues and problems concerned with the SALT II negotiations, thereby redeeming another campaign pledge, while simultaneously directing more of its attentions to the problems of the "Third World," especially the sets of relationships which exist between the "developed" (North) nations and the "developing" (South) nations. To a great extent, then, the Carter administration is apparently committed to a set of policies that both implicitly and explicitly repudiates the "balance of power" conceptual framework utilized by Kissinger under the last two administrations. To be sure, this transition to a "world order politics" approach has not yet been completed by the Carter administration and any judgment, thus, about its effectiveness must be tentative for the full implications of this transition and the possibilities for its success cannot yet be adequately discerned.

What can be discerned, however, is that the Carter administration has not been able to fully implement its conceptualization of a "world order politics" approach to the entire range of defense and foreign policy issues with which it currently confronted. As long as substantive agreement with the Soviet Union is absent on issues like SALT, the Soviet role in Africa, and the interpretation of the requirements of the detente process, it will probably remain impossible for the Carter administration to push ahead with its preferred approach to the reorganization of the international system. Thus, the importance of at least tacit Soviet agreement in a number of issue areas suggests that the Carter administration will be forced, if nothing else for a transitory period, to substantially upgrade the importance if not centrality of the Soviet-American relationship as a means to permit the implementation of its broader international objectives at some subsequent date when the conditions for their achievement would be more propitious.

CARTER'S DEFENSE POLICIES

The Carter administration, since it came into office, has initiated a number of policy changes in the national security sector which suggest that it has seriously attempted to adapt American defense policy to the conceptual framework described above. These changes allow one to discern the substantive content of the Carter administration's defense policy initiatives with respect to NATO and the Soviet Union. As a matter of convenience, these changes will be considered below in summary fashion and the primary focus will center on the SALT II negotiations with the Soviet Union, the perceived need to modernize and reorganize NATO, the problems presented by the stalled MFR/MBFR negotiations, and the contemporary problem of "Eurocommunism."

As the first post-Brzezinski Trilateral Commission Paper, <u>An Overview of East-West Relations</u>, has pointed out, it was by no later than the early 1970s that the Soviet Union began to achieve rough strategic parity with the United States.[19] This report notes, somewhat more significantly, that the overall build-up of Soviet armed forces' capabilities, which began in the early 1960s, has continued, unabated, to the present time; this build-up encompasses not only Soviet conventional, tactical nuclear, and strategic nuclear capabilities, but also includes dramatic improvements in Warsaw Pact capabilities. The continued build-up of Soviet-Warsaw Pact capabilities, and particularly the increase in Soviet strategic nuclear capabilities, poses a number of questions regarding Soviet motivations and intentions. This report considered three tentative, but not confirmable, explanations for the Soviet build-up: 1) that the build-up only reflected the Soviet military establishment's satisfaction of vested interests; 2) that it represented an attempt to keep up with American technological advances; and 3) that it manifested a political commitment to achieve strategic nuclear superiority as a means of making the American commitment to defend NATO less credible when coupled with Soviet-Warsaw Pact conventional superiority.[20] While any attempt to determine the Soviet rationale can only be speculative at best, there is virtually no disagreement that the Soviet Union has dramatically increased its overall strategic nuclear capability during the period when the United States has demonstrated unilateral restraint in its own weapons program both in terms of new weapons development and deployment (i.e., the cancellation of the B-1 bomber and slowdowns in the MX and Trident II missile programs).

During his presidential campaign, Carter was openly critical of the SALT agreements negotiations which were concluded with the Soviet Union under the Nixon and Ford administrations. Carter argued that Kissinger, in the SALT I agreement, had unnecessarily provided the Soviet Union with a strategic nuclear advantage in the form of an additional 600 launchers,[21] and that in the SALT I Interim Agreement (also known as the Vladivostock Accords, concluded in 1974) Kissinger had set too high a limit (2,400 delivery vehicles) for each side.[22] Upon assuming office, the Carter administration was faced with two immediate and urgent problems: 1) the unabated Soviet build-up; and 2) the fact that the SALT I Interim Agreement would run out in October 1977. The Carter administration response to these problems has been reasonably consistent with its conceptual framework.

SALT Proposals

In March. 1977, the Carter administration submitted two SALT II proposals to the Soviet Union for its consideration, which, if either had been adopted, would have been in effect until the end of 1985. Of the two proposals submitted to the Soviet Union, the Carter administration strongly advocated acceptance of what has since become known as the "deep cuts" proposal. This proposal was a dramatic departure from those negotiated with the Soviet Union by previous administrations, both in terms of its scope and in terms of its fundamental commitment to disarmament as a matter of principle. What Carter, in effect, proposed was a reduced quantitative limit on the number of launchers which both sides would have as well as controls on the qualitative "mix" of launchers. In essence, it was proposed that both sides reduce their total number of launchers by 400 to 600, and that strict limits on the number of MIRVed missiles and air launched cruise missiles and the number of large or "heavy" ICBMs be established.[23] This proposal would have required the Soviet Union to dismantle some 400 to 600 launchers in its strategic nuclear forces as it had already approached the numerical ceiling of the SALT I Interim Agreement, while the United States would have been faced with only a very small percentage reduction in its launchers-in-being. The Soviet Union rejected this proposal out of hand. The second proposal amounted to little more than an extension of the Vladivostock Accords, with the same numerical ceilings on delivery vehicles (2,400) without necessarily encompassing such weapons systems as the American cruise missile, the Soviet "Backfire" bomber, or other qualitative changes or developments for either side. Both proposals, it should be noted, would have limited Soviet strategic weapons production capacity, a capacity which far exceeds that of the United States through 1985.[24] A comparison of current Soviet and American strategic forces, as well as a projection for 1985, comprised of land based intercontinental ballistic missiles, submarine launched ballistic missiles, and heavy bombers for the period 1977 through 1985 is provided below.

SOVIET-AMERICAN STRATEGIC FORCES: 1977-1985
NO SALT II AGREEMENT

Soviet Union Strategic Forces

Weapon	1977	By End of 1985 Without SALT II Moderate	High
ICBMs	1490	1498	2492
SLBMs	850	1350	1680
Heavy Bombers	140	200	200
	2480	3048	4372

American Strategic Forces

Weapon	1977	In 1985 Without SALT II (Present Plans)
ICBMs	1054	1054
SLBMs	656	664
Heavy Bombers	349	341
TOTAL LAUNCHERS	2059	2059

Source: Congressman Les Aspin, "Salt II or No SALT," Mimeo, January, 1978, Figures B & C, pp. 3 & 4, respectively.

Thus, the Soviet rejection of Carter's proposals for a SALT II agreement was not, in some ways surprising. Given the existing production capacities of the United States and the Soviet Union, as well as the existing numerical differences as of 1977, with respect to strategic forces, the Soviet Union had neither a strong nor an immediate incentive to agree to the Carter administration's SALT II proposals.

The thrust of Carter's proposals, however, was clear. He attempted to place new and reduced quantitative and qualitative limits on the strategic arms race, limits which could be utilized in future SALT negotiations as a basis for strategic disarmament by stages. With the lapse of the SALT I Interim Agreement, it remains to be seen whether the Carter administration will still seek to fulfill its commitment to strategic arms control and disarmament, or whether it will shift its position and press for accelerated development of the MX missile, the Trident II missile, and other advanced technology weapons systems or weapons systems components,[25] which are potentially destabilizing, as a means of inducing the Soviet Union to agree to the type of SALT agreement that Carter desires. The fact that the Carter administration was willing to risk the expiration of the SALT I Interim Agreement without having negotiated a follow-on agreement is at least tentatively consistent with the shift from Kissinger's emphasis on the primacy of the American-Soviet relationship and the "balance of power" considerations that so dominated the two previous administrations. Whether this shift in negotiating position on the part of the United States will eventually result in the kind of SALT II agreement that the Carter administration desires, however, remains to be determined, for the Carter administration has modified its SALT II negotiating position once again in the period since negotiations with the Soviet Union broke down and the SALT I Interim Agreement formally expired. Nevertheless, under the conditions described above, and particularly in light of the now generally perceived vulnerability of the American land based ICBM force through 1985,[26] the Carter administration has continued its attempts to secure a SALT II agreement.

The failure of the Carter administration to secure a strategic arms limitation agreement with the Soviet Union in March 1977 did not result in the termination of the negotiating process itself. Throughout the Summer of 1977, and even after the expiration of the SALT I Interim Agreement, the United States actively pursued the achievement of a new SALT agreement, a process of negotiation which is still in progress. In the period since March, 1977, the Carter administration has sought to resolve its outstanding differences with the Soviet Union on the SALT II agreement through what amounts to a compromise between the two proposals previously offered. Any SALT II agreement that should emerge will quickly establish itself as an index of the strategic relationship between the United States and the Soviet Union and one which will tend to dominate American defense and foreign policy formation and promulgation through 1985. If substantial agreement on the outline of a new SALT agreement can be obtained, however, it is still unlikely that the Carter administration will submit the proposed agreement to the U.S. Senate before the Congressional by-elections are concluded in the Fall of 1978. This appears to be the most probable strategy for the Carter administration, for it is already anticipated that the administration will have a difficult time obtaining Senate ratification of the new SALT II agreement based on reactions to those parts of the proposed agreement which have become generally known.

In an excellent article on the proposed SALT II agreement, described by Richard Burt in a recent issue of Foreign Affairs, it has been noted that the proposal will consist of three separate parts: "a treaty lasting until 1985, a protocol lasting for three years and a statement of principles to guide negotiators during the next phase of the negotiations."[27] The tentative provisions of the treaty, which as summarized by Burt would include at least thirteen major items, do not resolve all of the outstanding differences or areas of disagreement between the Soviet Union and the United States. As presently envisaged, some of the major provisions of the treaty would provide that: the number of launch vehicles allowed for each nation would be set at 2,250 of which 1,320 may be MIRVed (Multiple Independently Targeted Reentry Vehicle) sea- and land-based missiles and long-range bombers equipped with air-launched cruise missiles (ALCMs); there may be no more than 1,200 sea- and land-based MIRVed missiles and only 820 ICBMs (Intercontinental Ballistic Missiles) on each side may be MIRVed (however the Soviets may MIRV all of their "heavy" missiles even though the United States does not possess any "heavy" missiles); the testing and deployment of long-range ACLMs will be limited to long-range bombers but there will be no limitation on how many ALCMs each bomber may carry. ALCMs will be limited initially to an effective range of 2,500 kilometers; no new MIRVed missiles with larger than already existing payloads may be deployed, even if they are developed; any missile tested with a MIRV configuration will automatically be counted as a MIRVed launcher; storage of additional missiles at silo sites will be prohibited; mobile ICBMs will not be affected, but the Soviet Union will not be permitted to deploy its SS-16 ICBM in a mobile mode due to its similarity with the mobile SS-20 IRBM (Intermediate Range Ballistic Missile); the Backfire bomber will not be covered by the treaty; and finally both sides will be committed to the non-circumvention of the treaty provisions and prior notice to missile testing will be provided and no interference with national means of verification, i.e., satellite reconnaisance, will be permitted.[28] The protocol, which is designed to be in force for a period of three years from the date of signing, is basically concerned with four provisions: 1) certain types of new missiles, which have yet to be precisely specified, will be banned for the purposes of either testing or deployment; 2) the upgrading of existing missile capabilities would be prohibited, subject to further negotiations; 3) the testing and deployment of ICBMs in a mobile configuration would be prohibited; and 4) ALCMs with an effective range greater than 2,500 kilometers may not be tested or deployed and cruise missiles with a range over 600 kilometers must be deployed on long-range bombers.[29] The statement of principles would attempt to outline remaining Soviet-American differences on strategic arms issues in order to provide a framework for the next round of negotiations, with the United States strongly advocating that consideration be given to overall reductions and qualitative limitations while the Soviet Union advocates that dual-capable (conventional and nuclear capable) systems in Western Europe be considered as well as the nuclear forces and capabilities of American allies in Western Europe.[30]

As Burt's summary of the major provisions of the proposed new SALT agreement demonstrate, it represents a compromise between the two proposals submitted to the Soviet Union in March 1977. It proposes a modest reduction in the number of strategic launch vehicles available to each side, it proposes some modest qualitative limitations on both extant and new weapons systems, but it does not fully resolve issues related to cruise missiles in general, dual-capable weapons systems stationed in Western Europe, or the Backfire bomber, all of which were deferred in the sense that they would be more comprehensively considered in the next round of strategic arms limitations negotiations, SALT III.

The mere fact that the Soviet Union and the United States may have substantially agreed upon the major provisions of the proposed SALT II agreement, however, does not mean that the agreement, as it is presently perceived, will be ratified. As mentioned earlier, it now appears that the Carter administration will have a difficult time in obtaining Senate approval if it can be obtained at all. The proposed SALT II agreement will encounter ratification difficulties inasmuch as "the agreement appears to countenance 1) an overall shift in the strategic balance in favor of Moscow; 2) the emergence of Minuteman vulnerability; and 3) the growth of serious strains within the Atlantic Alliance."[31] The first problem or difficulty considered reflects the increasing attention that the long-term Soviet-Warsaw Pact armed forces build-up and modernization is receiving in a period when the Soviet Union has attained rough strategic parity with the United States. In both the conventional and strategic nuclear arms areas, thus, there is an increasing perception that the Soviet Union and its allies may, if restraint is not exercised or if the Western nations do not adequately respond, gain political-military advantages from their increased overall military capabilities. This consideration is, of course, related to the fact that no matter what the United States and its allies do between now and

1985, the American land based Minuteman ICBM force will become vulnerable to the strategic forces of the Soviet Union. These two points, in turn, also touch on the third: the nation-states of Western Europe have always been extremely sensitive to fears that their defense interests could be "decoupled" from those of the United States. Somewhat more precisely, they fear that the United States, particularly as it becomes more vulnerable between now and 1985, may sacrifice the defense interests of Western Europe in order to secure some form of strategic arms agreement with the Soviet Union that would be compatible with the interests of the United States.

The difficulties of securing Senate ratification of the proposed SALT II agreement will probably be further exacerbated by a number of other factors. The Carter administration has not enjoyed a particularly good working relationship with a congress that is characterized by Democratic Party majorities in both Houses; moreover, it has long been known that Carter's defense policies have not been widely perceived as being appropriate even by members of his own party and doubts remain regarding this administration's understanding and capability to deal effectively with the contemporary American defense policy issues related to both NATO and the Soviet Union. Similarly, but in a different context, Carter will have to allay fears of any American "decoupling" of its commitment to the defense of Western Europe. This latter task may prove to be a very difficult one, particularly if the United States should act in such a manner as to limit Western European nations 'access to advanced weapons' technologies, such as the cruise missile and other forms of PGMs, that they are known to be interested in acquiring. As the experience of the "neutron bomb" or enhanced radiation weapon demonstrated (an issue that will be dealt with subsequently), the Carter administration may face difficulties in convincing the Western European nation-states that the proposed SALT II agreement will serve their defense interests as well as those of the United States. Thus, while the Carter administration's approach to the SALT II negotiations remains consistent with its proposals offered in 1977, it has modified its position somewhat in its search for an agreement that would be acceptable to the Soviet Union. Nevertheless, it is by no means certain that the modified American SALT II proposal will be ratified by the Senate, or, if the Senate elects to alter the proposal, that it would then be acceptable to the

Soviet Union. Regardless of what the contents of the final SALT II proposal considered, the Carter administration will undoubtedly encounter difficulty generating support for it both at home and abroad.

NATO: Changes and Continuities

The Carter administration's policies with respect to NATO demonstrate a number of different concerns all directed toward increasing the overall combat capabilities of the alliance. As has been true with virtually all previous administrations in the post-World War II period, the Carter administration has reconfirmed the basic American commitment to defend Western Europe from the Soviet Union and its Warsaw Pact allies. Unlike the last three administrations, however, the Carter administration is not preoccupied with Vietnam or divisive domestic political problems. Freed from such concerns, the Carter administration has been able to devote more of its attention to the widely perceived need to increase the defensive capabilities of NATO in order to confront the continuing increase in Soviet-Warsaw Pact capabilities.

Shortly after assuming office, Carter, in an appearance in conjunction with a North Atlantic Council summit meeting in May 1977, proposed that NATO initiate four new joint efforts designed to facilitate inter-allied cooperation and coordination. These four new efforts were to include: 1) a long-term defense program for NATO which would consider NATO needs through the 1980s; 2) a program of short-term improvements which was to improve NATO defense capabilities between 1977 and 1980, when the long term program would come into force; 3) the "two-way street" in defense expenditures which called for increased diversification of NATO weapons systems purchases; and 4) the preparation of a study on Soviet-Warsaw Pact capabilities and the prospects for East-West relations in both the short-term and long-term futures.[32] The thrust of the Carter proposals, thus, was to increase the participation of NATO member states in the alliance decision making processes in almost all areas of mutual defense interest or concern. These American initiatives reflect the Carter administration's commitment to multipolar diplomacy and reflected, as well, an attempt to redress or ameliorate the long-standing Western European criticism that the United States did not adequately consider the needs and/or problems of its Western European allies in making decisions affecting all member states and the alliance as a whole. These new efforts, however, may not come to fruition. Rather than serving as a vehicle for the effective coordination of NATO planning and decision making, these new initiatives may compound the different perceptions of the Western European NATO member states with respect to their responsibilities and obligations in providing for the alliance defense effort. Planning and burden-sharing considerations, moreover, will probably become even more complicated in the future. New weapons systems and advanced weapons technologies, for example, present a number of fairly obvious potential problems. Western European NATO member states have long desired access to American weapons systems and advanced technologies as a means of reducing their own research and development costs and as a means of permitting them to meet their defense requirements at reduced budgetary levels. While the United States has supported such efforts in principle, it has historically resisted, as the Carter administration is likely to do, the transfer of technology over which the United States has a virtual monopoly or which could be potentially destabilizing if it passed out of direct American or American-Western European national control. In the past, this was true largely in the areas related to strategic and tactical nuclear weapons. In the near future, however, conventional weapons systems, especially those employing advanced weapons technologies, may fall under similar types of constraint. For example, such considerations could easily emerge with respect to cruise missiles, other forms of PGMs, and CBUs (cluster bomb units) or new conventional weapons which have mass indiscriminate destruction capabilities. A corollary problem, of course, would touch on the concept of a "two-way street" in defense expenditures. It is unlikely that the United States, in support of this concept, would be willing to make large-scale purchases of Western European produced weapons systems or the components thereof for two reasons: 1) such purchases might create domestic problems for an administration if the American business community felt that its interests were being sacrificed for those of its Western European competitors; and 2) if the arms transfers in the form of "two-way" defense expenditures were based on co- or joint-production, the United States would again be faced with the difficult decision of how to limit the dissemination of various advanced weapons technologies without thereby offending NATO member states and raising, at least indirectly, questions about the degree of cooperation and credibility associated with the alliance. The conclusion which quickly manifests itself on the significance of the four new initiatives proposed by Carter to facilitate inter-allied cooperation and coordination is that nothing much will have really changed. Decisions made in the areas of defense planning and defense expenditures do not readily lend themselves to purely rationalized processes; such decisions have tended to be dominated by national political considerations in the past, and they will probably be so dominated for the foreseeable future, although initiatives similar to those recently proposed by the Carter administration will continue to be undertaken and widely supported, at least in principle.

In order to implement the Carter administration's commitment to increase the overall defense capabilities of NATO, the new administration has undertaken a number of initiatives either unilaterally or in cooperation with the NATO member states. In terms somewhat reminiscent of the much-ballyhooed Nixon-Kissinger "Year of Europe," 1973-1974, which was an abortive failure, the Carter administration has consciously decided to refrain from the disabuse of the media description or characterization of the current American defense budget as the "NATO budget." As a measure of its concern with the problems of the alliance, and as a means of visibly demonstrating its commitment to the defense of Western Europe, the Carter administration has deliberately highlighted those items in the current American defense budget that are designed to increase the capabilities of American armed forces committed to NATO, and, thus, indirectly to increase the capabilities of the alliance overall.

Budgetary considerations, moreover, were among the most important items on which alliance agreement was sought at the May 1977 North Atlantic Council meeting. Under the aegis of American leadership, the NATO member states, at this meeting, committed themselves "to aim at an annual increase in defense spending of about 3 percent, in real terms (compared with an estimated annual increase in spending of 5 percent by the Soviet Union)."[33] While the United States also supported this new spending level, problems have arisen in the interim period, for the new Carter defense budget projects that defense spending for the United States will increase "a little more than 2 percent over last year, but spending on NATO jumps more than 3 percent over last year. Whether this will satisfy the NATO pledge is uncertain."[34] Somewhat similarly, other nations, particularly the United Kingdom, have had recurrent difficulties in meeting their NATO defense spending commitments, a development which has always tended to exacerbate inter-allied disputes on the issues of "cost-sharing" and "burden-sharing."[35] Budgetary considerations, thus, raise questions in two areas. In the first instance, the Carter administration risks the credibility of its commitment to NATO unnecessarily because of the ambiguity surrounding the interpretation of how increases in the American budget can be considered as either meeting or failing to meet the pledged levels of defense budget increases agreed upon in May 1977. The second budgetary problem has been one with a long history. As NATO is presently structured there is no immediately available remedy at hand if any member state fails to meet its obligated budgetary commitment. If NATO planning and cooperation are to be placed upon a firmer footing in the future, both of these problems must be resolved as soon as possible, and they should be accorded a high priority by the Carter administration.

The Carter administration has also attempted to ameliorate some of the disaggregating tendencies within NATO which have manifested themselves over the course of the last decade. The obvious objective of this effort is to restore some semblance of political-military unity and cohesion to the alliance, thereby halting what some observers, such as Pfaltzgraff, have alluded to as its degeneration into little more than an American-West German defense arrangement.[36] The problems which have emerged within the alliance, however, do not readily lend themselves to quick and easy resolution. It is unlikely that France, even though it has increasingly participated in NATO exercises under President d'Estaing, will formally rejoin NATO's integrated military command structure in the near future. Without France, NATO will continue to have difficulties in establishing a defense-in-depth posture, a problem which would not be satisfactorily resolved even if Spain, at some future date, should apply for and be admitted to full NATO membership. The prospects for French re-integration, however, remain undercut by a number of differences and/or disagreements. First, the French do not perceive that the conditions which prompted them to initially withdraw from NATO's integrated military command structure have been significantly altered. Second, differences between the United States and France over the dissemination of nuclear technology have recently developed and exacerbated the already existing differences related to French participation in NATO. This latter issue, the sale and other dissemination of nuclear technology to nations which currently do not possess independent national capabilities in this area, has also created problems for West German-American relations. The friction created by the West German decision to export nuclear technology and facilities to Brazil, however, has not threatened to "spill-over" into issues related directly to NATO and the West German-American relationship in the context of NATO.

The Carter administration has also been searching for a means to bring about the resolution of the long-standing Greek-Turkish dispute over Cyprus and the economic exploitation of the Eastern Mediterranean. The withdrawal of Greece from NATO's integrated military command structure, coupled with the Turkish denial of basing facilities as long as the Ford-Kissinger arms embargo is in force, seriously undermines the defensive capabilities of NATO's southern flank. The United States is confronted, thus, with a paradox: if it lifts the current partial arms embargo on Turkey, it will further alienate Greece; if it does not lift the partial arms embargo, then the United States and NATO will continue to be denied use of Turkish bases that are deemed to be important to the Western European-American defense effort especially for intelligence collection purposes. Nevertheless, the Carter administration's recently announced policy will be to seek the lifting of the partial arms embargo and it has justified its proposed action as being dictated by NATO defense concerns. "The administration says lifting of the embargo is necessary to strengthen U.S. relations with Turkey and the NATO defense in the Mediterranean."[37] This policy shift by the Carter administration has also been described as a response to pressures emanating from other NATO member states to normalize relations with Turkey as the Soviet Union has sought to exploit this cleavage within NATO to its own advantage.[38] The full implications of this break with the policy of the Ford-Kissinger administration, if indeed it is successfully promulgated, on Turkish-American, Greek-American relations, as well as its implications for NATO, cannot yet be discerned. In any event, the question of the reintegration of Greece into NATO's military command structure will remain.

Confronted by the increasing military capacities of Soviet-Warsaw Pact armed forces, the Carter administration, like the two immediately preceding administrations, has no choice but to attempt by every means available to restore the credibility of NATO which can be severely questioned given the cleavages that presently exist in NATO. The nature of the differences that exist among various NATO member states, moreover, will be difficult to resolve with or without American pressures and incentives. Again, paradoxically, American efforts to resolve these differences may lead to the creation of new cleavages which could serve, in turn, to produce a further weakening of alliance cohesion, the common sense of purpose which it is supposed to fulfill, and/or antagonism directed at the United States for interfering in the internal and/or internecine disputes among NATO member states.

The Carter administration's commitment to improving the overall defensive combat capabilities of NATO can also be perceived in its most recent response to the Soviet-Warsaw Pact build-up. In an address by Carter to NATO's permanent representatives in January 1978, the United States committed itself to provide an additional 8,000 troops to NATO, mainly to be stationed in Northern Germany, as well as an additional wing of fighters, to be stationed in the United Kingdom. Unlike the two previous administrations, Carter has actually moved to reinforce American military capabilities in a most dramatic manner. It is unlikely that any other initiative could have impressed the NATO member states and, especially, the Federal Republic of Germany of the new administration's commitment to the defense of Western Europe as effectively as did this announcement. This move, when viewed with the May 1977, North Atlantic Council decisions to build-up the conventional combat capabilities of the alliance and the budgetary commitments to achieve this objective, will result in increased NATO capabilities in confronting the continued Soviet-Warsaw Pact build-up.

The importance of the American-NATO response to the Soviet-Warsaw Pact build-up, of course, is particularly relevant to a potential Central European conflict. The growth of Soviet-Warsaw Pact capabilities has raised questions concerning the adequacy of NATO's defense posture. This can be better appreciated if some of the dimensions of this growth are detailed and put in context.

> The Pentagon says that the U.S. is now outnumbered 5-1 in tanks, 4-1 in artillery pieces and 3-1 in submarines. At the end of World War II, the Soviet Navy consisted mostly of coastal-patrol boats and short-range subs; now the Russians possess a powerful blue-water fleet. They have also improved the quality of their army, sharpening their readiness, for example, so much that U.S. experts believe they could launch an attack on four to eight days notice, instead of the 30 days, as NATO once assumed.[40]

The implications of this growth are not difficult to extrapolate. The Soviet-Warsaw Pact armed forces, as compared to those of the United States and the NATO member states, clearly have been growing at a faster rate while they have simultaneously undergone a process of modernization. This poses two threats for NATO: 1) that the perceived shift and momentum associated with this build-up could be utilized in a massive conventional assault on NATO member states; and 2) that the newly developed Soviet-Warsaw Pact military capabilities could be politically exploited to further weaken NATO cohesion. These considerations underscore the importance of the Carter administration's new military force commitments to NATO. No recent administration, prior to Carter's, had been able to undertake such initiatives for a number of diverse but obvious reasons related to the American involvement in Vietnam and American domestic political constraints during the Watergate period. Nevertheless, the symbolic and actual significance of the new administration's commitment cannot be underestimated. These moves indicate that the growing disparities in NATO-American and Warsaw Pact-Soviet armed forces capabilities have been perceived by the new administration and that it is willing to take the necessary steps to redress these disparities.

These initiatives have also been complemented by a new American willingness, under the current administration, to address the issues of NATO standardization and interoperability in the context of increased inter-allied joint licensing ventures designed to reduce the per unit cost of various advanced weapons systems and equipment adopted for NATO-wide utilization through long production runs. Conceptually, standardization seeks to make future

NATO weapons systems and equipment similar, while interoperability seeks to make dissimilar NATO weapons systems and equipment compatible.[41] The practical problems that destandardization and non-interoperability pose for NATO can be seen in the fact that NATO forces in Europe now employ "23 different families of combat aircraft; 7 different families of main battle tanks; 8 different families of armored personnel carriers, and 22 different families of antitank weapons."[42] NATO, as opposed to the Soviet-Warsaw Pact forces which are standardized to a much greater extent, would be at a decided disadvantage in the event of actual combat in maintaining and resupplying such diverse sets of weapons systems and equipment. While previous administrations have all supported increased NATO standardization and interoperability in principle, the political-military reality has led the United States to remain the major supplier of NATO's major weapons systems and equipment. The Carter administration, with the May 1977, North Atlantic Council meeting and the recent decision to use a West German gun on the new XM-1 main battle tank, has indicated to the NATO member states that it is willing to be more flexible, in the interests of both the alliance and the individual nation-states, on the issues of standardization and interoperability.[43] The Carter administration's obvious intent, of course, is to facilitate the growth of inter-allied cooperation and coordination on defense problems and issues of mutual concern, while downplaying the prominence of the United States in alliance decision making and defense planning. The obvious limit to the flexibility that the new administration can exercise, however, is that Carter, like previous American presidents, will be extremely reluctant to provide NATO member states with advanced weapons and/or advanced weapons technologies that cannot be directly controlled by the United States or which the Soviet Union may insist, in the SALT or other negotiating formats, be prohibited from being provided to other nation-states. In both instances, NATO member states would be likely to criticize the Carter administration for either dominating the alliance structure or sacrificing their interests to the Soviet-American relationship. Also, in both instances, such actions would represent a contradiction of Carter's articulation of his administration's defense and foreign policy objectives. Thus, the Carter administration may well find itself in another paradoxical situation as a result of its position on the issues related to NATO standardization and interoperability.

The Neutron Bomb

In a similar vein, the Carter administration's proposal that the NATO member states inform it of their views on the production and deployment of enhanced radiation devices, the so-called "neutron bomb," before the United States would enter into production and deployment of this weapon in Western Europe, was designed to maximize allied participation and consultation. Unfortunately, disagreement about the nature of the weapon and a multiple set of domestic and NATO member state political considerations have clouded the decision as to whether to produce and deploy this weapon. The "neutron bomb" is basically an antitank weapon that owes its effectiveness to the fact that it unleashes a very intense, but short-lived burst of lethal radiation. Thus, it destroys an enemy force without necessarily employing the high levels of blast and thermal destruction typically associated with the use of nuclear weapons. It was designed, moreover, to counter Soviet-Warsaw Pact superiority in armor in the North Central German Plans Region (NORTHAG), for if the Soviet-Warsaw Pact armored forces were concentrated in an attempt to break through NATO's defenses, they would become extremely vulnerable to "neutron bomb" attack. In requesting NATO support for the production and deployment of this weapon, the Carter administration was clearly trying to diffuse responsibility for such a decision, for this weapon has been consistently criticized as immoral and irresponsible inasmuch as "it only kills people, but does not destroy property." The heads of the Western European governments have steadfastly resisted the invitation of the Carter administration of May 1977, to express their views on production and deployment. Aware of the domestic political problems that could arise if they openly endorsed the "neutron bomb," the heads of the Western European governments have insisted that the decision to produce this weapon must be one that the United States takes unilaterally.[44] For their part, they indicated that they wished to limit their views to consideration of deployment and its possible utility with respect to the SALT negotiations. "On their part, the allies--particularly West Germany--wanted to limit their pronouncements to eventual deployment and the prospect of negotiating the neutron weapons away with the Soviets after Carter took the production step by himself."⁴⁵ This already muddled issue became even more confused when Carter announced in April 1978, that he had decided against both the production and deployment of enhanced radiation weapons for the immediate future. Carter did not reject the "neutron bomb" option completely, rather he deferred the option to some indefinite date when the leaders of the Western European governments might find it politically feasible to support the production and/or deployment of this weapon. Carter indicated that he was making this decision because the leaders of the NATO member state governments had not responded to his invitation to inform him of their views on the production and deployment of this weapon. While it is true that these governmental leaders did not publicly respond to Carter's invitation for their views on this weapon, many analysts have concluded that Carter had secured the support of the West German government secretly and that West German Chancellor Helmut Schmidt was outraged when Carter deferred production and deployment after he had expended great effort to secure the support of the left wing of his Social Democratic party; Carter's decision, thus, was an acute embarrassment for Schmidt.⁴⁶

Carter's handling of this issue serves to illustrate a number of points. One, that even when the leaders of the NATO member states are consulted prior to the American production and deployment of a new weapon system, other constraints, and especially domestic political constraints, may prevent them from responding either quickly or publicly. This raises questions about the degree of allied cooperation that it will be possible to achieve. Two, Carter never fully explained the implications concerning the utilization of this weapon in a Western European context. The use of these weapons, instead of other tactical nuclear weapons, possessed at least one advantage beyond their obvious utility as an antitank weapon, namely, that if they were used in West Germany, casualties would probably be reduced overall and the West German industrial base might survive more or less intact. Three, in not being fully aware of the domestic political considerations of the Western European leaders, Carter unnecessarily undercut their leadership and raised questions about his own leadership in the handling of this issue, particularly since he did not make it publicly known that the production and deployment of this weapon might serve as a "bargaining chip" in dealing with other issues in the defense area of interest to both the United States and Western Europe, i.e., in the SALT II negotiations or in the MFR/MBFR negotiations. Thus, Carter's deferral decision has not resolved the controversy surrounding the production and deployment of this weapon; it has merely postponed it.

Eurocommunism

The Carter administration's position on the issue of the emergence of "Eurocommunism " also offers some comparisons with the two previous administrations and is related, albeit indirectly, to American defense policy. Kissinger, under both the Nixon and Ford administrations took an extremely strident view on the emergence of "Eurocommunism." To say the least, Kissinger was adamantly and virulently opposed to the emergence of communism in Western Europe and particularly so with respect to nations that were members of NATO. Kissinger felt that communist participation in or control over the governments of NATO member states would result in the weakening if not the collapse of the NATO collective security arrangements that had evolved over the course of almost thirty years. He felt that the perception of many American and Western European observers to the effect that "Eurocommunism" represented "a more polycentric, benign, nationalistic, enlightened and even anti-Soviet form of communism,"[47] was misplaced and totally wrong. Kissinger objected to communist participation in or control over NATO member state's government for several reasons. He felt that it was unlikely that the ideology of Western European communist parties could be successfully integrated into systems whose values and organizational principles were derived from traditional Western pluralist sources. Secondly, NATO, insofar as it was created in response to and directed toward a threat from the Soviet Union and Warsaw Pact nations, would be divided by internal contradictions to the extent that it would cease to be effective. Thirdly, Kissinger felt that the independence of Western European communist parties from either direct or indirect control by the Soviet Union could neither be satisfactorily established nor guaranteed. And, finally, even if NATO did continue to exist within a structure incorporating communist participation, its cohesion and ability to act in a crisis might be compromised and further complicated by the problems involved in allowing

"Eurocommunists" to have access to NATO defense plans, contingency plans, and on-going intelligence collection operations.

The Carter administration, at least initially, did not take such a harsh view of the emergence of "Eurocommunism." As long as the communist parties in Western European states, especially in France, Portugal, and Italy, did not threaten the withdrawal of their respective nations from NATO, a reduction of their nation's commitment to NATO, or gain direct control over the defense agencies of their governments, the Carter administration tended to avoid the public rhetoric and position of the previous administrations. At the end of Carter's first year, however, when faced with the presence of communists in the Italian coalition government and the threat of a "Leftist" victory in France, the Carter administration began to take a harder line on the emergence of "Eurocommunism." Two months before the French elections, Carter publicly warned the leader of the French Socialists, Francois Mitterrand, against forming an alliance with the French communists.[48] This warning to Mitterrand signaled a shift on the issue of "Eurocommunism" which was much more profound. On January 12 1978, the American State Department released a statement spelling out the Carter administration's shift on the "Eurocommunism" problem. It was stated that "We do not believe that the Communists share the 'profound democratic values and interests' of Western political systems."[49] It further went on to state that "the United States would like to see Communist influence in any Western country reduced."[50] The position of the Carter administration regarding "Eurocommunism," thus, over the course of its first year in office, apparently did a volte-face. It is unlikely however, that the Carter administration will ever adopt a position of shrill opposition to communist participation in Western European governments similar to that exhibited by Kissinger during the past two administrations. What is more likely, and this is particularly true with respect to the problems of NATO, is that the Carter administration, despite its commitment to open, multipolar diplomacy and its rejection of Kissinger's overall approach to international politics, will be forced to acknowledge that a high level of communist participation in NATO member states' governments would tend to be in fundamental contradiction of the NATO Charter. The choice is basically among one of three alternatives: 1) to maintain NATO more or less as it is; 2) to fundamentally alter NATO if "Eurocommunism" should wax rather than wane; and 3) to discard NATO and seek some new Western European collective security arrangement consistent and compatible with the changed Western European milieu. To date, the Carter administration appears to be predisposed to the maintenance of NATO as it presently exists.

Force Reductions

On the issue of the MFR/MBFR negotiations, the position of the Carter administration has been consistent with that of the several previous administrations since the mid-1960s. The early discussions on mutual force reductions in the Central European sector (Czechoslovakia, East Germany, Poland, the Benelux countries, and West Germany) were nonproductive. Indeed, this is where the issue remains today, stalemated. The United States, under the last two administrations has maintained that it would never agree to force reductions that were not reciprocal in nature and that these force reductions must ultimately result in the creation of equal and symmetric forces-in-being. This American position was first stated officially in 1972 by then President Nixon in a statement on American foreign policy. "Given the existing strategic balance and similar efforts by our allies, it is the policy of this government to maintain and improve our forces in Europe and not reduce them except through reciprocal reductions negotiated with the Warsaw Pact."[51] The Soviet Union and the Warsaw Pact position, conversely, has been that they will not accept reductions to equivalent forces-in-being, as this would force them to give up a numerical advantage in certain categories of personnel and equipment without receiving a quid pro quo from the NATO member states. Until recently these opposing positions remained fundamentally unaltered. The Carter administration has not repudiated the position of the two previous administrations on the MFR/MBFR negotiations. It has expressed a desire, however, that the NATO member states submit a new proposal to the Soviet Union and the Warsaw Pact nations for consideration, and it was suggested in January 1978, that such a proposal was prepared for submission.[52] Although no details of this proposal are known, it appeared likely that the Carter administration, in an effort to gain some momentum in the MFR/MBFR negotiations, would be willing to consider asymmetrical tradeoffs, involving perhaps American tactical nuclear weapons stationed in Western Europe for Soviet Warsaw Pact tanks, and intermediate range ballistic missiles stationed in Eastern Europe. The question of the production and deployment of American enhanced radiation devices might also be considered as an item to be introduced into these negotiations for the purpose of extracting some quid pro quo from the Soviet-Warsaw Pact nations.[53] If the Carter administration's new proposal did embody such elements, future MFR/MBFR negotiations would be established on a new basis encompassing "mutual" but "asymmetrical" and not necessarily "balanced" force reductions in the Central European sector and this would represent an important change in the negotiating position of the NATO member states on this issue.

Recently, however, Soviet intransigence in the MFR/MBFR negotiating process seems to have weakened. A new Soviet proposal, offered in early June 1978, for the first time accepts the concept of parity as an organizing principle of their negotiating position.[54] In essence, this change in the Soviet position may break the heretofore deadlocked negotiations. The level of parity established would be set at 700,000 combat troops for both NATO and the Warsaw Pact nations. There remains, however, a number of issues to be worked out and agreed upon before the change in the Soviet negotiating position can truly be viewed as a breakthrough. To begin with, both sides have come up with differing estimates as to the number of troops currently assigned to the Warsaw Pact, with the difference between the American and Soviet estimates ranging from 145,000 troops to 175,000 troops more than the 700,000 ceiling for the Warsaw Pact. The Soviet Union, perhaps in response to the Carter proposal submitted earlier this year, has also indicated a willingness to substitute reductions in NATO nuclear warheads and missiles for troop reductions, but the exact ratio of reductions being considered has not as yet been made public. Finally, while the Soviet Union has accepted the concept of parity, it may wish to advocate that reductions in forces-in-being not be done on a collective NATO-Warsaw Pact basis, but that "national allocations" be assigned. This position, if adopted, would be primarily aimed at West Germany and would undoubtedly be strongly resisted not only by West Germany, but by the United States as well.[55] The Carter administration has moved rapidly to accept the Soviet position on parity as a basis for the continuation of the MFR/MBFR negotiations. What remains to be seen, however, is how the Soviets will deal with the corollary issues discussed above, and how both the United States and the NATO member states respond to this and, perhaps, further changes in the Soviet negotiating position.

THE EUROPEAN PERCEPTION OF CARTER'S DEFENSE POLICIES

The Western European perception of Carter's defense policies are, at one level, virtually inseparable from perceptions of Carter. Over the period of the past 18 months, the Western European perception of Carter has varied widely. When he first assumed office there was nearly universal praise for his strong reconfirmation of the American commitment to the defense of Western Europe. As other issues arose, however, the perception of Carter gradually moved to a more critical assessment of his personal capacity for effective leadership. These critical assessments of Carter, and in some instances the policies of his administration in the defense and foreign policy sector, have tended to reflect some of the domestic criticisms of Carter. Thus, in order to gain a better understanding of the Western European perception of this administration's defense policies, their perception of Carter as President will be considered first.

Many Western European leaders have come to share a perception of Carter's capacity for effective leadership that is anything but flattering. While they have welcomed his interest in Western European problems and especially those concerned with NATO, they have also come to question his ability to carry out programs and policies that he wishes to promulgate. Carter is viewed, variously, as inexperienced in international affairs, unable to resolve the bureaucratic clumsiness of his staff, while pursuing too many diverse defense and foreign policy objectives at the same time, and lacking in a deep-rooted appreciation of the domestic political constraints and problems of Western European leaders, as well as being indecisive.

> ...both French President Valery Giscard d'Estaing and German Chancellor Helmut Schmidt found themselves in sad agreement that Carter has been a disappointment.
>
> They shared the view that the Western allies could no longer look to Washington for

leadership, that Carter was too inexperienced and indecisive. The signals from the White House, they agreed, were confused and inconsistent.[56]

This perception on the part of the leaders of the two most powerful nations of continental Europe hardly augurs well for the acceptance of Carter's leadership on issues related to their conception of their nations' national security interests or that of Western Europe as a whole. Fears concerning Carter's leadership qualities, if not his understanding of the issues at hand as well, reinforce Western European anxieties that the Carter administration may attempt to secure a SALT II agreement with the Soviet Union by sacrificing the defense interests of the NATO member states. "There has been suspicion that Carter, to strengthen detente with Russia, would accept an unequal treaty which could work against European interests."[57] Such suspicions, in turn, generate additional fears concerning Carter's leadership qualities, which tend to undermine the good impression that Carter made in the first few months of his administration when he indicated that dealing with the defense problems of NATO and Western Europe were going to be one of the primary objectives of his defense and foreign policy.

There has been mounting skepticism among Western Europeans in recent months over the quality of Carter's leadership in the U.S., as well as in the Atlantic Alliance. The President had his work cut out for him if he hoped to restore the confidence that he inspired among Allied statesmen at his first summit meeting in London last May.[58]

Confidence in Carter and his administration, in the defense and foreign policy areas, was further undermined by the Western European perception of the vacillating character of the policy positions advocated at various times by either Carter or his subordinates. Thus, the Western Europeans, among others, have had difficulty in comprehending how the Carter administration could effect transition so easily from the "hard line" taken with the Soviet Union in the SALT II negotiations in March 1977, to what many saw as a desire to make any accommodation with the Soviet Union by mid-1978 in order to reach a SALT II agreement. Similarly, the Western Europeans have had difficulty in understanding the extraordinary emphasis that Carter and his administration have accorded to human rights issues when other issues were perceived by them as clearly more important and pressing. In this context, they have also wondered what caused the administration to de-emphasize this issue over the course of the last year, when it is still being described as a cornerstone of the administration's approach to international politics.

In a somewhat similar sense, Western European leaders do not fully understand the reasons behind a number of actions initiated by the Carter administration since it came into office. They remain unconvinced that the present administration is capable of or has the will to deal resolutely with the Soviet Union; they do not understand why troops were to be unilaterally withdrawn from the Republic of Korea (and they fear that the same logic could be applied to American troops stationed in Western Europe); they are puzzled by the lack of a clear American response to the developments in Africa; and, in a period when Soviet-Warsaw Pact overall military capabilities are continuing to increase, they fail to understand why the United States has unilaterally decided to cancel the production and deployment of the B-1 bomber as well as a postponement on the neutron bomb, and has deliberately slowed the acquisition of the MX missile and the Trident II missile. As viewed from the Western European perspective, the Carter administration has undertaken these initiatives without extracting a <u>quid pro quo</u> from the Soviet Union and its allies. In brief, they do not understand what the Carter administration hopes to accomplish by these actions and they wonder what position Western Europe may be put in by any further initiatives of this nature.

> They question his competence to engage in superpower rivalry with the Soviet Union. They worry about the cumulative effect of unilateral pledges to withdraw troops from Korea, to reject military aid to post-Tito Yugoslavia and to maintain a low level of U.S. involvement in Africa.
>
> They don't understand why production of the B-1 bomber was halted and development of the neutron weapon was delayed without exacting matching concessions from the Soviets.[59]

Western European leaders particularly viewed the Carter administration's handling of the neutron bomb issues of production and deployment as yet another example of the confusing leadership being offered by the United States. While the United States obviously sought to diffuse the political responsibility for the production and deployment of this weapon, as well as to reinforce the administration's commitment to increasing the role and scope of participation of NATO member states in decisions of mutual interest, it was naive to expect that the Western European leaders would risk a weakening of their fragile political bases to publicly endorse such a controversial weapon without a clear indication, at least, of the American desire to add this weapon to NATO's arsenal. It must be noted, however, that not all of the Western European governments wanted this weapon to be produced or deployed. It is generally believed that the British and West Germans favored the incorporation of this weapon into NATO's arsenal, but that the Scandinavian nations, the Benelux nations, the Netherlands, and the French were opposed to both the production and deployment of this weapon.[60] Furthermore, the Western European leaders never felt that they really knew whether the United States wanted this weapon or felt that it was essential that it be incorporated into NATO's arsenal. Ambiguity over American intentions and desires characterized the entire episode.

In examining the Western European perception and reaction to the Carter administration's defense policy initiatives, as opposed to focusing on their perception of Carter, the impression is one that is much more favorable, the exceptions noted above notwithstanding. Broadly speaking, the leaders of the Western European governments generally feel that the Carter administration's strong identification of the defense interests of the United States with those of NATO is a long overdue but reassuring initiative. Specifically, they have been pleased by Carter's commitment to increase the defense budget of the United States both in absolute terms and in terms of the amounts alloted to meet its commitment to NATO. They were both surprised and pleased that Carter has decided to increase the number of American troops stationed in Western Europe and that he has addressed the long-standing problem of improper deployment of NATO personnel and weaponry in the north central plains region of the Federal Republic of Germany where any Soviet-Warsaw Pact attack would probably be initiated. The priority assigned to Western Europe by the Carter administration, inasmuch as it clearly is perceived by the United States as the most important of its regional collective defense commitments, has also been hailed as a positive step.

> Officials at NATO's dour barracks-like headquarters outside Brussels are particularly encouraged by the priority the U.S. has given to NATO in the $126 billion defense budget President Carter has sent to Congress. They see the U.S. freed from the trauma of Vietnam, once again placing the defense of Europe at the top of its defense concerns. They see President Carter's recent pledge to send 8,000 more troops to Europe as a tangible sign of this new priority.61

Similarly, the efforts and commitment of the Carter administration to dramatically increase inter-allied planning and cooperation in a number of ways has been perceived as a constructive set of initiatives. Institutionally, NATO has long been characterized as an organization that has been dominated by the United States. This widely held Western European view has, in the past, exacerbated French-West German differences on alliance defense posture, led at least indirectly to France's decision to withdraw from NATO's integrated military command structure in 1966, indirectly contributed to the fall of the Erhard government in West Germany, and has generally proved to be a view that has done more to increase allied dissensus rather than to contribute to allied consensus.

The approach of the Carter administration, thus, to these problems has been especially appreciated by the NATO member states. This is true because Carter's initiatives are broadly conceived. They cover questions related to NATO short-term and long-term planning. They encompass questions related to projections of NATO defense expenditures, including the level of national commitments in the form of regular defense expenditure increases, and the cost- and burden-sharing problems that have long been a source of Western European friction and American frustration. In conjunction with these efforts, moreover, the Carter administration has demonstrated that it will tentatively be more receptive to Western European concerns and interests in coproduction, joint licensing, and other forms of ensuring that the United States does not serve as either the exclusive or primary supplier of weapons and/or weapon technology to NATO member states. Such an approach will obviously go some distance to ease both political and military concerns of the Western European nation-states which have tended to intensify other differences among them in their individual and collective relationship with the United States. These problems, in turn, and at one level or another, are related to another set of issues that have been of great concern to both the NATO member states and the United States, the issues of standardization and interoperability. The flexibility demonstrated by the Carter administration on these issues will go a long way toward resolving some of the enormous logistical problems that the maintenance of incompatible national weapon systems and equipment have presented for NATO. While all of these initiatives have had a positive effect on the NATO member state-American relationship, the test of these initiatives, as well as those discussed above in different contexts, will be in their effective implementation and in the continuing American support of them. This, as previously noted, is the area where the leaders of the Western European governments have expressed their greatest reservations, the capacity of the Carter administration to adopt a policy, to remain consistent in its application, and to offer effective leadership and guidance as problems, disagreements, or grievances arise.

The above discussion notwithstanding, the leaders of the Western European governments have been disappointed in the Carter administration's handling of a number of issues related to NATO. In particular, they have felt that Carter has not moved quickly or decisively to bring some sort of resolution to the problems posed for the alliance by the Greek-Turkish dispute. Since the United States is directly involved, they believe that the United States must assume the initiative before the Soviet Union and the Warsaw Pact nations can exploit the situation to their own advantage. Specifically, given the strategic position of Turkey, the importance of its contribution to the manpower resources of the alliance, and the importance of NATO and American bases located in Turkey for intelligence collection purposes, they wish to have the partial arms embargo limited from Turkey.

Carter, however, has not had the necessary majority in Congress to bring about this policy reversal. The Western European leaders are aware of this consideration, but they see Carter's failure to achieve this objective as perhaps another indication of his weak leadership qualities given the importance that they attach to the normalization of Turkish-NATO relations. However this issue is settled, the Carter administration would then presumably move to placate Greece as well, and thus effect both nations' reintegration into NATO's military command structure at the earliest possible date.

The leaders of the Western European governments have also had misgivings about the Carter administration's determination to deal with its energy and balance of payments problems which they see as potentially affecting American defense and foreign policy promulgation, if the unfavorable position and vulnerability of the United States in these areas is not meaningfully addressed by both short- and long-term readjustments. In so far as these weaknesses and vulnerabilities continue to exist, they also have an impact on NATO member states, for they encourage the United States to advocate policies that the Western European states are either unwilling to adopt e.g., (the "heating-up" of the West German economy), or that they feel would increase their own domestic and/or international political problems. In brief, they are unwilling to undertake any actions at the present time to aid the United States in these areas unless or until they perceive that the Carter administration recognizes the magnitude of its problems and initiates policy changes in these areas which they feel will contribute to the resolution of these problems rather than their avoidance.

Not surprisingly, then, the Western European perception of the defense and foreign policy initiatives of the Carter administration is mixed. In some areas discussed above, there is a clear consensus that Carter is moving in the right direction, and thus meeting the defense requirements of both the United States and Western Europe. Substantial areas of selective disagreement about policy alternatives as well as how policy can or should be implemented remain, however, and these areas of concern are also clearly related to Western European assessments of the ability of Carter to offer effective leadership across the broad spectrum of the defense and foreign policy agenda that this administration has set for itself. In a more parochial sense, where the Western European governments have perceived a mutuality of interests with the United States, they have applauded and supported initiatives taken by the Carter administration, particularly in the NATO context. In areas where this mutuality of interests and perceptions have not developed, conversely, they have not hesitated to criticize this administration and to seek an explanation for unilateral actions which they feel have served no constructive purpose. Without a doubt, the leaders of the Western European governments would like to see the Carter administration limit the number of items on its defense and foreign policy agenda, to pursue those that remain with greater diligence, to relate policy means and ends in a more comprehensible manner or at least in a way that they can better understand them, and to continue to expand the base of inter-allied consultation and cooperation in all policy areas of mutual interest.

CARTER'S DEFENSE POLICIES: IMPACT AND PROSPECTS

The Carter administration's defense policy initiatives, with respect to the Soviet Union and NATO, have not been without impact. Carter's initial rejection of the Nixon-Ford/Kissinger conceptual framework and approach, predicated upon an emphasis of "balance of power" politics which stressed the primacy of Soviet-American relations, and his adoption of a "world order" politics conceptual framework and approach, which deemphasizes the primacy of Soviet-American relations while placing a premium on multipolar diplomacy directed toward Western Europe and the "Third World," has led to the tentative emergence of a new pattern of American foreign and defense policy. At the same time, it has led to some confusion as to the ultimate objectives of American foreign and defense policy.

The tough negotiating position of the Carter administration vis-a-vis the Soviet Union in the SALT II talks, consistent with the Carter administration's criticism of the two previous administrations, represented the first indication of the new administration's strong commitment to the decreasing emphasis on Soviet-American relations as central to American foreign and defense policy making as well as its willingness to risk the failure of securing a SALT II agreement in order to secure the kind of SALT II agreement which it desires. The Soviet rejection of the administration's SALT II proposals and the expiration of the SALT I Interim Agreement, coupled with the continuing build-up of Soviet and Warsaw Pact military capabilities, however, will undoubtedly lead to increased pressures on the Carter administration to consider an acceleration of programs such as the MX missile, the Trident II missile, the cruise missile, and other weapons systems incorporating advanced technology as a means of inducing Soviet concessions and/or cooperation in concluding a SALT II agreement. It does not appear likely that the new administration, despite its initial failure to secure the SALT II agreement before the expiration of the SALT I Interim Agreement, will alter its negotiating position substantively by making concessions that would be totally inconsistent with its objectives of both controlling the strategic arms race and reducing the overall strategic nuclear capabilities of the Soviet Union and the United States. Given the Soviet capability, by 1985, to achieve at least a strong numerical superiority in strategic launch vehicles (which has been described by Congressman Les Aspin as possibly being in the magnitude of a 2:1 ratio, or 4,372 Soviet launchers to 2,059 American launchers),[62] it is apparent that the Carter administration will seek to conclude some type of SALT II agreement with the Soviet Union. To fail to do so would be: 1) potentially destabilizing with respect to Soviet-American political-military relations; and 2) potentially destabilizing for Western Europe, which might perceive a fundamental shift in the overall military balance taking place and feel constrained thereby to make political concessions or adjustments to reflect this shift.

The Carter administration's defense policy initiatives directed toward NATO, while consistent with the "world order politics" approach, are also clearly related to actions taken by a number of previous administrations. NATO has always tended to be viewed as the foundation of American foreign and defense policy with respect to Europe. In this sense, the Carter administration's initiatives do not represent any sharp break with the policy of previous administrations. The new capacity and willingness of the Carter administration to reinforce NATO's military capabilities, in the post-Vietnam and post-Watergate era, however, cannot be discounted as merely a transitory development nor as a temporary adjustment to the Soviet-Warsaw Pact military build-up. Carter's policy initiatives reflect, at a higher level, a perceived need to maintain both the strategic and a regional (especially European) military balance between the United States and its allies and the Soviet Union and its allies. The Carter administration's dramatic decision to increase the level of its own commitment to NATO, its efforts to establish regularized increases in the annual defense budgets of all NATO member states, and its attempts to reestablish and reinforce the political cohesion and unity of purpose of NATO, have demonstrated the importance that is attached to NATO's problems and the need to maintain a credible NATO defense posture by the new administration. Somewhat similarly, the new administration's commitment to increased inter-allied consultation and cooperation, on issues ranging from questions of the degree of standardization and interoperability desired to sharing of defense costs and burdens, the introduction of new, advanced weapons and weapons systems, and joint decision making on the evolution of NATO strategy and tactics, are all consistent with the emphasis on multipolar diplomacy associated with the "world order politics" conceptual framework and approach.

Having noted the broad outlines of the Carter administration's defense policy initiatives vis-a-vis NATO and the Soviet Union over the course of the last year and the broad outlines of the Carter administration's conceptual framework and approach as it has differed from that of previous administrations, it is now possible to make some tentative judgments as to the effectiveness of the Carter administration with respect to defense policy formation and promulgation.

Although there have been few articles written by established scholars regarding the Carter administration's foreign and defense policy changes and initiatives, there is one notable exception, an article by Stanley Hoffmann, entitled "The Hell of Good Intentions," which was recently published in Foreign Policy. The Hoffmann article, inasmuch as it summarizes the major criticisms leveled at the Carter administration's performance which have appeared in other scholarly journals and publications, will be utilized in an attempt to assess the new administration's performance, touching on a number of points with respect to its record in the area of national security policy.

Hoffmann argues that the "good intentions" of the Carter administration have been inadequate as a measure of its performance, and that more is expected from policy than just "good intentions." In expanding on this point, Hoffmann offers several sets of criticisms which he feels tend to substantiate his position. In attempting to break quickly and cleanly with the Kissinger era, Hoffmann feels that the Carter administration has neglected to develop an overall strategy as a basis for the articulation and conduct of foreign policy. Initially, thus, he sees the policy making process, under the Carter administration, as being flawed in three ways: 1) no coherent set of policy positions has emerged, and the Carter administration has been forced, therefore, to spend an undue amount of effort on discrete problems, specific objectives, and daily tactics; 2) no clear set of priorities has emerged nor has a time frame been developed for priorities, once established, to be accomplished; and 3) no statement of just what the administration's objectives are has been articulated, only a list of objectives that have not been related to any overall strategy. Furthermore, Hoffmann views these difficulties as being compounded by Carter's operating on two different levels: 1) the level of high principles; and 2) the level of pragmatic politics with, however, no established link existing between both levels of operations and often resulting in the propensity for contradiction between these two levels. The policy making processes under the Carter administration, thus, according to Hoffmann, should be altered to avoid such problems as: 1) the aggregation of issues rather than their integration; 2) the inadvertent linkage between human rights objectives and other policy concerns; 3) the overconcentration on issues and functions, rather than on countries; 4) the lack of centralized control over the direction of policy; 5) the danger of sending conflicting signals to other international actors; 6) the lack of effective coordination with Congress on substantive policy issues and problems; and 7) the failure to build an adequate base of domestic public support for the administration's policies.[63] Other of this administration's critics, as their views have become publicly known, tend to share these criticisms either in whole or in part with Hoffmann.[64]

The above criticisms can be applied as well to the specific area of defense policy initiatives of the Carter administration during the course of the last year. To date, the Carter administration has not articulated how the diverse measures and initiatives which it has promulgated are to fit together into a coherent whole nor how they are related in terms of priorities and objectives. Indeed, although American foreign and defense policy is clearly in a period of transition under the new administration, the overall pattern of international politics, especially as they relate to NATO and the Soviet Union under the rubric of "world order politics," which the new administration wishes to have made manifest remains unclear. In the absence of a clearly defined and well understood overall American strategy for the formation and promulgation of American foreign and defense policy initiatives, confusion on the part of the Soviet Union and the member states of NATO as to American intentions has been an obvious problem with which the new administration has been confronted. That this is a problem of large dimensions has been demonstrated by the Soviet reaction to the American SALT II proposals, the Western European reaction to Carter's request for a statement of views on the production and deployment of enhanced radiation weapons, and continuing NATO member state uncertainty regarding the limits of their role and impact on defense policy issues and problems encompassing both Soviet-American strategic arms negotiations and NATO-Warsaw Pact relations and negotiations. These difficulties have been further compounded, as has been evident for almost a year now, by the Carter administration's preoccupation with the human rights issue. Somewhat paradoxically, both the Soviet Union and the NATO member states have criticized the new administration for stressing the human rights issue to the extent that progress or the opportunity for progress on other substantive issues and problems may have been sacrificed. Confusion about the linkages or lack of linkages among these diverse issues has also had its domestic counterpart inasmuch as neither the Congress nor the American public fully understands just what it is that the Carter administration seeks to accomplish or how it seeks to accomplish the realization of those initiatives already undertaken in light of Soviet intransigence and Western European confusion on the direction and implications of American foreign and defense policy postures.

While the above comments suggest the dimensions of the problem and/or conflicts to which the Carter administration must address itself, they do not suggest that the substance of the Carter administration's defense policy initiatives will necessarily have to be dramatically altered. It would appear to be very improbable, moreover, that the administration's defense policies are likely to experience any dramatic change, at least as of this point in time. The Carter administration, while it may be forced to become somewhat more flexible in the SALT II negotiations with the Soviet Union, still remains steadfastly committed to both strategic arms control and, ultimately, to strategic arms limitation and/or reduction. Similarly, the Carter administration remains committed to reinforcing and building up the defense capabilities of NATO as a means not only of maintaining the regional balance of military forces in Europe, but also as a means of putting pressure on the Soviet Union and the Warsaw Pact nations to make further concessions in the MFR/MBFR negotiations whose deadlocked state has recently been broken. In support of these dual objectives, the Carter administration will probably continue to stress the need for Western European unity and cohesion and will make every effort to reduce the influence of Western European communist parties in NATO member states. It is also likely that continuing attempts will be made to resolve the long-standing questions regarding the NATO status of Greece and Turkey, and to push for increased inter-allied consultation and cooperation on all matters of general interest, including NATO defense budget appropriations, increased standardization and interoperability, consensual decisions with respect to the introduction and deployment of new weapons and weapons systems, and increasing the combat capabilities of the NATO armed forces.

The Carter administration, thus, like any other new administration, has encountered difficulties in its early tenure in office, especially in articulating its policies and establishing an agenda for their achievement in terms of their priorities. The criticisms and comments made above notwithstanding, it would appear that the single most important change which needs to be undertaken touches upon the evolution and dissemination of an overall strategy for the administration's foreign and defense policy initiative; this would not necessarily suggest or require that the initiatives already made be dropped or even modified, but rather that they be related, in Brzezinski's terms, to some form of "architecture" that can be readily discerned by both the Soviet Union and Warsaw Pact nations as well as the member states of NATO. If this could be accomplished, American foreign and defense policy initiatives would become more understandable and more defensible, thereby significantly enhancing the chances for their realization as a domestic and Western European base of support for them could be built.

NOTES

1. On these points, and especially the third, see David T. Johnson, "U.S. Forces for Europe and the MFBR Talks," in Current Issues in U.S. Defense Policy, eds. David T. Johnson and Barry R. Schneider (New York: Praeger Publishers in cooperation with the Center for Defense Information, 1976), p. 18.

2. Stanley Hoffmann, "The Hell of Good Intentions," Foreign Policy, no. 29 (Winter 1977-1978): 4.

3. Ibid.

4. Ibid.

5. Tad Szulc, "Washington Dateline: Springtime for Carter," Foreign Policy, no. 27 (Summer 1977): 187.

6. "The Notre Dame Address," The Review of Politics, no. 39 (July 1977): 293.

7. Ibid., see pp. 293-296 for a fuller consideration of these points.

8. Ibid., p. 292.

9. Ibid., see pp. 292-293 for a discussion of the development of these new, largely normative considerations in international politics.

10. Thomas L. Hughes, "Carter and the Management of Contradictions," Foreign Policy, no. 31 (Summer 1978): 36.

11. Terence Smith, "Carter Calls on Soviets to end Confrontation or Risk 'Graver' Strain," New York Times, June 8, 1978, p. A1.

12. Ibid.

13. Craig R. Whitney, "Soviet Calls Attitude of Carter 'Strange,' Reaffirms Detente," New York Times, June 8, 1978, p. A1.

14. Szulc, p. 191.

15. On these committee responsibilities, see John E. Endicott, "The National Security Council - Formulating National Security Policy for Presidential Review," in American Defense Policy (4th ed.), eds. John E. Endicott and Roy W. Stafford, Jr. (Baltimore, MD: The Johns Hopkins University Press, 1977), p. 319.

16. Richard Burt, "Probing the Brzezinski Factor," New York Times, December 25, 1977, Sec. 4, p. 1.

17. Tom Mathews, Eleanor Clift, and Thomas M. DeFrank, "Zeroing in on Zbig," Newsweek, January 30, 1978, p. 50.

18. On this description, see Szulc, p. 179 and Hoffmann, p. 14.

19. This point is considered in Jeremy R. Azrael, Richard Loewenthal, and Tohru Nakagawa, An Overview of East-West Relations, The Triangle Papers: 15 (New York: The Trilateral Commission, 1978), pp. 37-38 and in Congressman Les Aspin, "SALT II or No SALT," (Mimeo: January, 1978), p. 1.

20. See Azrael, Loewenthal, and Nakagawa, pp. 38-40 on this point.

21. For these figures, see Richard T. Ackley, "Strategic Arms Limitation: The Problem of Mutual Deterrence," in Foreign Policy and U.S. National Security, ed. William W. Whitson (New York: Praeger Publishers in cooperation with the BDM Corporation, 1976), p. 223.

22. Ibid.

23. For these figures, see Aspin, Figure D, p. 5.

24. With respect to this conclusion, see Aspin, passim.

25. The points on these advanced weapons systems are discussed in Counterforce Issues for U.S. Strategic Nuclear Forces, Congressional Budget Office

(January, 1978), pp. 31-51.

26. On this point, see Congressional Budget Office, Planning U.S. Strategic Forces for the 1980s, Background Paper (June 1978), p. ix and passim.

27. Richard Burt, "The Scope and Limits of SALT," Foreign Affairs, no. 56 (July 1978): 756.

28. Ibid., pp. 756-758 for a summary of the treaty provisions.

29. Ibid., pp. 758-759 for a discussion of the protocol provisions.

30. Ibid., pp. 759-760 for a consideration of the statement of principles.

31. Ibid., p. 767.

32. For a brief discussion of these four new Carter administration efforts, see Atlantic Community News, ed. June Haley (Washington, D.C.: The Atlantic Council of the United States, May, 1977), p. 1 and Atlantic Community News, ed. June Haley (Washinton, D.C.: The Atlantic Council of the United States, January, 1978), p. 2.

33. Atlantic Community News, ed. June Haley (Washinton, D.C.: The Atlantic Council of the United States, January, 1978), p. 2.

34. "Study Warns of Arms Costs if U.S.-Soviet Pact Fails," New York Times, April 4, 1978, p. 11.

35. On these points, see Atlantic Community News, ed. June Haley (Washington, D.C.: The Atlantic Council of the United States, October, 1977), p. 3 and Herbert Schandler, "Europe: The Problems of Consensus," in Whitson, p. 60.

36. See Robert L. Pfaltzgraff, Jr. The Atlantic Community: A Complex Imbalance (New York: Van Nostrand Reinhold Co., 1969), p. 37 and U.S. Congress, House of Representatives, Report to the Committee on International Relations by the Foreign Affairs and National Defense Division, Congressional Research Service, Library of Congress, NATO Standardization: Political, Economic, and Military Issues for Congress, 95th Cong., 1st sess., March

1977, p. 19.

37. Lisa Meyers, "Turkey Arms Plan Faces Fight," Chicago Sun-Times, April 5, 1978, p. 40.

38. Ibid.; see also, Bernard Weintraub, "NATO Working to End Arms Ban on Turkey," New York Times, January 11, 1978, p. 10.

39. On this point, see Loye Miller, Jr., "U.S. To Boost NATO Force by 8,000," Chicago Sun-Times, January 11, 1978, p. 4.

40. Kim Willenson, Fred Coleman, Lloyd H. Norman, and David C. Martin, "Russia's Reach," Newsweek, June 12, 1978, pp. 30-31.

41. On this point, see U.S. Congress, House of Representatives, NATO Standardization, p. 40.

42. Ibid., p. 40.

43. For a brief discussion of this decision, see Michael Getler, "U.S.-German Gun Pact Reported," Chicago Sun-Times, January 24, 1978, p. 20.

44. On the Western European decision that the U.S. must unilaterally make its decision on the production of the "neutron bomb," see June Haley, ed., Atlantic Community News (Washington, D.C.: The Atlantic Council of the United States, October, 1977), p. 2.

45. Walter Pincus, "Carter Gets Bonn's Neutron Bomb OK," Chicago Sun-Times, April 5, 1978, p. 42.

46. Rowland Evans and Robert Novak, "Carter's Neutron Decision Undermines Germans," Chicago Sun-Times, June 30, 1978, p. 58, discuss this point.

47. Robert L. Pfaltzgraff, Jr., "The American-Soviet Relationship in Global Perspective," in American Defense Policy (4th ed.), eds. John E. Endicott and Roy W. Stafford, Jr. (Baltimore, MD: The Johns Hopkins University Press, 1977), p. 8.

48. On this point, see Jonathan Kandell, "Carter Warns Chief of French Socialists on Tie to Communists," New York Times, January 7, 1978, p. 1.

49. Quoted from Rowland Evans and Robert Novak, "Our Man in Italy Nudges Carter to Get Tough," Chicago Sun-Times, January 25, 1978, p. 48.

50. Ibid.

51. Johnson, p. 25.

52. On this new proposal, see June Haley, ed., Atlantic Community News (Washington, D.C.: The Atlantic Council of the United States, January, 1978), p. 2.

53. This possible tradeoff is considered in Azrael, Loewenthal, and Nakagawa, p. 49 and Kenneth H. Jacobson, "Mutual and Balanced Force Reductions: The Problem of 'Balance,'" in Whitson, pp. 312-313.

54. Evans and Novak, "Carter's Neutron Decision Undermines Germans", p. 58.

55. Ibid., Evans and Novak, "Soviets Now Accept Idea of Equal Troop Ceilings," Chicago Sun-Times, June 14, 1978, p. 66.

56. Jack Anderson, "If Carter Could See Himself as Europe's Leaders See Him," Chicago Sun-Times, June 19, 1978, p. 38.

57. U.S. News & World Report, "Verdict From Experts on Jimmy Carter's First Year," January 9, 1978, p. 15.

58. Ibid.

59. James Hoge, "Europeans' Confidence in Carter Leadership Wanes," Chicago Sun-Times, Views Section, p. 3.

60. On the divergent NATO views on the neutron bomb, see June Haley, ed., Atlantic Community News (Washington, D.C.: The Atlantic Council of the United States, May, 1978), p. 2.

61. Takashi Oka, "NATO Gets Good Reports," Christian Science Monitor, February 3, 1978, p. 6.

62. See Aspin, passim, but especially Figure D, p. 5, on this point.

63. Hoffmann, *passim*.

64. See, for example, Karen Koshner, "Dole Assails Foreign Policy as 'a Mess,'" *Chicago Sun-Times*, January 23, 1978, p. 10; Loye Miller, Jr., "Carter's Second Year: Time for a Change," *Chicago Sun-Times*, January 15, 1978, Sec. 2, p. 1; and Joseph Kraft, "The Balance Sheet One Year Later," *Chicago Sun-Times*, January 20, 1978, p. 50.

7
The United States, China and Japan

George P. Jan

INTRODUCTION

International politics and defense policies can be studied profitably by examining the major powers' perceptions of their potential adversaries. Indeed, many nations go to war because of the misperception of the leaders of at least one of the belligerent states. If the leaders of both adversary nations misconceive each other's power and intentions, a war is a very likely development. If a leader on the brink of war believes that his adversary will attack his country, the chance of war is fairly high. If the leaders of both countries share this perception about each other's intent, war becomes a virtual certainty. A leader's misperception of his adversary's power and intentions is perhaps the quintessential cause of war. The defense policy of a country is determined to a great extent, by that country's perception of the power and intentions of its potential enemy or enemies. It is not the actual distribution of power that precipitates a war. It is the way in which a leader thinks that power is distributed.[1]

In a larger sense, according to Lewis F. Richards and Kenneth E. Boulding, it is one nation's image of the hostility of another, not the "real" hostility, which determines its reaction. The image is the total cognitive, affective, and evaluative structure of the state or its internal view of itself and its universe.[2] Decision-makers do not respond to the "objective" facts of the situation, whatever that may mean, but to their "image" of the situation. It is what they think the world is like, not what it is really like, that determines their behavior. They act according to how the world appears to them, not necessarily according to the way it "is."

The perceptions which are important in international systems are those which a nation has of itself or self-perception, and of those other bodies in the system which constitute its international environment. In the study of perceptions, there are three important groups to be considered. The first group is the central decision-makers in government who actually make authoritative decisions for the people. The second group is the mass of ordinary people whose perceptions can affect the decision-makers and are also influenced or even manipulated by the decision-makers. This is particularly true in democracies such as the United States and Japan. The third group is the elite members of the society who are outside the government. Their perceptions can influence the perceptions of the government decision-makers as well as those of the masses.

This paper is an abridged version of a larger study of this subject. It is confined to the examination of the perceptions of the central government decision-makers and those of the masses as reflected in public opinion polls. The perceptions of the Chinese masses were not examined because of the difficulty of collecting such data. Furthermore, this paper will be limited to an assessment of American perceptions of China and Japan, and Chinese and Japanese perceptions of the United States. As stated earlier, other perceptions are important, but our concern here is primarily United States defense policy vis-a-vis the two major powers in the Far East. Finally, the time frame for this study is January 1977, through the Summer of 1978; the first years of the Carter administration.

AMERICAN PERCEPTIONS OF CHINA AND JAPAN

Cultural and geopolitical connections with Europe have dictated a distinctly European perspective to American foreign and national security policy. This changed little until after World War II. The defeat of the Kuomintang and the establishment of a Communist system in China awakened, in a dramatic way, American policy makers to the problems of security in the Asian area. Indeed, the Korean War was one manifestation of this concern.

Equally important, the demise of colonial empires and the concomitant rise of independent states throughout Asia and the Far East created a new security environment. Increasingly American policy became deeply involved with new Asian politics. This deep concern, following after a degree of success in Europe with the Marshall Plan and NATO, set the stage for the Vietnam involvement. Subsequently American defense policy seems to have developed directions similar to the pre-Korean period. While various administrations have stressed the fact that America is a Pacific power, historical, cultural and economic ties with Europe continue to affect American policy. Nonetheless, the emergence of a potentially powerful Communist China and a modern democratic Japan have changed the security alignment throughout Asia and may necessitate a more important role for the United States in the area.

Beginning with the announcement of the Guam Doctrine in 1969, the United States began its military disengagement from Asia which is now being accelerated by the Carter administration. Given the visible commitment to Europe and the increasing focus of defense policy on the area, it is difficult for the present administration to credibly articulate an Asian policy, regardless of policy pronouncements.

The Leadership's Perceptions

Carter's basic Asian policy was outlined in his speech to the Foreign Policy Association on June 23, 1976 during his presidential election campaign. In this speech he stated that "the United States is both an Atlantic and Pacific power and our commitment to the security of Western Europe and of Japan are inseparable from our own security. Without these commitments and our firm dedication to them, the political fabric of Atlantic and Pacific cooperation would be seriously weakened and world peace endangered."[3] He further stated:

> As we look to the Pacific region, we see a number of changes and opportunities. Because of potential Sino-Soviet conflict, Russian and Chinese forces are not jointly deployed as our potential adversaries but confront one another along their common border. Moreover, our withdrawal from the mainland of Southeast Asia has made possible improving relationships between us and the People's Republic of China.[4]

Most of the major decisions of the Carter administration toward Asia seem to be based on the four premises enunciated in this speech. These are: (1) The danger of war and the threat from the Soviet Union and China in Asia have been reduced because of the Sino-Soviet conflict; (2) The cessation of the Indochina War and the withdrawal of American forces from the mainland of Southeast Asia has enhanced the chances of the improvement of Sino-American relations; (3) Japan is our most important ally in Asia; (4) Our gradual military disengagement in Asia is safe and desirable because it will further reduce tension between the United States and the two communist giants.

Carter prides himself in the faithful fulfillment of his campaign promises. In the same foreign policy speech of June 23, 1976, he pledged a phased withdrawal of American ground forces from South Korea over a time span to be determined after consultation with both South Korea and Japan. Shortly after assuming office, Carter announced his plan to withdraw American ground troops from South Korea in four to five years. Contrary to expectations, this decision was made without real consultation with Japan. As a matter of fact, the Japanese were faced with a <u>fait accompli</u> in this matter.

It is useful to compare the Asian policy with that being pursued in Europe. While there are plans to withdraw American ground forces from South Korea, there are planned increases of American troops in Europe. The reasons for withdrawing troops from South Korea is based on the assumption that South Korea will be able to defend itself with a $3 billion U.S. assistance program designed to strengthen the South Korean military, in addition to commitment of American naval and air support. One can reasonably argue however, that the same justification can be applied to the withdrawal of ground troops from Europe.

These changing priorities are reflected in the defense budget request for the fiscal year of 1979 which contains a $1 billion increase in weapons for the army, mostly for use in Europe. The emphasis on defense in Europe flows from a 1977 interagency study that found "serious deficiencies" in the ability of the Atlantic alliance to cope with a Soviet attack in Europe. The study concluded that Soviet-led Warsaw Pact forces had a 2-to-1 edge in tanks and other equipment and that Western stocks of ammunition were low. These findings were used as the basis for a presidential directive, issued in August 1977, calling for an enhanced capacity of United

States forces to respond to an attack that comes with little warning. At the same time, Carter committed himself to a 3% increase in defense spending to foster greater integration of allied military activities in West Europe.[5] Carter's ambitious NATO defense program, which was endorsed by the NATO meeting in Washington in May 1978, will greatly improve NATO's combat readiness over the next ten to fifteen years at an estimated cost of $60 to $80 billion dollars.

The increase of American troop commitment in Europe is a sharp contrast to the general reduction or projected reduction of American forces throughout Asia. In addition to the projected withdrawal of ground troops from South Korea, American military strength was reduced in the following Asian countries and territories since 1969: Guam from 15,000 in 1969 to 9,000 today; Japan (not including Okinawa) from 38,000 to 18,000; Okinawa from 43,000 to 28,000; Taiwan from 9,000 to 1,000; The Philippines from 27,000 to 16,000; and Thailand from nearly 48,000 during the Indochina war to only about 120 today. The reduction of U.S. forces in Thailand was largely due to the demands of the popularly elected government of Thailand (1973-1976) that American forces leave the country. (The Thais, like many other Asians, feel that the United States is abandoning its responsibilities in Asia, retreating into a semi-isolationist posture and ignoring the Communist threat in Asia.)

Although most of the American troops in these countries were withdrawn before the present administration, the President either accepted this policy or plans to further withdraw American troops from Asia. The Carter administration's long-range policy is the gradual reduction of American military strength in the West Pacific area, including Japan over a long period of time. This was disclosed by Harold Brown, Secretary of Defense, to the Japanese in November 1977.[6] The Carter administration does not perceive any serious threat of aggression in Asia from either the Soviet Union or China. Furthermore, because of China's presumed backwardness and internal problems, it is not considered an immediate threat to any country in Asia. The administration apparently does not believe that China seriously intends to liberate Taiwan by force in the near future despite Peking's repeated threats to do so. Additionally, Peking's insistence on the three conditions for the normalization of Sino-American relations has made it more difficult for the Carter administration to improve relations between the two countries. The three conditions demand the United States to: (1) sever diplomatic relations with Taiwan; (2) withdraw all American armed forces and military installations from Taiwan and the Taiwan Straits area; and (3) abrogate its mutual defense treaty with Taiwan.[7] Although Carter is committed to improving relations with Peking, he is unwilling to abandon American commitment to the peaceful existence of Taiwan.[8]

This policy is also reflected in the Carter administration's reluctance to sell defense-related technology to China. According to Presidential Review Memorandum 10, the sale of defense-related technology to China would lead to a "fundamental reassessment" of Soviet policies toward the United States and an increase of tension between Moscow and Peking.[9] The policy now being pursued closely follows the guidelines of this memorandum. However, after Brzezinski's trip to China in May 1978, there seems to be a gradual modification of this policy.

As to Carter's perception of Japan, as mentioned earlier, he regards Japan as the most important American ally in Asia. Japan's security is thought to be inseparable from that of the United States and West Europe.[10] Thus, President Carter places Japan in a special category among the Asian nations. This is consistent with the concept of the Trilateral Commission (founded by David Rockefeller and Zbigniew Brzezinski, and of which the then governor Jimmy Carter was a member).

Although Japan is considered a special ally, Carter's treatment of Japan appears short of the true spirit of equal partnership. A number of measures have been taken by the United States which had great significance to Japan. Yet the United States failed to meaningfully consult Japan before the decisions were made. The withdrawal of American ground troops from South Korea is a case in point. Another example is the decision to ban the export of enriched uranium to Japan which uses it for its nuclear fuel reprocessing plant. This threatened the Japanese economy and infuriated the Japanese government. The chairman of Japan's Atomic Energy Commission, Sosuke Uno, suggested that American officials were dealing with Japan in bad faith in the dispute over nuclear reprocessing and warned that this controversy would threaten to disrupt Japanese-American friendship.[11]

Following the policy of limiting the number of nations capable of producing plutonium, the United States withheld approval of a Japanese reprocessing plant, thereby exercising an effective veto power over the project. This decision was also apparently made without adequate prior consultation with Japan. The problem was finally resolved in September 1977 by the conclusion of an agreement between the two countries permitting the Japanese to open their newly built Tokai Mura plant north of Tokyo on a controlled experimental basis for two years while conducting intensive research into alternative recycling methods.[12] This incident seems to indicate that the United States has again made decisions affecting Japanese interests without adequate consultation with Japan.

The lack of an equal partnership relationship between the two countries is also reflected in trade relations. The United States has huge trade deficits with a number of countries, such as West Germany, Saudi Arabia and Nigeria, to name only a few. While the United States has not openly interfered with the domestic economic policy of any of these countries, it has done so with Japan, demanding the acceleration of its economic growth and the liberalization of its trade policies. Apart from the fact that Japan is dependent on the United States economically and militarily, the vestige of historical patron-client relationship between the two countries may be influencing current relationships.

Nevertheless, the United States expects Japan to play a greater role in world affairs, especially in Asia. The President supports Japan's aspiration for a permanent seat in the Security Council of the United Nations.[13] Fully aware of Japan's reluctance to expand its armed forces, Carter nonetheless urges Japan to increase its defense spending. In 1977, Japan spent only 0.88% of its GNP for defense. The defense budget for 1978 called for slightly over 0.9% of Japan's GNP.[14] The President's view is shared by many Congressional leaders. For instance, Senator John H. Glenn, chairman of the Subcommittee for East Asia of the Senate Foreign Relations Committee, told a press luncheon in 1977 that the Japanese Self-Defense Forces should up grade their equipment and modernize their weapons, especially in acquiring early-warning aircraft. He also argued that Japan should have a balanced force that could support American military commitment in this area. Glenn further stated that the self-imposed limit on defense expenditure, not over 1% of Japan's GNP, was unrealistic. He stated "It is difficult for many of our people to see why Japan cannot spend a greater portion than one per cent of GNP."[15] One result of this concern over defense policy was the establishment in July 1976, of a United States-Japan Subcommittee for Defense Cooperation under the United States-Japan Security Consultative Committee.

Despite the Carter administration's desire for greater Japanese military strength it does not expect Japan to play a bigger military role in Southeast Asia.[16] Nor does the United States want to see Japan developing nuclear weapons. In January 1978, the United States made public a declassified CIA study of 1974 which saw the strong possibility of Japan going nuclear in the early 1980s.[17] In this regard, it is difficult to reconcile the Japanese people to the idea that they can rely on American nuclear protection to accept a non-nuclear status.

American Public Opinion

What are the opinions of the American people toward Asia in general and China and Japan in particular? Is the policy of the Carter administration toward this area consistent with American public opinion?

In a public opinion survey conducted by the Foreign Policy Association in May 1976, the results concerning China, Japan and Korea were as follows:[18]

TOTAL NO. OF BALLOTS: 5463

	Pro	Con	No Response
a. Maintain United States military forces in South Korea at current level; in case of invasion from the north, use them to help defend South Korea	2,488	2,198	777
b. Gradually remove United States military presence from South Korea	2,946	1,894	623

c. Renounce bilateral defense treaty with South Korea and remove United States military forces as quickly as possible	662	3,623	1,178
d. Continue to treat security of Japan as vital to United States security	4,399	622	442
e. Continue to furnish nuclear umbrella for defense of Japan provided Japan does not develop nuclear weapons	3,724	895	844
f. Press Japan to increase its conventional defense forces	2,201	2,374	888
g. Renounce defense treaty with Taiwan and give full diplomatic recognition to People's Republic of China	1,410	2,788	1,265
h. Adopt a "Japanese formula" in relations with Taiwan and give full diplomatic recognition to China	3,470	977	1,016
i. Support a policy looking toward the eventual independence of Taiwan	3,787	814	860

The results of a Foreign Policy Association poll on China conducted in April 1977 were as follows:[19]

TOTAL NO. OF BALLOTS: 5,032

	Pro	Go Along Without Enthusiasm	Con	No Opinion
1. With regard to the People's Republic of China (mainland				

China) and the Republic of China (Taiwan), the United States should:

a. Continue present policies: i.e., maintain full diplomatic relations with Taiwan; liaison office in Peking, defense treaty with Taiwan; encourage trade with both.   42%   26%   19%   13%

b. Give full and unconditional recognition to the People's Republic of China; sever diplomatic relations with Taiwan and renounce bilateral defense treaty with Taiwan.   13%   20%   53%   14%

c. Give full recognition to People's Republic of China on condition that it provides firm assurances it will use peaceful means only to resolve the status of Taiwan.   51%   23%   14%   12%

d. Give full recognition to People's Republic of China while giving Taiwan guarantees United States will use force, if necessary, to defend it against aggression by Peking.   18%   25%   40%   17%

2. If Taiwan declares itself a new, sovereign and independent nation, the United States should:

a. Refuse to recognize it.   12%   14%   51%   23%

b. Establish full diplomatic relations with it but allow existing defense treaty to lapse.	34%	29%	18%	19%
c. Establish full diplomatic relations and maintain defense treaty in force.	23%	22%	34%	21%

The American people's image of China has been unfavorable except for the period immediately after the Nixon visit to China in 1972. A survey conducted in March 1977 by the National Opinion Center of the University of Chicago showed that China was the second "most disliked" country next only to the Soviet Union. On a +1 to +5 and -1 to -5 scale, China scored 54% minus points and 36% plus points with 10% answering "Do Not Know."[20]

Although the American people have no particular liking of China, before 1971 they perceived China as a growing military power which was more threatening than the Soviet Union to world peace. As of this writing, there has been no survey on the same issue since 1971. Table 7.1 shows the American people's changing perception of China's power. Figure 7.1 shows the American people's perception of threat regarding China and Russia.

The American people's perception of Japan in recent years has been generally favorable. A Gallup poll conducted in 1973 showed that on a +1 to +5 and -1 to -5 scale, Japan scored 70% plus points and 22% minus points with 8% expressing no opinion.[21] A 1977 poll on the same scale showed that Japan scored 62% plus points as the fourth "most liked" country among the American people. It received 28% minus points with 10% answering "Don't Know."[22] This is quite a reversal from the extremely unfavorable American image of Japan during and immediately after World War II.[23]

In spite of American people's favorable image of Japan, there is a gradual decline of their willingness to defend Japan with American forces. A Gallup poll conducted in 1975 showed the following results to the question of "if Japan is attacked":[24]

	Use Troops	Send Supplies	Refuse to get Involved	Don't Know
1975	16%	36%	40%	9%
1971	17%	34%	38%	11%

Table 7.1 American Expectations of Chinese Power
(Poll conducted in December, 1976)

Start of:	Increase	Decrease	Don't Know
1977	59%	16%	25%
1976	65%	11%	24%
1968	48%	27%	25%
1967	54%	27%	19%
1966	58%	21%	21%

Source: Gallup Opinion Index. Princeton, N.J.: American Institute of Public Opinion January 1977, p. 7.

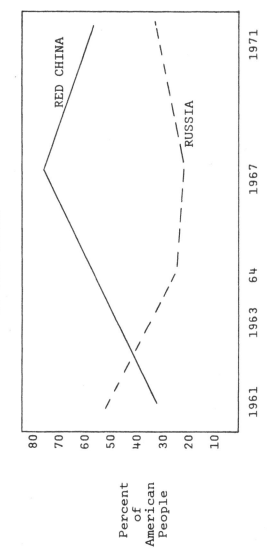

Figure 7.1

These poll results showed that only a very small percentage of the American people, 16%, wanted to defend Japan with American troops if Japan was attacked. A substantial number of them, 40%, refused to get involved even if that country was attacked.

Summary

On the basis of the above public opinion polls, the present administration's overall Asian policy seems to be consistent with the mood of the American people. The reluctance to abandon Taiwan is supported by the majority of the American people. Although the American people consider the security of Japan vital to the United States, and desire to continue the security treaty with Japan, they seem unwilling to defend Japan with American forces. They are almost equally divided on the issue of pressing Japan to increase its conventional force. The chief American concern in Asia appears to be the continued expansion of Soviet naval power in the area and the threat this poses to American naval forces and lines of sea communications. As a counter to this, the United States has attempted to enlist the help of China and Japan on the presumption that they have parallel interests in limiting Soviet power.

CHINA'S PERCEPTION OF THE CARTER ADMINISTRATION

The foreign policy of China is closely linked to the factional struggles among the leaders of the Communist Party of China (CPC). Before the Cultural Revolution (C.R.), the Chinese communist leaders were able to present a facade of unity of purpose and action to the Chinese people and the world, although there were policy differences on both domestic and foreign issues. During the C.R. from 1966 to 1969, policy differences were debated publicly.

In the area of foreign policy, there were three groups. The first group was composed of the moderates led by Premier Chou En-lai. The moderates perceived that the Soviet Union posed a far greater threat to China than did the United States. Because of the international situation and the relative weakness of the Chinese military force, they urged China to isolate the main enemy--the Soviet Union, by driving a wedge between it and the

United States. They believed in the tactical importance of diplomacy and did not perceive the United States as an offensive threat to China. They advocated the normalization of relations with the United States to cope with the Soviet threat.

The second group was composed of many military leaders led by Defense Minister Lin Piao. They rejected the moderates' analysis of the international situation and concluded that, since the United States would inevitably extend the Vietnam War into China, it posed the greatest threat to China's national security. The Soviet Union, however, was not yet irreversibly hostile to China, and therefore, if China did not provoke the Soviets, the confrontation that the moderates predicted could be postponed or prevented. The military leaders strongly opposed the moderates' move to normalize Sino-American relations because, in their view, it would only dramatize the extent of China's commitment to opposing the Soviet Union. This might provoke the Soviet Union into applying even greater pressure against China. They wanted to follow a cautious policy of gradually building up the People's Liberation Army (PLA) in order to increase its ability to cope with the Soviet threat while continuing to explore means of defusing the crisis.

The third group was composed of the radicals led by what is now known as "the gang of four."[25] The radicals urged China to oppose simultaneously both superpowers. They did not want to appease the Soviet Union nor did they want to cooperate with the United States. They advocated a strategy of militant confrontation with both superpowers. They emphasized self-reliance and joined the military in opposing the moderates' bid to improve relations with the United States.

Chairman Mao Tse-tung's real position on the China-United States-Soviet triangular relationship was difficult to ascertain because of the lack of reliable data. On the basis of available public statements, Mao seemed to have been hostile to both the Soviet Union and the United States throughout the C.R. period. It was possible that he played the role of an elder statesman and arbitrated and moderated the factional debates on Chinese foreign policy. Although domestic policy and personal power struggles were the main concern during the C.R., foreign policy was certainly a major factor contributing to the schism among the Chinese Communist leaders.

Throughout the C.R. period, the official theme

on United States-Soviet relations was that the two super-powers colluded with each other to encircle China and to monopolize nuclear weapons. But at the same time they contended with each other for world hegemony.[26]

It is only since the middle of 1971 that we find Mao strongly endorsing the policy of the moderates. He invited the American ping-pong team to visit China in April 1971, and agreed to the Nixon visit to China the same year. In 1972 he personally hosted Nixon, thus officially sanctifying the policy of improving Sino-American relations. The joint Shanghai Communique between Nixon and Chou En-lai laid down the basic policy of the normalization of Sino-American relations. From that point on, Mao firmly supported the moderates' policy of improving relations with the United States to counterbalance Soviet pressure.[27]

What changed Mao's mind in dealing with the United States? The Nixon Guam Doctrine of 1969 of military disengagement in Asia and his gradual withdrawal of American troops in that area probably convinced Mao that the United States had no political and territorial ambitions on the Asian continent. The military conflict between China and the Soviet Union along the Sino-Soviet border in 1969 increased China's apprehension about Soviet threat to China's national security. The official statements and the concrete measures of the Nixon administration apparently convinced Mao that the United States posed no immediate threat to China. The moderates' policy of improving Sino-American relations proved to be sensible and profitable, convincing Mao to give his support to the moderates although he still had differences with them concerning domestic policies.

After 1971, China deemphasized its theme of United States-Soviet collusion to encircle China. Subsequent to the Nixon visit to China in 1972, China dropped this theme altogether. The total withdrawal of American troops from Indochina in 1975 fully vindicated the validity of the policy of the moderates. After Chou En-lai's death in January 1976, the radicals were briefly in control of the Chinese government until their arrest in October of the same year, one month after Mao Tse-tung's death. The radicals did not stay in power long enough to affect major foreign policy changes.

Perceptions of the Present Leadership

The present Chinese leadership of Hua Kuo-feng

and Teng Hsiao-ping is basically following Chou En-lai's domestic and foreign policies. The moderates are now in power, but not all the radicals have been purged. There seems to be serious differences between Hua Kuo-feng and Teng Hsiao-ping with regard to the extent of purge of the radicals. After all, Hua Kuo-feng himself was closely associated with the "gang of four" before Mao Tse-tung's death. We can expect the survival of many followers of the "gang of four" in Chinese politics for some time to come. But for the present, their influence on Chinese foreign and domestic policies is very limited.

The premise of the Chinese moderates is that the two super-powers will continue their competition for world hegemony. The fundamental conflict between them is irreconcilable. China pointed out that all American-Soviet disarmament talks failed.[28] Even SALT I did not prevent the arms race between the two super-powers. Peking also predicted that SALT II negotiations would fail and the nuclear armament race between the two would continue.[29]

China now emphasizes the contending theme either out of conviction or wishful thinking. China fears progress in the SALT negotiations. Any achievement in the disarmament talks is viewed by Peking as detrimental to Chinese interest. Although the limitation of nuclear weapons by the United States and the Soviet Union will make it easier for China to catch up with the two super-powers in nuclear development, China seems to be more concerned about Soviet-American collusion against China than its nuclear inferiority.[30] Moreover, the Peking leaders now feel that the Soviet Union has caught up and is surpassing the United States in nuclear might. The Soviet Union is seen as the most dangerous threat to world peace.[31]

China is also seriously concerned about the apparent appeasement of the Soviet Union by the West, especially the United States. The Chinese liken the appeasement of the Soviet Union today to the Munich tragedy of the 1930s.[32] China praised some leaders and newspapers in France and West Germany for their opposition to United States appeasement to the Soviet Union. In particular China cited their criticism of the United States Presidential Review Memorandum 10 as disclosed by the American press in August 1977. This memorandum, among other things, seemed to indicate that the United States was willing to give up one-third of West German territory in the event of a Soviet attack.[33]

In his report to the Fifth National People's Congress on February 26, 1978, Hua Kuo-feng reaffirmed the validity of Mao's theory of the "Three Worlds." He also perceived that the two superpowers were "locked in a fierce struggle for world domination" and war is bound to break out sooner or later. The Soviet Union, he stated, is bent on subjugation of China. Hua Kuo-feng reiterated China's belief that appeasement of the Soviet Union would hasten the outbreak of war. Accordingly he stated that China's attitude toward a world war is "First, we are against it; second, we are not afraid of it."[34]

The new Chinese leadership is concerned with the present administration's Chinese policy, envisioning a regression of Sino-American relations under the Carter administration. This was pointed out by Teng Hsiao-ping who regarded the visit to China by Secretary of State Cyrus Vance in August 1977 as a retreat from the Ford-Kissinger promises. The Chinese leadership also felt that efforts to establish normal diplomatic relations between the United States and China suffered a setback during the Vance visit. Teng alleged that President Ford promised in December 1975 that if he was re-elected he would break diplomatic relations with Taiwan and establish relations with Peking.[35] Although Ford denied any such promise, he admitted that he did suggest the "Japanese solution" as a "possibility."[36] The Carter administration has suggested to Peking that full diplomatic relations be established between the United States and China with a U.S. liaison office in Taiwan. This proposition was rejected by China.[37] The Brzezinski visit to China in May 1978 and his interest in greater Sino-American cooperation to counter Soviet expansion seems to have improved the atmosphere of Sino-American relations although the Taiwan issue remains unresolved.

Summary

To sum up, the Hua-Teng leadership in China is unhappy with the Carter administration's unwillingness to abandon Taiwan and its appeasement of the Soviet Union. It sees the danger of the Soviet Union surpassing the United States in military might, thus changing the balance of power in favor of the Soviet Union. The Hua-Teng leadership does not feel that the United States is an immediate threat to China, nor does it see the probability of Soviet-American reconciliation in the near future. China perfunctorily attacks both super-powers, but its real fear is the Soviet Union. To counterbalance Soviet military pressure on China, it would like to see continued American military presence in Asia, although it officially demands the withdrawal of American troops from South Korea. China desires continued Soviet-American tension so it can manipulate the situation diplomatically to China's advantage. In all probability, China will continue its policy of trying to improve relations with the United States despite its frustration over the Taiwan issue.

JAPAN'S PERCEPTION OF AMERICAN DEFENSE POLICY

Trade and defense are the two current major problem areas between the United States and Japan. Here we are concerned with the problem of defense. Since the end of American occupation of Japan in 1952, the keystone of Japanese national defense policy has been the military alliance with the United States. This is based on the United States-Japan Mutual Security Treaty, which was signed in 1951, revised in 1960, and will come up for revision in 1980. Under the terms of this treaty, the United States provides a "nuclear umbrella" and maintains air and naval bases on Japanese soil. Because of this arrangement, Japan has been able to avoid heavy defense expenses. Up to the present time, Japan has been spending less than 1% of its GNP for defense purposes in contrast to the 10 to 15% for the two super-powers, and about 5% for the middle powers such as Great Britain, France and West Germany. The Japanese government has consistently stated that it intends to continue the American alliance despite criticisms from leftist groups, especially the Japanese Socialists and Communists. At the same time, there are signs of a revival of nationalistic feeling among the Japanese people. The trend is in the direction of a more independent foreign policy. For many Japanese, the reliance on American protection is a sign of inferiority. This sentiment has been growing since Japan achieved its great economic power status in the 1960s.

Perceptions of Japanese Leaders and Parties

Despite the desire to achieve foreign policy

independence, Japan, under the control of the Liberal Democratic Party (LDP) since 1955, has continued to base its defense policy on the United States-Japan Security Treaty and still looks to the United States for protection against possible aggression from the Soviet Union and China. This position has not changed despite American military withdrawal from Indochina in 1975. For instance, Japan's White Paper on defense for 1976 stated that Japan intended to continue relying on the United States for its primary military security and planned no major arms build-up of its own.[38] The Japanese White Paper on defense for 1977 characterized the situation in Northeast Asia as a "tripolar balance," the United States, the Soviet Union and China. The three powers were compelled to be prudent in action because of the need to take into account the response of the two other powers. For this reason, the White Paper concluded that "confrontation in our area is less likely to become aggravated than in Europe." And "No major change in the international environment is anticipated for the present."[39]

The same White Paper noted that two matters deserved Japan's attention. One was United States withdrawal of ground troops from South Korea and the other was an increase of Soviet military strength in this region. This would affect the control of the sea by the West, especially the United States. The White Paper did not anticipate any large conflict for the time being, but it did not rule out minor conflicts.[40]

On the issue of American withdrawal of ground troops from South Korea, the 1977 White Paper basically echoed the American concept that if American air forces continued to stay in Korea and the modernization of the South Korean forces could be achieved, the withdrawal of American ground forces from that country in the near future would not seriously affect Korea's ability to deter aggression. This is different from the perception of the 1976 White Paper which noted that the security in the Korean Peninsula was largely maintained by the military balance involving the 43,000 American troops stationed there.[41]

But it is quite obvious that the Japanese government is very much concerned about the withdrawal of American ground troops from South Korea. After the "Nixon shocks" of 1971, which included the devaluation of the dollar and the abrupt announcement of the Nixon visit to China, the decision to withdraw American ground troops from South Korea by

Carter without real consultation with Japan, once again caused the Japanese government to question American reliability. Furthermore, Japan perceives a gradual decline of United States military strength in the Pacific and the expansion of Soviet military force in the same area. This has caused debates among Japanese decision-makers with regard to the build-up of Japanese military forces.[42]

Fumihiko Togo, Japanese ambassador to the United States, pointed out that the political stability in the Far East depended on "the capacity and will of the United States to maintain the balance of power in that part of the world." He declared that both in Korea and in Southeast Asia a continued American presence and commitment were vital to the maintenance of peace. He particularly expressed concern that the American withdrawal of ground forces from South Korea and the accompanying strengthening of South Korean forces should be carried out in such a way as not to upset the "precarious balance" on the Peninsula.[43] This is a reflection of Japan's uneasiness about American withdrawal of ground troops from South Korea.

Some opposition parties in Japan also support the LDP's basic defense policy. The Komeito, the third large party in Japan, which had been opposed to the United States-Japan Mutual Security Treaty, made a policy shift in 1977 in favor of keeping the treaty. It did not want to terminate the treaty hastily, creating a security vacuum that might tempt third country aggression. The Komeito also favors the maintenance of the Self-Defense Force, another reversal of its early stand on this issue.[44] The head of the New Liberal Club (NLC) also favors the maintenance of the United States-Japan Mutual Security Treaty and the improvement of the quality of Japan's defense capacity.[45]

The Democratic Socialist Party (DSP) has traditionally favored a phased dissolution of the United States-Japan Mutual Security Treaty. It perceives the diminishing need for this treaty in a multipolar world. It wants to improve relations with the United States, the Soviet Union, and China, and urges Japan to give greater assistance to Asian nations. It is in favor of international disarmament including nuclear weapons.[46] Although the DSP sometimes called for an early withdrawal of United States military bases and troops from Japan, it rarely opposed the treaty in a militant fashion as did the leftists.

Among the major political parties in Japan, only the Japan Socialist Party (JSP) and the Japan Communist Party (JCP) are consistently and militantly opposed to the United States-Japan military alliance.

While the Japanese government showed some concern about American disengagement in Asia, its manifestation has been very subdued and indirect because Japan does not desire public confrontation with the United States. This attitude perhaps has something to do with, among other things, the postwar patron-client relationship between the two countries, reflected in Japan's dependence on United States military power and economy.

The different perceptions of America's role in Asia has been expressed less subtly by semi-official and private groups. For instance, at a general meeting of the Japan-South Korea Parliamentarians' Association in Tokyo in 1977, the participants issued a joint communique expressing "serious concern" about the planned United States military cutbacks in South Korea because it contained a risk of bringing new instability to the Korean Peninsula and the rest of the Far East as well. They appreciated the United States military presence on the Peninsula, saying it had so far played the role as a deterrent against another war. Most Japanese participants at the Association meeting were members of the LDP, including Foreign Minister Iichiro Hatoyama.[47]

In the fourth American-Japanese Assembly held in Japan in September 1977, the two sides differed sharply on the withdrawal of American troops from South Korea. The Japanese side was concerned about upsetting the equilibrium on the Korean Peninsula and the stability of Asia because of the withdrawal. The American side did not share this view at all.[48]

Japanese Public Opinion

The Japanese public is divided and uncertain about the value either to Korea or to Japan of the American troops' presence in the Korean Peninsula. A 1976 poll showed that 50 percent of the more highly educated Japanese (college/university graduates) felt that maintaining American troops in Korea was important both to Japan and Korea. Only 30 percent of those at the lowest level of formal education had this opinion.[49] The same survey showed that Japanese confidence in the United States defense commitment dropped from a plurality of 43 percent in late 1975 to an almost even split (35 percent confident--31 percent not confident) in late 1976. As of the end of 1975, the majority of the Japanese people still opposed the use of American bases in Japan to defend South Korea from a North Korean attack.50

Carter's decision to withdraw American ground troops received lukewarm attention from the Japanese press. Several editorials regarded this as a step toward reduction of tension. Some Japanese were concerned that the United States may drag Japan into the Korean conflict. They felt that Carter's projected withdrawal of American ground troops would mitigate this danger.51

As shown in Table 7.2, the Japanese saw a greater increase in Russian and Chinese power than the United States.

Table 7.2
Japan's View of Power Expection in 1977

	Increase	Decline	Same/Don't Know
United States	14	11	75
Soviet Union	22	3	75
China	23	10	67

Source: <u>Gallup Opinion Index</u>, January 1977, pp. 4-9.
(This poll was conducted in December 1976.)

The Japanese people feel less threatened by war. A survey conducted in Japan in 1975 for example, showed that the number of Japanese people who felt the danger of war declined from 52% in 1969 to 44% in 1975. Correspondingly, the number of Japanese people who felt there was no danger of war increased from 23% in 1969 to 34% in 1975.52 American-Soviet detente policy, the improvement of Sino-American relations, and the normalization of Sino-Japanese relations apparently were major reasons for these shifts in attitudes.

With regard to national defense, most Japanese seem to desire the status quo, i.e., to keep the United States-Japan Mutual Security Treaty and the Self-Defense Force. A survey in 1975 showed that 54% of the Japanese people favored the maintenance of the present defense arrangement, which compared with 41% in 1969 and 41% in 1972. By comparison, 9% favored armed neutrality (strengthening Japanese military forces and abrogating the United States-Japan Mutual Security Treaty), with 13% in 1969 and 11% in 1972. Only 10% were in favor of non-armed neutrality in 1975, compared to 10% in 1969 and 16% in 1972. About one-third of those surveyed did not know the answer or gave other answers.[53] By 1976, 56% favored the maintenance of the present defense arrangement; 7% favored the revision of the constitution to rearm Japan; 16% favored the abrogation of the Japan-United States Mutual Security Treaty, the abolishment of the Self-Defense Force and the adoption of a policy of non-armed neutrality; and 21% gave no answer or other answers.[54]

In his administrative policy speech before both houses of the Diet, on January 31, 1977, Premier Takeo Fukuda stressed the importance of United States-Japan relations. He said "Of fundamental importance to our nation's foreign policy is the Japan-United States relationship.... There is no change whatsoever in my Government's basic policy for firmly maintaining the Japan-United States Security Treaty. At the same time, it is only natural that we should endeavor to build up a foundation of our own defense capability."[55] But in the so-called "Fukuda Doctrine" proclaimed in Manila in August 1977, Fukuda pledged that Japan would remain a pacifist nation and contribute to the peace and prosperity of Southeast Asia and the world.[56] A survey of December 1977, showed that the region the Japanese people were most interested in was Asia (42%, based on a multiple entry system).[57]

Summary

The Japanese government and people do not perceive any immediate threat to their national security by any external force. They feel that the United States-Japan Mutual Security Treaty is adequate to protect Japan and want to continue this military alliance. They do not seem aware of the fact that by now only a small percentage of the American people are willing to defend Japan with American forces if Japan is attacked. Nor do they pay much attention to the "escape clause" in the security treaty--Article 5 of which requires congressional approval for the United States to take action.[58] They do not seriously doubt American willingness to defend them if they are attacked, although there is a growing feeling of uneasiness and concern because of the gradual but steady American military withdrawal from Asia since the Indochina War. This feeling has been accentuated since Jimmy Carter became President, despite the administration's repeated assurance that the United States would maintain a military, political and economic presence in the Asia-Pacific region.[59]

CONCLUSION

The Carter administration's defense policy in Asia is based, in part, on its perception of the reduced threat from the Soviet Union and China because of the Sino-Soviet dispute and internal struggles and backwardness of China. The present administration does not see the probability of Soviet or Chinese invasion of any Asian countries in the immediate future. On the other hand, it does see a serious military weakness of the NATO countries in West Europe and a greater danger of Soviet aggression in Europe. With limited military manpower and available funds for national defense, President Carter has decided to gradually withdraw American ground forces from Asia to further reduce tension and strengthen United States military forces in West Europe. His perception appears consistent with the mood of the American people regarding United States military commitment to defend Asia. The President does not see any danger to the security of South Korea and Japan even after the withdrawal of American ground troops from South Korea.

American defense policy in Asia may serve adequately for the United States provided two conditions continue. First, the Chinese leadership continues its present policy. This is unpredictable. The Hua-Teng leadership is certainly not immune from internal and external pressures. Intra-party struggles and international changes may affect its foreign policy, altering its policy toward the two super-powers. Second, United States military disengagement in Asia remains limited so as not to mislead the Soviet Union and China into believing that the United States has abandoned Asia. If the United States should appear to have abandoned Asia the two Communist powers may be tempted to change their policies in that part of the world with the possible destruction of the present precarious balance of power.

As for United States-Japan relations, the

Carter administration pays lip service to Japan as an equal partner. In practice, it often ignores Japan in making decisions concerning Asia. The Japanese government and people still show deference to the United States partly because of their economic and military dependence on the United States and partly because of the lingering patron-client psychology developed during the period of American occupation. The present administration presumes that this relationship will remain. But this is changing. If Japan no longer perceives the United States as a reliable ally to protect its national security or if there develops serious conflicts between the two nations over economic or other matters, the Japanese may pursue a more independent policy. In such a case, the development of a nuclear force by Japan cannot be entirely ruled out, although all indications in Japan today seem to oppose nuclear armament.

If the LDP loses its majority in the Diet, which may be a probability, Japan may have a coalition government dominated by centrist forces, which may not be as pro-American as the LDP administrations. This will not enhance United States-Japan relations. Any major conflict between the Carter administration and the Fukuda administration will accelerate the continued decline of the popularity of the LDP. Growing Japanese nationalism may also have a bearing on Japan's policy toward the United States. A change of Japanese public opinion may have the same effect. To counter such possibilities, the Carter administration needs to improve its communications with the Japanese government, treat Japan as a truly equal partner and convince the Japanese that they can rely on American military forces to defend them in case they are attacked by external forces.

Soviet global military strategy is based on clearly defined political objectives. Every part of the world is linked to its overall planning. The Soviet Union makes moves only in areas where it thinks the resistance is the weakest. South Korea in 1950 and Africa today are cases in point. The greater concentration of Soviet military forces in Eastern Europe can justify Carter's emphasis on our NATO alliance; but this does not warrant the substantial reduction of our military forces in Asia or weaken our resolve to defend Asia.

FOOTNOTES

1. For a detailed study of this subject, see John G. Stoessinger, <u>Why Nations Go To War</u> (New York: St. Martin's Press, 1978) Second Edition, pp. 229-233.

2. Kenneth E. Boulding, "National Images and International Systems" in Harold Karan Jacobson and William Zimmerman, (eds.). <u>The Shaping of Foreign Policy</u> (New York: Atherton Press, 1969), p. 161. Originally published in <u>Journal of Conflict Resolution</u>, III:12 (June 1959), pp. 120-131.

3. <u>The New York Times</u>, June 24, 1977.

4. <u>Ibid</u>.

5. <u>Ibid</u>., March 24, 1978.

6. <u>The Japan Times</u>, (Tokyo), November 18, 1977.

7. <u>Peking Review</u> (Peking) No. 10, March 10, 1978, p. 39.

8. <u>The Japan Times</u>, August 19, 1977.

9. <u>The New York Times</u>, June 24, 1977.

10. <u>Ibid</u>., June 24, 1976.

11. <u>Ibid</u>., May 18, 1977.

12. <u>Ibid</u>., September 2, 1977.

13. <u>The Japan Times</u>, March 23, 1977.

14. <u>Ibid</u>., September 17, 1977.

15. <u>Ibid</u>., September 1, 1977.

16. <u>Ibid</u>., November 18, 1977.

17. <u>Ibid</u>., January 28, 1978.

18. <u>Great Decisions '76 Opinion Ballots</u> (New York: Foreign Policy Association, July, 1976) Topic 4.

19. Great Decisions '77 Opinion Ballots (New York: Foreign Policy Association, June, 1977) Topic 6.

20. World Opinion Update (Williamstown, Massachusetts: Survey Research Consultants International, Inc., Vol. 1, Issue 1, September, 1977), p. 15. For a more detailed study of American people's opinion about China, see George P. Jan, "Public Opinion and American Policy Toward China, 1949-1977," a paper delivered at the Tri-State Modern China Seminar, 1977-1978, at the University of Pittsburgh, Pittsburgh, Pennsylvania, November 19, 1977.

21. Gallup Opinion Index (Princeton, New Jersey: American Institute of Public Opinion, June, 1973), p. 18.

22. World Opinion Update, p. 15.

23. For a detailed study of American image of Japan during and immediately after World War II, see George P. Jan, "Public Opinion and American Policy Toward the Sino-Japanese War, 1937-1945," a paper delivered at the annual meeting of the American Association of Chinese Studies in November, 1976 at Washington University in St. Louis. It will be published by Asian Profile in 1978.

24. Gallup Opinion Index, July, 1975, p. 18.

25. The four radical leaders are Wang Hung-wen, Chang Chun-chiao, Chiang Ching and Yao Wen-yuan.

26. Chun-tu Hsueh and Robert North, "Peking's Perception of Soviet-American Relations," in Chun-tu Hsueh, Dimensions of China's Foreign Relations (New York: Praeger Publishers, 1977), pp. 53-54.

27. For a detailed analysis of factionalism and Chinese policy toward the United States and the Soviet Union during the Cultural Revolution period, see Thomas M. Gottlieb, Chinese Foreign Policy and the Origins of the Strategic Triangle (Santa Monica, California: The Rand Corporation, 1977).

28. Peking Review, No. 5, February 3, 1978, pp. 24-25.

29. Ibid., No. 30, July 22, 1977, p. 29.

30. For a detailed study of China's attitude toward the SALT negotiations, see Michael Pillsburg, SALT on the Dragon: Chinese Views of the Soviet-American Strategic Balance (Santa Monica, California: The Rand Corporation, 1975).

31. Peking Review, No. 29, July 15, 1977, pp. 4-10.

32. Ibid., No. 50, December 9, 1977, pp. 6-11. Also see Foreign Minister Huang Hua's speech at the United Nations, Ibid., No. 41, October 7, 1977, p. 35.

33. Ibid., No. 6, February 10, 1978, pp. 23-25.

34. Ibid., No. 10, March 10, 1978, pp. 13, 14, 35-39.

35. The New York Times, September 7, 1977.

36. Ibid., September 8, 1977.

37. Ibid., September 7, 1977.

38. Ibid., May 28, 1976.

39. The Japan Times, August 1, 1977.

40. Ibid.

41. Ibid.

42. The New York Times, August 1, 1977.

43. Ibid., October 31, 1977.

44. The Japan Times, January 14, 1978.

45. Ibid., January 25, 1977.

46. Ibid., April 9, 1973.

47. Ibid., February 17, 1977.

48. Ibid., September 2 and 3, 1977.

49. United States Information Agency survey in December, 1977 based on a national adult sample of 1,585 persons. See World Opinion Update, p. 4.

50. Ibid.

51. The Japan Times, June 3, 1977.

52. Chosa Geppo (The Monthly Review) (Tokyo: Cabinet Research Office of Japan, December, 1976), p. 42.

53. Ibid., p. 56.

54. Ibid., p. 60.

55. The Japan Times, February 1, 1977.

56. Ibid., August 19, 1977.

57. Ibid., May 13, 1978.

58. Kiyoaki Murata, "Japan's Defense Delusion" Ibid., December 30, 1977.

59. Carter's most recent assurance of this American policy was made during Fukuda's U.S. visit in May, 1978. See The Japan Times, May 13, 1978.

8
The Presidency and Defense Policy: Questions for the Future

Sheldon Simon

INTRODUCTION

The purposes of this concluding chapter are to highlight and elaborate some of the themes and issues raised by other authors in this volume; to see if there are some critical points in common over the kind of defense policy which has emanated from Washington in the early period of the Carter Administration; and to compare the defense policy <u>process</u> under recent Presidents with an <u>ideal-typical</u> analytical framework for the creation of defense policy.

Since defense policy is the product of a political process, it is sensible to begin by examining that process. Ideally, defense policy should grow out of strategic concepts. That is, policy should be among the last stages[1] of a linear process which commences with an articulation and ordering of America's foreign policy values (stability, equality, development, human rights, the expansion of international commerce) some of which may even be in conflict with each other. After ordering these values, goals should be identified for their realization. <u>Goals</u> in this case refer to specific conditions in world politics necessary for the realization of values--for example, naval control of certain key trade routes in order to effect the value of expanding international commerce. Only after goals are identified should <u>strategies</u> be formulated. Strategies themselves are complex concepts, consisting of political, economic, and military components designed to attain the goals identified in the preceding stage of the process. The military component of the strategies should include specific force levels and combinations appropriate for the desired goals. Only then should the question of budget be addressed.

While the foregoing is a brief statement of how the ideal-typical defense policy comes about, in reality, the process is more frequently turned on its head. Force levels are based on budgetary constraints and the pulling and hauling of international and domestic priorities in Congress. Only after force levels are known do deployments occur and strategies for their use are devised. National goals are often lost in the shuffle.

To further complicate the process, strategic policy is not made in a blank international environment. It is affected by the policies of the countries and events in the regions in which it operates. Effective policies cannot be carved in granite but must adjust as the environment changes. Alterations in regional political leaderships, economic growth or decline, and outside great power activities--to name only a few--should lead to strategy adjustments over time.

POLICY ANALYSIS

Thomas Fabyanic, Vincent Davis and Larry Korb all address themselves to these overall processual concerns. Davis, as an intellectual historian of American strategic studies, has composed a witty rendition of how the scholarly community intersects with the policymaker. And the correlation he finds between presidential elections and scholarly writings on coping with the bureaucracy suggests that intellectuals have their own strategy for getting appointed by incoming administrations. Davis also quite rightly takes his academic colleagues to task when he points out that while scholarly attention focuses on crisis decision making (because of the large amount of data available over a short period of time) the bulk of bureaucratic activity in defense policy is ignored since it is "routine" and protracted.

Davis's examination of the Carter administration defense policy is perplexing in light of the strategic policy criteria mentioned at the beginning of this chapter. He argues that Carter has no strategic policy both because of a lack of experience in national-level politics and foreign affairs and a dysfunctional decisional style. Davis illustrates this position by ascribing vacillation in U.S. policy toward the USSR to White House indecision rather than any calculated response to changes in Russian policy. Another example of the administration's almost passive defense policy decisions can be seen in the May 1978 congressional refusal to support the turnover of $800 million worth of American military equipment to ROK forces in Korea. The effect of this negative congressional action was to provide an excuse for the President to retain approximately the same number of U.S. ground forces in South Korea (30,000) as were there at the time of his inauguration and pledged force reduction. The point is, however, that a strategic decision--such as the retention of ground forces in the ROK--should have been made on politico-military grounds and not as a stopgap reaction to congressional obstruction. This criticism may be directed, however, as much at congressional efforts to share defense policy initiatives with the presidency in the wake of Watergate and the Indochina War as it is a complaint against Carter specifically.

On the other hand, some strategic gains may have been won by the President in the Spring of 1978 when he was able to convince Congress to approve his package sale of military aircraft to both Israel and such Arab moderates as Egypt and Saudi Arabia, despite domestic political objections from the traditionally strong pro-Israel lobby. The President's victory was based at least, in part, on strategic arguments about the necessity of building American rapport with regimes committed to such desiderata as an Israeli settlement and the protection of the flow of oil from the Persian Gulf.

Underlying Davis's argument is the belief that the American public will no longer accept any strategy which may require a lengthy U.S. involvement in hostilities in other lands, particularly if those lands are part of the Third World and hence not seen as traditional allies and cultural progenitors of this country. Thus, large defense budgets with significant ground force components are artifacts of the past. A general antipathy toward defense spending plus Carter's own skepticism about the military's utility in foreign policy imply that military force levels have at best reached a plateau. Without a sense of clear and present danger transmitted by the President to the public and with the growing costs of merely replacing obsolete technology in all services, prospects for a leaner (some would say less capable) military over time seem inevitable. These reductions are already apparent in the Navy where recent cost overruns have led to budget cuts which have denied funds to build a Nimitz-class nuclear carrier, the Aegis missile-equipped strike cruiser, and the procurement of a number of fighter aircraft. One could argue that none of these systems should be built on strategic grounds. But the decisions not to fund appear to have been made essentially on the basis of financial and managerial considerations.

As Korb notes, the defense budget signals intentions to both ally and adversary. But, as he might also have pointed out, given the cost and long lead time for new high technology weapons systems, decision to go with a particular system may lock the military into certain force structures and capabilities relevant at the time the decision was made but potentially irrelevant when the systems are deployed years later. Or, available systems may be used in an inappropriate fashion simply because they are available. A notorious example of the latter was the Air Force use of the B-52 during the Vietnam War as a tactical precision bomber when, in fact, it was developed as an area strategic bomber. The result was the destruction of large amounts of land and people, friend and foe alike.

Korb presents a very useful and highly detailed comparison of the Ford and Carter defense budgets. But with respect to the earlier stated criteria for strategy, additional analysis is necessary to judge those budgets. Specifically, the nature of American goals under Carter, how they relate to those of potential adversaries and their capabilities, and whether American force decisions are sufficient in this respect. Korb does point out the importance of domestic priorities for this administration, demonstrating that the defense portion of the total Federal budget seems to be going into a shallow decline. He provides much of the information needed to infer American strategic goals for selected world regions, for example, against the USSR in Central Europe. And, most importantly, Korb has addressed the strategic effects of major reductions in systems such as the B-1 bomber and M-X missile as well as the slowdown in Trident deployment. His discussion is incomplete, however, without an analysis of how these developments might affect Soviet calculations and military policies. Illustrative of this is Korb's well documented decline in U.S. naval capability over the next five years across several ship categories. Such a diminution of capability should have implications for the Carter Administration's view of the Navy's strategic role vis-a-vis potential adversaries. These implications are not spelled out in Korb's paper.

Complicating defense decision processes are promises that may be given to particular constituencies to "buy" their support on other parts of the defense package. Korb notes that these promises may be necessary in order to put a politically viable defense budget together; but he does not go on to show how they affect strategic planning. Along the same lines, while Korb argues persuasively that Carter is leading us toward a real decline in defense spending, he provides no way of assessing whether such a development is "good" or "bad." In short, Korb does not provide a <u>strategic analysis</u> of the defense budget. The partial exception to this criticism is the author's very apt discussion of superpower nuclear policies. However, a broader-gauged analysis would compare expenditures at the superpower nuclear level with other kinds of defense challenges. An example would be to ask whether there was a tradeoff between expenditures on Trident versus additional conventional naval capability with a different kind of mission?

Korb contends that a stagnant defense budget is unwise because it communicates a sense of weakness and passivity to allies and adversaries. He may be right. But might there be a counter-hypothesis that defense spending is a Richardson-like action-reaction cycle? If one side appears to reverse direction, the other might follow, assuming its external behavior is based on changes in the environment rather than being solely a product of internal political imperatives. If not--that is, if the Soviets march to a different drummer--then we would seem to be on track for an open-ended arms race to the detriment of both superpowers, where billions are spent to retain deterrence at ever higher levels of sophistication, while neither side obtains a real increase in security.

Finally, Korb briefly raises an intriguing prospect the implications of which could lower deterrent costs and possibly stabilize SALT negotiations. He argues that the United States is not exploiting its particular strengths in missile accuracy but relying instead on a point-by-point defense against areas of Soviet strength (much the way cold war containment policy required the United States to respond at those points on the globe where Soviet probes were supposedly occurring). By elaborating Korb's idea, might it not be possible to move away from costly counterforce planning as a deterrent to the targeting of more vulnerable Russian social support systems such as power facilities and water supplies without which urban life would come to a halt? Such a targeting policy would avoid the moral condemnation directed at the earlier MAD concept with its hostage populations but would retain MAD's lower technological costs. Its deterrent effect should be strong because it threatens the complete disruption of urban industrial society.

U.S. SECURITY AND MILITARY CAPABILITY

While the first four chapters of this volume deal with general defense policy concerns from a domestic American perspective, with Doris Graber's essay the book moves into the problems of projecting American military force globally. She grapples with the crucial issue of employing American power through intervention. Graber's very perceptive analysis is somewhat marred by her operational definition of "intervention" for it includes nonaction, such as nonrecognition of a new regime, as well as more standard actions. In short, the definition appears so inclusive that most state interactions could be subsumed, diminishing the concept's analytical utility.

Moving on to her findings, Graber (as Davis) is pessimistic over future public acceptance of American military intervention to either aid ally or friend under communist attack. She makes a particularly effective case for this view by noting that opposition to an interventionary American policy now comes from the elite which had previously almost always supported a strong, forward American strategy.

On the other hand, some of Graber's generalizations about specific regional intervention opportunities are questionable. She speaks of Indonesia as a possible surrogate for American anticommunist policies in Southeast Asia, but ignores the fact that Indonesia's regional political behavior is now circumscribed by its membership in the Association of Southeast Asian Nations (ASEAN) which is attempting to pursue a policy of accommodation toward Indochina, China, and the USSR. Moreover, it is difficult to envisage scenarios in which Indonesian forces would either be welcomed or deployed beyond their home islands. Nor is South Korea necessarily an example of permanent dependency on the United States. Its remarkable economic growth over the past 15 years has permitted it to diversify trade and investment partners. And, it has even embarked on a military production program which will lead to virtual self-sufficiency in the manufacture of most armaments by the early 1980s.

Graber does provide an excellent taxonomy of types of intervention and examples of their success and failure. But again, some inferences are questionable. If, as she suggests, clandestine intelligence has not led to important benefits, then how can its decline significantly weaken American intervention capabilities?

Finally, Graber points out--as do other contributors to this volume--that American intervention decisions are reactive to Russian probes. However, whereas in the 1950s and '60s the United States had the domestic political support to pursue a containment policy, its _political_ ability to do so in the late 1970s is problematical. At a time when the Soviets seem to be exploiting targets of opportunity in Angola and the Horn of Africa with an augmented air and sealift capability, the Americans seem to be boxed out of participation. As the Russians accelerate their support for "national liberation movements", the West displays a diminished ability to block them.[2] However, this need not be seen as an inevitable loss to an ascendant USSR. The forces of nationalism in the Third World still dominate. Although the Russians may be testing their capabilities for direct Third World military intervention, it is unlikely that Soviet military personnel will be any more acceptable over time to host countries than their Western European and American predecessors. Third World nationalism is a difficult force to manipulate, especially where, as in Africa, it is compounded by tribal animosities.

The region of primary concern to both the United States and the Soviet Union is, of course, Europe, where the world's two best organized and equipped alliances have faced each other for 30 years. Jim Linger reminds his readers that no administration can begin with a clean slate; that it inherits commitments and policies from its predecessors which are frequently deeply embedded in international arrangements. Changes occur at the margin.

Linger believes that the Carter Administration has developed a tougher policy on SALT II which sets it apart from its precedessors. However, the arguments of the Korb and Davis papers suggest that Carter's rhetoric is not borne out in his policy recommendations.

Linger is virtually the only author who raises the question of <u>Soviet</u> military policy motivations, intimating that <u>there</u> may be goals other than the quest for strategic superiority inherent in Russian thinking. Unfortunately, he drops this line of thought as speculative. I say <u>unfortunately</u> because if Soviet intentions or motivations are precluded from analysis, then American policy must be based exclusively on Soviet capabilities. At least some of the latter are oriented toward the maintenance of control over Eastern Europe and the Russian confrontation with China. By focusing only on capabilities, the United States is forced into a "worst case" posture, increasing its own capacities, thereby providing additional reasons for the Soviets to respond in kind.

There is some evidence that Carter is trying to break out of this syndrome. By holding such new weapons systems as the B-1, M-X, and Neutron Bomb in abeyance, the President is signalling his intention for meaningful arms control negotiations. He is also providing the Soviets a comparable opportunity to demonstrate restraint on, for example, the production of Backfire bombers and the deployment of medium-range SS-20 missiles. Those who are skeptical of Soviet intentions, such as Paul Nitze, however, point to the fact that Russia has increased defense expenditures four to five percent annually despite internal economic difficulties, while NATO has been unable to get three percent across the Alliance.[3]

Linger highlights NATO's perennial problems and weaknesses vis-a-vis the Warsaw Pact, including the lack of weapons standardization and interoperability. But he points to Carter's policy initiatives as an attempt to revitalize America's own commitment to NATO and motivate its other members to agree to regular increases for Alliance forces.

An additional issue Linger might have addressed in his thorough and well-balanced chapter is the question of a NATO nuclear strategy. One of the ironies of the Alliance position over these many years is that it has come to rely on battlefield nuclear weapons as a substitute for understrength divisions without really thinking through questions of population protection and collatoral damage if such weapons were ever employed. The neutron bomb controversy goes to the heart of this issue.[4]

Of all contributors, George Jan is the author who takes the most system-dependent view of defense policy, arguing that nations make defense decisions primarily on the basis of their perceptions of others' power.

Jan explains the background for a lower American military profile in Asia, noting both the region's reduction in military priority to Washington in the wake of the Indochina War and the large scale withdrawal of American forces after 1973. Jan's argument is not entirely persuasive, however. It could be countered that a lower American military presence in Asia does not represent a diminution of the region's importance to the United States but rather that, in the aftermath of Vietnam, there are few security challenges which would require the presence of large numbers of U.S. troops. By contrast, in Europe, NATO faces the best-equipped and largest concentration of Soviet forces in the world.

Jan states that the Carter Administration believes that the PRC cannot "liberate" Taiwan by force. The accuracy of that belief is questionable. China probably could occupy Taiwan successfully, but only at considerable military and political cost, including the destruction of its new relationships with the United States and Japan as well as a potential escalation of the Sino-Soviet conflict into open warfare. Hence, the low probability that China will, in fact, choose a military course of action for Taiwan in the foreseeable future. Moreover, there may be some ambivalence in Peking's view of the U.S. commitment to Taiwan and the presence of the Seventh Fleet in the South and East China Seas. Publicly, of course, China must articulate a tough rhetorical position; but given its overriding concern with Soviet military growth in the Pacific, the American commitment to Taiwan is an indication of U.S. staying power in East Asia and hence desirable.

Jan imputes a kind of racism to the United States in its economic pressure on Japan, pointing out that the same intensity of concern is not manifested toward West Germany with which Washington also runs a substantial balance of payments deficit. This allegation appears to be somewhat overdrawn, however, and does not take account of the facts that U.S. investment and trade access to the

FRG is nowhere near as encumbered as access to Japan and that Japan is a more important trade partner than is Germany. In short, the stakes are larger, and so is the pressure.

With respect to SALT II, China's position may be more complex than Jan intimates. While he is correct in noting that Chinese statements assert the talks will fail, there is, nevertheless, a distinct possibility that China's negative position could change as its own capabilities develop. Indeed, China has already benefited from SALT I which forestalled a large ABM buildup and hence gave the PRC a better chance to develop its own deterrent. Similarly, if the United States and Soviet Union slow their military-technological growth as a result of SALT II, China also benefits.

Survey data provide the base for some of Jan's most interesting findings, for example, the paradoxical development of diminished American public opinion support for the use of U.S. forces should Japan be attacked coinciding with increased Japanese public approval of the Mutual Security Treaty. In the future, it would be useful to obtain survey data showing how the Japanese view the Far Eastern clause of the Treaty which could be interpreted to commit Japan indirectly to support American military operations in the East Asian region. Japanese reticence over the possibility of military involvement beyond the home islands should clash directly with this Treaty provision.

One final disagreement with Jan. He foresees that the loss of a Liberal Democratic Party majority in the Diet will lead to a leftist coalition government composed of the Japan Communist and Socialist Parties and that such a coalition would completely undermine the U.S.-Japan security arrangement. While it is undoubtedly true that a JCP-JSP government would abrogate the Treaty, the probability of such a government coming to power is minimal. First of all, the two left parties have been unable to cooperate effectively at the national level. Secondly, electoral trends do not portend a clearcut shift to the left. Instead, a new combination of conservative and liberal parties, including the LDP, New Liberal Club, Komeito, and Democratic Socialists are a more likely coalition should the LDP lose its majority in the Diet. This latter combination would have little difficulty in retaining the American security connection.

CONCLUSIONS

In conclusion, the contributors to this book have found Carter's first 18 months a mixed bag in the realm of defense affairs. They agree that the United States is in a period of global military retrenchment and express concern that the USSR appears to be trying to take advantage of this lower American profile. This concern remains somewhat amorphous, however, since it is not tied to strategic concepts. Thus, we have no way of judging whether a lower U.S. military presence in, for example, Asia is sound for there is no strategic policy based on political, economic, and military goals (and potential challenges to them) from which to assess the "right" level of military forces. The same complaint can be made for the NATO front. While the United States appears to be redressing its recent neglect of the Atlantic Alliance, without a strategy based on the overall European balance, it is difficult to develop force agreements among the allies and an agreement for the use of battlefield nuclear weapons.

As for the Third World, there appears to be no American security policy at all, other than the general congressional rule of avoiding direct military involvement. In these areas particularly, a lack of presidential leadership is apparent; and congressional government appears to be in the ascendancy for better or worse.

NOTES

1. The final stages being implementation and feedback for subsequent policy modification.

2. R. Judson Mitchell, "A New Brezhnev Doctrine: The Restructuring of International Relations," World Politics (30,3) April 1978. Especially pp. 380-382.

3. See Paul H. Nitze, "A Plea for Action..." New York Times Magazine, May 7, 1978; and Drew Middleton, "NATO Viewing Carter Policies with Unease," New York Times, May 9, 1978.

4. For a specific examination of these questions and the neutron bomb, see R.G. Shreffler, "The Neutron Bomb for NATO Defense: An Alternative," Orbis (21, 4) Winter 1978. pp. 959-973.

A Final Word

Sam C. Sarkesian

The views expressed in this volume support the prevailing perspective that present national security policy is vacillating, ambiguous, and lacks clearly defined purposes and national objectives. While there appears to be a cohesive and focused policy with respect to NATO-WARSAW confrontation in Europe and the Soviet Union, the United States appears to be in a policy vacuum in other parts of the world. That is, there appears to be a perceived gap between the rhetoric of policy, and United States capabilities and military posture, indicating an inability of the United States to relate policy pronouncements, objectives, capabilities and intentions. Equally important, the national security policy process seems to be dominated by concern for political image rather than policy effectiveness. The administration seems to be speaking with a number of voices, none of which project a credible image of national security policy.

It would be presumptuous to suggest specific policies, programs, and procedures to correct what we see as weaknesses in the national security policy process. In this respect, we recognize that the analysis on national security policy by those outside of the national security establishment and not privy to state secrets, may be based on incomplete information and result in faulty assessment. Nevertheless, what is perceived to be the direction of national security policy process deduced from unobtrusive sources and bringing to bear of mature judgment and scholarly assessment can provide useful alternative and independent perspectives. It is in this context that we suggest some general directions for national security policy.

There needs to be developed a systematic and rational national security process that provides for input from alternative sources while retaining a sense of direction and manageability. While we recognize the need to retain domestic consensus, we also recognize the necessity for relatively closed policy making structures. Only a President who is confident of his own capabilities and aware of the sensitivities of other political actors (both domestic and foreign) is in a position to orchestrate and balance the apparent contradictions between a democratic policy process and the necessities of national security.

There should be a more effective correlation between military posture, capabilities, and pronouncements on national security. Once a policy is articulated, there ought to develop consequences, that is people must see that the policy pronouncement has been followed by some program designed to accomplish policy purposes. Our national security policy therefore; must be clearly linked to what can or cannot be accomplished by the prevailing military posture and seriously consider the political constraints on commitment of the military instrument. If policy is to be actively pursued, then the military instrument must be so postured as to be able to achieve policy goals.

There must also be some sense of history in assessing the present international environment. This simply means that there are historical continuities, antagonisms, and necessities that should be a basic part of the national security dimension. While not necessarily determining what future policy should be, these historical considerations should form a basic part of the assessment made by the national security establishment. Too often, advisers around the President seem to be more concerned about the political image than historical realities, thus creating an unpredictable national security behavior pattern which can damage U.S. relationships with its allies and generate behavior on the part of potential aggressors which may be disadvantageous to the United States.

What may be the most apparent weakness of our national security policy process is the lack of a "firm hand" and a dominant voice. The present administration does not give the appearance of firmness nor confidence in its ability to deal with the national security environment. Regardless of what the policies are designed to accomplish, a basic part of the total credibility of the administration's national security policy is in its perceived ability to develop a sense of direction and cohesion.

One positive note emerges from these assessments. The administration appears to have developed a more cohesive policy and a sense of direction with respect to its commitment to NATO. The defense budget and the focus of the military instrument give clear indications that the build-up of conventional capability and at least the maintenance of strategic effectiveness is primarily focused around our European commitment. It is clear, however, that there is little capability or indeed, intention of pursuing national security goals around the periphery of Europe without a major mobilization or escalation of crises into strategic proportions.

While not addressed categorically, the papers both directly and indirectly assess the administration with respect to the four national security requisites: sense of national purpose and national objectives; identification of intentions of potential aggressors; lead time in policy implementation; and linkage between domestic policy and national security policy. By and large, the assessments here convince us that in the aggregate, the administration is not doing well. While there are some positive indicators, the general thrust indicates a failure to respond effectively to these requisites in national security. Specifically, national security policy of the United States in the first two years of the Carter administration has become characterized as rhetorical, diminished in credibility, and is generally viewed as ineffective. Having said this however, we must note that these weaknesses are not insurmountable. Nor do they necessarily mean an imminent collapse of the United States as the leading world power. Nonetheless, without corrective action, these assessments may well be harbingers of considerably diminished American power in the 1980s.

What is accomplished (or not accomplished) in national security is a reflection of the President's own political style and leadership ability. The best of policies and programs are considerably eroded by a President who is unable to inspire confidence, provide a firm sense of direction, and manage his staff in developing cohesive policies. In sum, national security policy is in no small measure a direct reflection of the President's leadership. At the end of the two year period, Jimmy Carter has not yet been able to succeed as an active-positive President, in the national security area.

About the Authors

VINCENT DAVIS is the Director of the Patterson School of Diplomacy and International Commerce and the Patterson Chair Professor at the University of Kentucky. He received his Ph.D. from Princeton and served there as a faculty member. He also was a faculty member at Dartmouth, the Graduate School of International Studies in Denver, and a visiting professor in the Nimitz Chair at the Naval War College. Immediately after his graduation from Vanderbilt University in 1952, he served four years as a carrier pilot in the U.S. Navy. Author of many books and articles in the foreign and defense fields, and often a consultant for U.S. Government agencies in these fields, he was also the President of the International Studies Association during 1976-77.

THOMAS A. FABYANIC is a career officer with the U.S. Air Force, with the rank of Lieutenant Colonel. His flying experience included tactical airlift operations and combat missions in the F-4 Phantom during the Vietnam war. He received his graduate degree from St. Louis University and was an Assistant Professor of History at the U.S. Air Force Academy. He has also served as a Research Associate at the Institute of War and Peace Studies, Columbia University. Currently he is a faculty member at the Air War College, Maxwell Air Force Base.

DORIS A. GRABER is Professor of Political Science at the University of Illinois at Chicago Circle. She received her Ph.D. from Columbia University with a specialization in International Law and International Relations and worked for the U.S. Department of Defense prior to her academic career. Her books include <u>The Development of the Law of Belligerent Occupation</u>; <u>Crisis Diplomacy: U.S. Intervention Policies and Practices</u>: <u>Public Opinion</u>, <u>The President and Foreign Policy</u>; and <u>Verbal Beha-</u>

vior and Politics. She has published articles dealing with U.S. intervention policies in the Political Science Quarterly, the Western Political Quarterly, the Yearbook of World Affairs, the Encyclopedia Americana, and the Dictionary of American Foreign Policy.

GEORGE P. JAN is a Professor of Political Science and Chairman of the Asian Studies Program at the University of Toledo. Born in Peking, he received his Ph.D. degree from New York University. He is the author, co-author or editor of several books including Government of Communist China and International Politics of Asia. He is also the author of more than one hundred articles and professional papers on Asian affairs. Dr. Jan is a member of Phi Beta Kappa, Pi Sigma Alpha, and Phi Kappa Phi and many other honorary and professional organizations. Recipient of numerous research grants, he has also taught at several universities and lectured widely in many parts of this country and abroad. He was the editor of a daily newspaper and a weekly magazine in China.

LAWRENCE J. KORB is Professor of Management, U.S. Naval War College and an Adjunct Scholar of the American Enterprise Institute for Public Policy Research. He is currently a consultant to the Office of the Secretary of Defense, the National Security Council, and the Office of Education. He specializes in national security organization, process and policy and is the author, co-author, and editor of numerous articles, monographs, and books on these subjects, including The Joint Chiefs of Staff; The First Twenty Years. He also served as President of the ISA, Section on Military Studies.

JAMES A. LINGER is an assistant professor of Political Science and History, at St. Xavier College, Chicago, Illinois. He received a Ph.D. in Political Science from the University of Chicago. He has held a number of positions with the Inter-University Seminar on Armed Forces and Society and has participated in numerous professional meetings dealing with comparative politics, international politics, arms control and disarmament, and military sociology. He is currently a preceptor in the Divisional Masters Program at the University of Chicago and has several publications forthcoming.

SAM C. SARKESIAN is Professor and Chairman, Department of Political Science, Loyola University of Chicago. He received his Ph.D. from Columbia University in the City of New York. He served in the U.S. Army for over 20 years as an officer and enlisted man, performing duties with Special Forces, Airborne, and Infantry units in Germany, Korea and Vietnam. He includes among his publications, The Professional Army Officer in a Changing Society (1975), Revolutionary Guerrilla Warfare (1975) and several other books, articles and papers on similar subjects. He has served as Executive-Secretary and Associate Chairman of the Inter-University Seminar on Armed Forces and Society and was elected President of the Illinois Political Science Association for the 1977-1978 term.

SHELDON SIMON is Professor and Chairman of Political Science at Arizona State University. He is author or editor of four books on Asian and Third World security concerns and has written some 30 articles on similar topics for such journals as Asian Survey, Orbis, Pacific Affairs, China Quarterly, Current Scene, and International Perspectives.

Index

NOTE: This Index is principally concerned with entities, major political actors, and material of substantial importance to the various articles; generally no source references or names have been included. Please refer to the detailed notes at the end of the respective chapters. Additionally, information contained in the various tables and figures are not referred to in the Index, since the titles are listed separately in the front matter of this volume, page vii.

American Allies 37
Assured Destruction-
   Damage Limiting 31
Arms transfer 46, 133
All Volunteer Forces
   218, 219
American-West German
   Defense Arrangement
   259

Balance of Payments
   276
Bureaucracies 13, 15,
   53
   U.S. Army 60
   U.S. Navy 60
Bureaucratic and Decision-making Studies
   59

Camp David 79, 82
Carter Administration
   Defense capability
   272
   Defense strategy 282
   Defense policy weaknesses 330
   Image Building 229
   NATO commitments 256

   National security requisites 332
   Open policy process 246
   Policy needs 330, 331
   Role of the President
     in policy 332
   Use of the military 228
   U.S. and Africa 222,
     223
Carter-Ford Defense Budgets
   Outlays 142
   Priorities 145
   Budget titles 147
   Readiness 150
   Strategic areas 150-153,
     175-179
   Combat categories 153
   Service projections
     157-166
   Strategic weapons 179-
     181, 183-185, 190
   Central Europe 190
   NATO 191, 194
   Budgetary impact 196
Carter, Jimmy E., President
   Annapolis speech 90
   Appointment process 64,
     65

Brzezinski and defense policy 239
Decision-making style 66, 68
Divine inspiration 81
Foreign and domestic policy 61, 69, 89
Foreign Policy Association speech, 1976 291, 292
Image building 77
Intervention policy 215, 218
Kissinger and defense policy 239
Leadership 76
Long range impact 23
Personality 22, 62, 99
Policy perspectives 19
Promise and performance 63, 73, 80, 95, 96
Circular Error Probability 32
Communist China
 Emergence 291
 Foreign policy 302, 303
 Attitude on SALT 305
 Views on the West 305
 Fifth National People's Congress 306
 Taiwan 306
 Views on Carter 306
Competitive Balance 30
Congress 15, 74
 The President 75
 Views on Japan 295, 296
Cuban Missile Crisis 10, 35

Defense Budget (U.S.) 97, 98
Analysis 141
Changing priorities 292
Congress 170, 173
Europe-Asia comparison 292, 293
FY 79 138, 139
FY 78 138, 139
Implications 166
Levels of spending 168, 175
Defense Policy 4, 28
 Asia 313
 Criticisms 242, 279, 280
 Ethical and moral content 18
 Goals 319
 Images and perceptions 289, 290
 Impact 278
 NATO 237
 Post Vietnam orientation 237
 Process, Ideal/Typical 319
 Soviet Union 237, 238, 247
 Strategies 319
 Western European views 276
Department of Defense 84
Department of State 84
Detente 243
Deterrence 30, 44

East-West Confrontation 47
Economic Problems 72, 73
Eisenhower Doctrine 204
Essential Equivalence 36
Eurocommunism 266
 NATO 267

Flexible Response 31

Good Neighbor Policy 207
Graduated Deterrence 31
Greek-Turkish Dispute 260
Groupthink 9

Guam Doctrine 216

Human Rights 221, 222, 229

Intelligence Community 85
 Reorganization 87
International Security Assistance and Arms Export Control Act of 1976 220
Intervention 38, 45, 203
 Africa 222, 223
 Collective and individual 201
 Costs 216
 Covert 217
 Effectiveness 213, 214
 Europe 224
 Meaning 200, 202
 Post World War II 205
 Pre World War II 205
 Public opinion 210, 211, 221

Japan
 Role in Asia 295
 US-major problems 307
 Liberal Democratic Party 308
 White Paper 308
 Views of parties 309, 310
 Public opinion 310, 311, 312
Johnson, Lyndon B., President 8

Kennedy, John F., President 10, 36, 209
Korea 325
 U.S. withdrawal 308

Looking at "Them" Research 54
Looking at "Us" Research 54, 55, 58

MFR/MBFR Negotiations 268
 Soviet proposals 269
Massive Retaliation 30
 Soviet 30
 United States 30
Mayaguez 114, 117
Middle East Conflict 46
Military Instrument 4, 13
Mondale, Vice-President 87
Mao Tse-tung 303, 304
Murphy Commission 57

National Command Authority 31
National Interests 2
National Purpose 6
National Security
 Meaning 2, 4
 President 2, 4, 6, 7
 Requisites 6, 332
 Domestic policy 7, 18
 Process 7
 Political actors 8
National Security Council 82, 111
 Committees 112, 117
 Interdepartmental Groups 112
 Lack of experience 134
 Process 126
 Strengths 126
 Subcommittees 112
 Weaknesses 121
National Security Structure 121, 244
 Committees 245
 Collegium 246
National Security System
 Nixon-Ford-Kissinger 114
National Security Decision Memoranda 119
National Security Establishment 12
National Security Study Memorandum 114

National Security Policy
 Democratic criteria 23
 Major needs 330, 331
 Major weaknesses 331
NATO 133
 Advanced weapons 257
 Criticisms of Carter 264, 265, 270, 271, 275
 Cost sharing 259
 Nuclear strategy 326
 Standardization 262
 Warsaw Pact 330
Neutron Bomb 71, 134, 264, 273
Nixon Administration 8
Nixon Doctrine 204
Nonintervention and U.S. Policy 206
Notre Dame Address, 1977 240, 241
NORTHAG 264
North Atlantic Council 258, 263

Organization of American States 209
Oil Resources 220, 321

Panama Canal 225, 226
Peaceful Coexistence 68
Policy
 Substance 5
 Ends 5
 Process 6
Power Projection 39
Presidency
 Imperial 1
 Limits 1, 11
President
 Center of policy process 17, 332
Presidential Decision Memorandum 131
Presidential Directive 119, 134
Presidential Elections 54, 57
Presidential Review Memorandum 117, 119, 124, 131, 132, 134
PRM 10 294
Public Opinion
 Views on Japan 296, 297
 Views on China 297, 298, 299

SALT I 249, 250, 251
SALT II 247, 248, 249, 252, 281, 282, 326, 328
 U.S.-Soviet disagreements and agreements 253
 Ratification 255
Sino-Soviet Dispute 304
Southeast Asian Nations (ASEAN) 324
Soviet Air Forces 42
Soviet-Cuban Activities 210
Soviet Intervention 212
Soviet Naval Forces 35, 39, 40
Soviet Policy in the Middle East 208
Soviet Union 32
Strategic Impotence 37
Strategic Issues 29
Strategic Nuclear Deterrence 47
Survivability 32, 33

Taiwan 327
Third World 247, 321
Triad 33
Trilateral Commission 248
Trio 10
Truman Doctrine 204

Unilateral Disarmament 98
United Nations
 Article 2   209
 Resolution 2131   209
United States Air Power 42
 Airlift capability 42
 Operational limits 43
 NATO 43

U.S. and Africa 90, 246
    Staff conflicts 90-95
U.S. and Japan
    Equal partnership
        294, 295
    Mutual Security
        Treaty 309, 312,
        328
U.S. and U.S.S.R. Relationship 67, 88
United States Army 46
    Force employment 47
United States Naval
    Forces 39, 41

Vietnam 1, 11, 327
Vital Interests 38

Wake Forest Speech 219
Warsaw Pact 248, 261
    Comparison to NATO 262
    Superiority 264
War Powers Act, 1973 220
Watergate 1, 11
Western Europe
    Perceptions of Carter
        273, 274

Year of Europe 258